FUTURE SOCIAL CONSUMER BEHAVIORAL CHANGES

JOHN LOK

Contents

Preface

Introduction

Nowadays, we are experiencing new economic development period. Many countries societies will have significant unpredicted change, however, we will difficult to predict whether what our societies will change or how and why we future societies will have these possible changes. I write this book aims to explain whether what some social changes will be causes to influence our daily living in possible future development. Due to we are experiencing new economic development period, so we ought to attempt to predict whether what our societies will be influenced to change by new economic development. However, I predict that human is facing old economic society change. Why do we shall experience old economy society?

What are our social customer and economic problems ususally we will encounter in our lives. Can economists apply any economic theories to attempt to solve any economic or customer problems absolutely? Do economists apply any economic theories to solve any problems in any economic environment or suitations or they need find the suitable economic theories to solve the suitable environment of economic or customer problems? I shall attempt to apply new economy theory to explain below industries how develops to change in order to achieve customer purchase or entertinment desire to their products or entertainment service.

Telephone broadcasting entertainment service change. Nowadays, television brodcasting competition is serious because internet invetion, it brings online broadcasting business chance. Any young and old television audiences can apply laptop or desktop computer or mobile electronic platform to watch any television entertainment programs anywhere conveniently when they leave homes. So, online broadcasting can bing one kind of new watching television audio visual content entertainment activities to attract any watching television age audiences choose to watch online broadcasting from computer or mobile electronic platform conveniently.

It brings one competitive problem to traditional television watching audiences to cause them to choose other new watching television channel to watch any television entertainment programs. Then, it may bring television product buyers number reduces when they feel mobile or computer electronic platform can bring more convenient and new audio visual content entertainment enjoyable feeling when they watch any broadcasting entertainment programs from online channel. Moreover, some television entertainment programs are needed to make decision either they only concentrate on either online broadcasting or traditional offline television broadcasting both channel. So, they need to have strategic plan to design the different kinds of entertainment programs in order to satisfy any television entertainment audiences feel these both online and offline channels can let them feel new audio visual content enjoyable feeling. Then, they won't reduce television audiences number when their any television entertainment programs can adapt online broadcasting market changes to let television audiences still choose to watch their television entertainment programs when they leave their homes and apply mobiles or laptops electronic platforms to choose to watch themselves productive television entertainment programs in any places any times. Then, their television entertainment programs won't reduce audiences number, due to online broadcasting channel creates.

I shall explain how to apply behavioral economic method to preidct normal basic income consumption client group's habitual spending behavior as well as how to apply behavioral economic method to predict how labor market changing behavior and predict when labor market changes will occur in order to solve shortage of labor or job supply shortage challeges. I shall explain how can apply behavioral economy method raises basic stable income consumer consumption desire. I shall explain behavioral economy method to explain what is the mean of basic stable income consumption great of small amount desire, how to apply life-cycle advertisement method to predict of consumer behavior, and explain how to apply behavioral economy method to raise electricity consumption from electricity user individual habit

I shall explain how to apply behavioral economic method to build consumer confidence is as a predictor of consumption spending. I shall also explain what confidence in consumption survey means and I shall apply behavioral economy method to explain how and why to apply survey to gather data in consumption market. It can measure how much degree of confidence of overall clients to the brand of product or service as well as how to build consumer confidence to buy the brand of product or consume the brand of service as well as I shall also explain what a confidence indicator means and how to apply confidence indicator to predict how many potential consumers will choose to buy the brand of product or consume the brand of service.

On employee productive efficient raising method aspect, I shall explain how to apply behavioral economy methods to influence employee individual psychology to achieve to raise productivity of long term incentive invention. I shall apply behavioral economy method to explain why increasing salary is short term incentive productivity method,how to improve the design of incentive structures to encourage productivities organizations, how to build employees and managers kindly co-operational relationship method, explain whether bonus method can encourage service performance to be raised as well as how to apply behavioral economy method to explain how to predict human motivation natural behaviors.

In the final, I shall apply behavioral economic method to explain that why under-level productive efficiency is not represent low production number to the manufacturer as well as low-consumption desire is not represent less consumer demands or customers lose confidence to the product. The most importance, you can learn how to apply marketing strategies to analyze to solve your further problems to threaten your business. Besides, you can learn how to use strategy to analyze any business case study to prepare your studying. I shall give reasons to explain why I shall apply this kind of marketing strategy to solve every problem to every company case study. Hence, students can understand what reasons to be judged to make these strategic decision more clearly.

In my this book it divides two parts, in first part I shall attempt to indicate some customer problems and they can apply which kinds of economic theories to solve. I also apply demand and supply theory to explain the developed countries' low wage growth reasons why causes. . In my this book seond part, I shall recommend my readers some strategies to let television broadcasting makers how to design their television broadcasting entertainment programs to adopt broadcasting market changes in order to raise new audio visual content broadcasting competitive effort.I hope my readers can enjoy to judge whether these economic theories are the most suitable to solve these customer and labor market problems in our societies.

In second part, it is concerned how to apply marketing and behavioral economy and organizational behaviour theories and concepts to predict marketing behavior. I shall indicate some different marketing and economy and organizational behavioural theories or concepts to predict marketing behavior Also I shall compare to explain what advantages and disadvantages between any one of my solvable suggestions and the any one of the company's choice of solvable method to any one of these case study challenges to aim to let any reader to judge whether how to choose the solvable method is better. This book is one teaching book to give some behavioral economy concepts how to apply to solve the individual company's actual case studies challenges and predict marketing behavior to sample enterprises.

In my this book, I shall discuss whether China will become future world factory leader, what factors may help China to develop its world factory mission as well as what is the main factor help it to implement this world factory mission in sucess; future whether what new form of public transport tool invention will influence our traditional public transport tools, e.g. train, tram, bus catching need. How does this kind of new public transport tool replace all traditional public transport tools in our future public transport catching need? Whether future oil need will be influenced to reduce if one kind of new energy invention? Does global oil industry become decline or experience decline life cycle stage if this kind of new energy can be invented in possible? What our society will be influenced to change to be better or worse if artificial intelligence will replace any social tasks?

Readers can make analysis whether any above issues occur how to influence our future social development to be improved better or worse. I hope my readers can judge new economic society whether is better to compare traditional old economic society or worse to compare traditional old economic society. Our technology will assist our society to develop or it can bring negative impact to influence our future social development. Readers can have more clear answers after you read this book.

Prologue

Chapter of table

    Chapter 1

    Electronic vehicle and non -manual driven vehicle invention how to bring negative impact to passengers' public transport needs

    Electronic vehicle persuades future designing transport system needs

● Designing transportation system advantages
Electronic vehicle invention causes future underground train transportation needs to know passenger behaviour reasons

● Electronic vehicle invention casues passengers feel impact of undergrouund train transport to their working time efficiency
    ● Electronic vehicle invention causes underground train MTR passengers to feel catching time reducing .

    Artificial Intelligent In Road Transportation Strategy
How artificial intelligent vehicle may interact intelligent transportation tools
● Why can (AI) machine learning system main factor to influence driving consumer individual desires ?
● Non-manual driving transportation tool market development
● Why temperature control can be applied to intelligent transportation tools
● How technological technology influence intelligent transportation market development
AI safe immediate response system
Factors influence public transport service industry reaches life cycle decline stage

Chapter 2
Economic recession or boom how influences consumer behavior when the business had been experiencing decline life cycle stage
● COVID -19 disease how influence businesses may experience either growing life cycle stage or decline life cycle stage.
● How recession influences the role of advertising changes?

Applying business development strategy to raise the educational robotic manufacturer sale number in recession period
● How to develop organizations in growth stage?
● How to apply business development strategy to help educational robotic manufacturers to enter traditional education market ?
● Future educational robotic are applied on development teaching maths market
Learning behavioral economy to solve social challenges
● Why do some social challenges may influence customers number ?
Organizational life cycle stage decision making strategy
● Why do managers feel difficult to make
decisions?
Computer technological firm merger cooperational strategy
● IBM and Apple merger strategic advantages and
disadvantages

Chapter 3
How airport service strategy influence future tourism industry development
● New and old economic theories explain oil is not main factor to influence tourism income
● What are the characteristics of birth life cycle stage to tourism industry ? p.100-151
● What characteristics to space tourism growth stage?
Airport service life cycle stage improvement strategy
How can processes improvement management strategy influence airport service performance?

Chapter 4
Factors influence oil industry development recession

● How to raise global gas users need desire ? p.152-200
Chapter 5
New economic society influences human right marginal
social cost and benefit social analysis need
● Environment Economy-Pollution and illness influences c
consumer behavior p.331-345

● How artificial intelligence impacts energy consumers using behaviours

● Is the low income and rising price of modern fuels both factors best to influence Nigeria householders choose to use energy efficiently?

● Urbanization level and income per capita both tangible factors as well as temperature (weather variation factor) will have close relationship to influence China householder energy consumption or useful needs at home every day

● Does season factor influence New Zealand householders' energy consumption behaviors at homes

● Employment rates or gross domestic product macro economic variation factor, residential space size factor, and the government's implementation of energy labeling schemes provide significant impacts on Taiwan residential electricity consumption .

New economy society why and how changes to old economy society

● Reasons new economy society will experience old economy society

● How to recover new economy society p.346-346

Electronic vehicle and non -manual driven vehicle invention how to bring negative impact to passengers' public transport needs

Nowadays, since electronic vehicle invention, it brought competition to fight traditional gas vehicle martet. Electronic vehicle is only needed to be charged battery, then battery will bring energy to push the electornic car to be driven fastly. So traditional vehicle market is experiencing decline life cycle stage. When, electronic vehicle is popular to be accepted to every drivers. In fact, when we drive cars on the roads, our cars will have gas emission to polluate our sir. Earth warmth is dramatically increasing. The main reason is that global air is polluted, e.g. frequent driving activities will bring air pollution when gas emission is caused. Hecnce, environment vehicle is only needed to charged battery. Every time battery charged can bring one day driving time power or enerty to let drivers to drive . So, basing on environmental protection and battery long time driving both reasons, it brings strengths to electronic vehicle to persuade global any drivers to choose to buy electronic vehicle more than traditional gas vehicle. I shall research these questions: These questions may concern: Will the gas vehicle be influenced to experience the decline life cycle stage rapidly when the electronic vehicle is accepted to be popular to drive ? Can traditional gas vehicle avoid decline life cycle stage comes as well as if traditional gas vehicle real prepares to experience decline life cycle stage ? Can it re-grow to change to enter growth life cycle stage again? Can new electronic vehicle market influence traditional gas vehicle market to shorten time to experience decline life cycle age rapidly?

In our driving history, cars invention had helped us do not need to spend long walking time to go to anywhere conveniently. In fact, due to technological limit, e.g. bus, taxi, tram, train must use gas to be energy to push them to be driven on the roads. When car invention period, or it may call car market birth life cycle stage period. In the 1800 year beginning , human does not know what car function or why we need car. When cars had been invented, it is global whole car industry borth life cycle stage period. This period its characteristics are: In societies , people accepted car tools to drive on the roads. Many people feel to spend money to buy cars, it is waste money, because they may choose to catch any kinds of public transport tools, e.g. bus, train, tram, taxi, ferry, undergroundtrain to arrive any destinations conveniently. So, from 1800 year to 1900 year, global whole car industy had been still keeping in the growth life cycle stage. Because in global society, many people hasd been general accepting public tranposrt tools, their fee are vey cheap and passengers can spend short time to catch them to go to anywhere, they can provide long transport service time for office working people, student from morning to evening time. Hence, this 100 years period, global car sale number could not significant increase, because public transport tools could bring convenience to any one when they needed to leave homes to arrive far away destination in short time.

Hence, global car industry ought not develop rapidly, because many people could not accept to spend money to buy cars to replace to catch any public transport tools. But after 1900 year, global whole gas vehicle industry began to experience growth life cycle stage. Because global many people had jobs to do, unemployment ratio begain to reduce. In society, rich people number began to increase. It based on theseboth factors: families began to consider to attempt to buy any kinds of cars in order to attempt to buy any kinds of cars in order to let them to feel enjoyable to drive to go to anywhere. So, from 1901 year to 2000 year, it may be global whole gas vehicle market growth life cycle stage . In this period, global car buyers number had been increasing significantly . In average, global every family may own at least one car, even more. It depends on whether how many members number, the family has and whether the family has how many member(s), he/she has own one car licence. Moreover, in society, many people began to accept second hand cars, because second hand cars must be chaper to compare new cars as well as it is real one good choice for the low income car buyer social consumer groups in society. So, in this global vehicle market growth life cycle stage, instead of new car buyers number had been increasing significantly, the second hand car buyers number had also been increasing significantly in the same time. So, global new cars and secod hand car buyers number had increased rapidly every year, because global population is increasing. It also caused many working people did not like to spend long time to queue to wait public transport tools, it is another factor to persuade people chooce to buy cars to drive to go to offices or schools or anywhere in their relax time, e.g. holiday, sunday. So, this 100 year, may be global whole car industry growth life car cycle stage.

After 2000, it may be global car industy mature life cycle ctage , many car manufacturers begun to innovate any kinds of traditional cars to change to advanced engine function, auto-window, auto dooe functions , navigation road locaion search function, even non-manual driven artificial intelligent car invention. So, after 2000 year, due to global car buyers begun to pursue comfortable drivin feeling. They need to pursue comfortable driving feeling. They need to buy unique design of cars, or more functions of cars to drive on the road . Hence, global different unique function and styles of cars purchase needs had been significant increasing. Moreover, car prices had also been increasing more, due to more different unique functional and styles of car purchase needs had been increasing in order to satisfy the rich or high income car buyers group. So, after 2000, it may be global car market 's mature life cycle stage.

But, I believe that global car market's mature life cycle stage can not keep long time. The main reason is because the electronic car invention. After 2000 year, since one kind of new transport tool of electronic car invention, it influences many gas car owners or non car owners feel interesting to learn how to drive electronic cars and feel whether what advantages that electronic cars can satisfy their driving needs. IN special, environmental protection awareness drivers must believe electornic cars can reduce air pollution when they choose to drive them on the roads , due to none gas emission effect to pollute our earth air. When they choose to drive electronic cars, due to they only need to charge battery, then their electronic cars can be driven on the roads in short time rapidly. Even, report also indicated driving electronic cars accident occurrence chance may be also influenced to reduce to compare driving gas cars usually. So, electronic vehicle market may be future main competitor to global traditional gas vehicle market.

May electronic vehicle invention influence future gas vehicle shorten time to experience to decline life cycle stage rapidly? How gas vehicle market may avoid the shorten time to experience decline life cycle stage if electronic vehicle market may influence its development in global car manufacture industry? I shall attempt to solve these challenges as below:

IN fact, electronic vehicle innovation is not long time , so the global electronic vehicle manufacturing and sale market is experiencing birth life cycle stage. Can electronic vehicle market reduce to shorten time to experience growth, even mature life cycle stages. It depends on these factors:

The factors may affect battery electronic vehicle energy consumption and driving behavior impact. They may include whether environment protection awareness will increase or decrease to global nay one gas car owners or non car owners. Because if global environment protection awareness increase, it will influence gas car owners or non car owners (potential either battery electronic vehicle energy or gas vehicle energy car choice buyers), begun to feel their frequent driving gas vehicle behaviors may bring air pollution or global warming, temperature rises weather disaster occurrence in the future. They alsoknow battery electronic vehicle energy consumption price may be cheap to same to gas vehicle energy consumption. Moreover, they may feel that if they change to drive battery electronic vehicles, it may help them to minimize environmental air pollution impacts of the end of life stage and brings positive impacts on improving climate change and air quality for our future. So, if many car owners or non car owners feel that they have responsibility to protect our climate environment pollution. Then, battery electronic vehicle buyers number will have possible to increase rapidly in short time. Due to the significant impact of gas vehicle and battery electronic vehicle their life cycle analysis can be utilized to analyze the advantages and disadvantages to cause car buyers make comparison between them and gas vehcile and battery electronic vehcile both kinds vehicles are highly complex supply chain choice in the automobile industry nowadays. Moreover, due to carbon intensity of this stage was calculated from emission factors at the global car manufacture industry. Hence, emission factor may be one important influential factor to influence any one makes car purchase decision or either gas or battery electronic car purchase decison.

For example , in our societies, if many people own environment protection awareness, then global gas vehicle buyers number may be influenced to reduce, even the owning gas vehicle families may be influenced to choose to buy battery electronic cars to replace their gas cars. They may sell their gas vehicles to any one, even to steel manufacturers easily. Hence, gas vehicle on steel existence number may also reduce ot they can disappear in our road in short time rapidly. If batttery electronic vehcile can be popular to accept to drive on the road to any one driver in our societies. Then, battery electronic cars may be influenced to increase driving needs to any one driver. it's sale number may also influenced to increase rapidly. Consequently, it may have chance to experience to growth life cycle stage from birth life cycle stage in short time rapidly in global whole electronic car manufacturer and sale market.

Then another influential factor concerns how owning car consumers feel the charge of the battery energy use of resources in comparison to conventional gas energy use of resources to driving cars. In combination with the regional electricity mix these factors influence the energy materials for a specific car market. For these first life cycle phases a range of values is possible to battery electronic car market. If in our societies, there are many people choose to use battery charge energy resource to drive electronic cars, their prices are very reasonable to compare gas vehicles or they feel gas will face rapid shortage challenge, if global any one only likes to drive gas vehicle. Then, they may be influenced to choose to buy the battery electronic vehicles to replace gas vehicles. Hence, enery resource used to car my also be one main factor to influence any one car buyer individual either battery electronic car or gas vehicle purchase choice.

Hence, it implies that the life style environmental impacts and energy resource used both impacts of battery electronic cars are a topic of increasing relative importance of the vehicle production stage and the maximum impact on climate change (ingc02/km) that is observed by many climate scientists, their observation to climate change good or bad change effect may influence global battery electronic vehicle needs. So, how clean are battery electric cars, it will be one popular topic for environmental scientists to environmental protection awareness car owners and non car owners. T o analysis hoe to cause electric car life cycle changes. The arrival of the electric car has brought with it an array of life cycle factors that influence the carbon emission level to any one country's environment.

Influence of national electricity grid over the use phase, so it implies that if the country feels carbon emission level is high , due to gas vehicle may bring carbon emission to pollute air to the country. Although, factory's carbon emission or airplane carbon emisson may be one factor to influence the country's air pollution level to be increase. The year has high carbon emission level, it considers gas vehicle air carbon emission level whether it is high or low in the year. So, if the country's gas vehicle car owners number is sudden increasing rapidly. Consequently, it will evaluate that the car increasing number may influence the country itself carbon emission level to be high and it may cause air pollution seriously.

Hence, battery electric car industry life cycle whether when it can experience growth life cycle stage or mature life cycle stage from birth life cycle stage, it depends on what carbon emisson level to any one country. If this year has many countries believe their high carbon emissin level is due to gas vehicle 's carbon emission causes. Then, this high carbon emission level report factor may raise many car owners or non car owners consider environment protection awareness and it may also influence many car buyers choose to buy battery electric cars to replace gas cars to drive on the road frequently in this year.

Also in order to avoid themselves countries' air pollution is more serious. Hence, global carbon emission rise or fall level and any one environmental protection awareness psychological both factors may influence future battery electric car market development. They may have close relationship to influence any one traditional gas vehicle owner to buy one new battery vehicle vehicle to replace it to drive on the road, or any one potential car purchaser makes final battery electric car or gas vehicle decision absolutely. On conclusion, above these factors may explain whether it is possible that battery electronic vehicle invention may influence future gas vehicle market changes to decline life cysle stage from mature life cycle stage. It depends on whether environmental protection awareness to car owners increasing or decreasing number , carbon emission level whether it is high or low, gas energy resource facing shortage factors to influence future electronic vehicle need.

Electronic vehicle persuades future designing transport system needs

● Designing transportation system advantages

Nowadays, transportation and economic development have close relationship. Economic development stimulates transportation demand by increasing the numbers of workers commuting to and from work, customers traveling to and from services areas, and products being moving by lorries on the roads between products and customers. According to Bailey, Mokhtarian and Little (2008) indicated "transportation route is past of distinct development pattern or road network and mostly described by regular street patterns as an important factor of human existence, development and civilization. The route network combined with increased road transportation investment result in changed levels of conveniently reflected through cost benefit analysis, savings in travel time, and other benefits. " These benefits are noticeable in increased catchment areas for services and facilities , shops, schools, offices, banks and leisure activities.

What are the crisis of neglection to care transporation system ? Why do any countries need to design road transportation system? For example, the Japan country lacks design road trsnaportation system effectively. So, the crisis of road traffic fatalities will raise and the econominc influence will be changed. The crisis indicates more than 7,000 people die annually as a result of motor vehicle crashes in Japan. Driving when under the influence of alcohol is the leading cause of motor vehicle crash fatalities in both developed and developing countries. So, alcohol is the most serious factor to raise personal risk when drivers are driving in Japan. However, a number of studies have shown that deterring drink driving is an important way to cause fatalities. There is a demonstrative need for social change in Japan.

Japan has recently strengthened its already strict laws in order to reduce the number of alcohol related road fatalities. Those deforms lowered the legal blood alochol contant limit increased, the penalties for offenders. The Japan road traffic legal needs. Any driving a motor with a alcohol limit of 0.03 or higher Japan's maximum sentence is up to 3 years imprisonment or a fine not exceeding 500,000 yen dollars. Is law impact to reduce drinking alcohol to drive in Japan? What are economic influence of the crisis of road traffic fatalities in Japan?

The rational choice theory of offending suggests that offenders are active decision makers who influence a large number of variables into decision whether or not to commit an offence. On the cost-benefit analysis, it is the punishment a possible jail, large fines worth is the reward the convenience of driving home without the expause of a taxi and innovenience to the alcohol drivers in Japan. Instead of law reforms when it detects alcohol in the air exhaled from the alcohol and other offenders and it educates children about the dangers of drinking and it also explains why alcohol driving can also threaten drivers' life when who are drinking alcohol and driving behaviour in the same time in Japan.

On the economic influence hand, implementation of the policy deregulating alcohol sales and alcohol production did not appear to increase traffic fatalities among adult or teenage males or females in Japan. We found that male adult fatalities demonstrated a statistically significant decline following enactment of the deregulation policy in 1994 year. So, Japan implement law to threaten alcohol drinking behaviour is useful. It can influence the alcohol availability and consumption, alcohol production and sales, the 24 hours operated convenience stores or liquor discount stores incomes to be reduced. Even, Japan overall GDP is also reduced from the deduction of liquor alcohol production and sale, also the occurrence of traffic accident fatalities chances will be also reduced.

The Japanese economy has entered a rapid process of liberalization since the mid-1990 year. Many sectors previously under direct government control are now regulated by the competitive market place. The Japanese alcohol beverage market has changed. The entry of cheaper import alcohol products resulted in a encouragement of alcohol consumption to Japan drinking drivers and an raising of increasing of more import alcohol products supply to Japan. Although, it is beneficial to Japan GDP growth. But it also raise the occurrence of chance to traffic accidents rate to cause alcohol drinkers to be death or hurt when who choose drinking alcohol to drive at the same time in Japan. So, alcohol import can bring more consumption, but it can also raise many traffic accidents occurrence in Japan in the same time.

In conclusion, alcohol is not good for health to drink when the consumer often buys alcohol at drink habitually. So, if many Japanese, including the alcohol driving consumers and the alcohol non drinking consumers both who often buy different countries alcohol to drink daily. It will cause their bodies to be unhealth for long term in Japan. It is possible to increase Japan's government's medical expenses to assist the low income or poor people in the future. So, although alcohol import can raise Japan GDP growth in the short term, but it also raise Japan government's medical expenditure to the low income or poor Japanese long term in the future, So it's economic benefit will not good in the future if Japan still import much alcohol to sell in its country.

Many commercial users depend on road transport facilities, with movement of products and services from place to place on the roads, aspect of global and urban economic survival. Hence, developments of various transportation modes have become important to physical and economic developments. For example, urban locations with such relative advantages are found where different transport routes with high degree of connectivity, within the intra and inter urban road networks. On similarly, commercial activities like banking, retail/wholesale businesses and professional services can take advantage of nearness to concentration of activities attracted consumers service providers. This partly caused increase in demand for commercial space and its effects on commercial property values along commercial roads can be rose. However, some countries' roads need to provide pedestrian movements more than the businesses activities, e.g. shorten the time of lorries parking on the road to let pedestrian movements on the narrow road. If the country government did not consider the roads need to let more pedestrian movements or shorten the time of lorries parking on the road. It will cause traffic jam or traffic density of the individual roads. Hence, governments need to concern the locations of commercial property buildings and the relationship between the explanatory variables of the design road networks.

What are construction of roads design networks benefits? In fact, construction of roads increased substantially with the opening up of residential environments that also is getting much benefits from increasing demand for spaces in commercial properties. Many private companies, retail stores, commercial banks aggregate in the main roads of cities, which get advantage of opportunities afforded by locations near central of cities to attract many pedestrians concerning their businesses existence. This led to high concentration of vehicular and pedestrian movements. Specially along the access main roads in the central of cities. The main roads exhibits linkages to form networks of minor routes along which commercial properties locate. If commercial users are displaced residential users, causing sites to be at the highest and best uses with increases in the values of commercial properties. However, it seems road network development is affected by the compact nature of various routes that sometimes causes volume of traffic jam. Thus, demand for transport can't be treated solely as a derived demand road. Improved main and minor roads access an city or rural areas is a necessary (but not sufficient). Precondition for increased productivity, the UK Standing Advisory committee On Trunk Road

Assessment (SACTRA, 1999) noted "various ways in which transport can affect economic growth, for example benefits include through reorganization and rationalization of production, distribution and land use: reducing labor costs by expanding catchment areas etc."

What is land use and road transport design system relationship? Land use refers to the whole range of human activity and of the built environment, and to some aspects of the natural environment. This is a way relationship between land use and road transport. Governments need to design how to use land and how to design road transportation systems. e.g. where are built the main roads and/or where are built the minor roads are the most suitable locations in the cities or rural areas ? If the main roads is located in the not suitable locations at the centers of the cities or rural, it will case the increasing traffic volumes and levels of congestion, including air pollution, noise, ground water pollution from run-off , loss of soil functions and loss of bio-diversity to natural environment. By influencing the spatial structure of locations in the urban environment, so land use planning can help to mitigate any negative effects resulting from land use changes.

Modelling and land use transportation interactions has become an important aspect of road design transport planning. On the one side, for example, design roads in urban centers, it can increase land use and it can also reduce employees or students catching buses or driving cars' time spending to go to workplaces or schools users. Hence, the land use and roads designing transportation can give benefits to residents and employment people to reduce time to wait buses or taxies etc. public transportations to go to workplaces or schools or shopping centers etc. anywhere. It seems to assist bus companies or taxi drivers to earn more income, On the other side, designing urban transport systems is also important . Increased densities mean more destinations become within convenient walking and cycling distances and consequently the use of these modes tends to be higher. Also in dese cities public transport systems are able to offer higher levels of service and operate more economically, when the provision of sufficient road space to meet potential demand becomes impractical. It aims to reduce the danger of driving or walking in urban areas. The transport modes (that is walking, cycling, public transport) and the extent of car dependence is less, due to driving users dependency is less on rural roads. Hence, building main roads can concentrate on designing convenience to pedestrian walking to close to their houses on the streets. However, poor transport design and land use can cause to spend too expenditure not only transport costs on governments and transport users both and also the costs of providing other services. These include the usual utilities and also education and health services as well as negative externalities , such as greenhouse gas emissions. Most such studies concluded that there are significant financial and economics cost advantage of inner city redevelopment compared with fringe development.

However, such policies won't necessarily be successfully, in particular because of the two ways road problem, they may result in additional private investments and employment opportunities flowing into the region, buy may equally result in population and employment opportunities flowing out of the target region because of the improved access to other centers. Hence governments need to analyze how to arrange the land use to assist the property developers to choose where are the suitable locations to build offices or factories or shopping centers or houses at capital or urban cities to adapt to whose the growth of living population. For example, to judge where the land use whether where main roads or junior roads are built where are the suitable locations to satisfy the lorry drivers to park their lorries are the safe locations ; to design the minor roads to let the pedestrians to feel no danger to walk on the streets when the cars are driven to near to the streets on the minor roads. Thus, the factor of choosing where the land use to design the main or minor roads areas, sizes and lengths and of the minor or major roads can influence the drivers and pedestrians feel safe or dangerous when who are driving whose cars on the roads or who are walking on the streets to arrive the offices, schools, cinemas, church, houses etc. destination.

Designing road transportation networks how to assist economic growth ? I feel it is not all transport investments will be equally effective in enhancing economic growth. Designing road transport investment is a necessary, but on its own not sufficient requirement to earn significant economic growth at either a national or regional level. There are conditions under three categories: economic conditions, investment conditions and political conditions. In fact, although in some circumstances, transport investment may be a necessary condition for enhancing economic growth, it is rarely on its own a sufficient condition. Other factors including the broader policy environment, need to be present if the investment is going to be successful in addressing regional economic objectives. My some suggestions the following key aspects as being most relevant including:

a. Scale economies for example, where these dominate, lower transportation costs through improved accessibility may encourage increased concentration of firms in core regions, until the point that diseconomies set in.

b. Size of the local market.

c. Local land and labor conditions.

d. The nature and scale of transport improvements.

e. The nature of backward and forward linkages

in the country 's local economy.

In any countries, road transportation improvements don't guarantee increased economic development. To increase economic development, an improvement needs to assist any lorry drivers to drive in short trips to reduce transportation costs and shorten time driving on the road or to make transportation more reliable, e.g. reducing the numbers of traffic jams on any roads. A proper economic climate must also exist as well as other support services. With these factors to influence transportation improvements can become catalysts for economic expansion. However, road transportation improvement that intends to induce job creation, when employers need many lorry drivers to help them to transport products and to move products on the roads often. So, the employers need to employ many transportation workers and lorry drivers to help who to transport their products to send to clients, due to the transportation time is shorten and work efficiency is rasied, so the transportation times are also increasing every day when the road transportation roles are improved. On the other side, improving transportation can raise productivity when many customers need to buy many products and the lorry drivers may drive whose lorries to transport many products between factory and office or between factory to the client's home or between the shop and the client's on the road in the short time fast.

I recommend one model links in an overall road transportation network includes these four modes.

I. Maximizing use of the existing road highway system.

II. Extending or improving the multi-lane divides system local roads and connectors.

III. Continually improving the entire road highway network in response to business activities demand.

The improvement of modern road transportation successful factors include:

● How to improve the highway network

modernization includes obsolete interchanges and other segments of the road, transport network of new designs to improve the life and service of pedestrian walking streets, rebuilding certain in main or minor roads. To the extent that labor markets operate more efficiently and more jobs are created to raise economic expansion if our governments can improve road transportation system to design to satisfy business users demand when lorry drivers need to move or transport whose products on the streets, but who will not influence pedestrian are walking on the streets. Hence, excellent transportation design network can subsequent plan efforts, it can also rise economic efficiency, community and social effects, it can also encourage transportation users to attempt to drive lorries to transport products a lot of times in one day fast and who can also avoid traffic jams occurrence on the road easily. On the one side, economic development is a concept referring to the material aspects of community welfare. There are numerous factors need of development: growth in income and wealth, equitable distribution of income, decreased infant mortality rates, increased literacy rates. On the other side, economic growth means which is sustainable increase in community income and /or wealth. (wealth is the net of resources that generate income). It seems the link between transportation facilities and economic growth has close relationship. Good transportation facilities support economic growth by lowing the transportation costs of users of the transportation network, such as roads. Direct users benefits are reductions in travel, times and fuel consumption, increased reliability and increased safety in the movement of people and products, users' transportation costs are reduced, resources are used for other purpose.

The relationship between transport and economic development occur in two directions, in the sense that (i) land use and economic development are major drivers' of demand for transport (in terms of quantity , type, location and mode); and (ii) transportation investments and other initiatives (such as regulations, pricing) can influence levels, patterns and locations of economic development. The principal role of road transportation is to provide access between spatially separated locations for the business and household sectors, for both commodity (lands transportation) and person movements. For the business sector, this involves connections businesses and their input sources between business factories and other business shops and between business and their markets. For the households sector, it provides people with access to workplaces and education facilities, shops and social recreation, community and medical facilities etc. on the roads. I feel different countries' road transportation system can be self funded in the sense that the majority of the costs of transportation system investment operation and maintenance are either paid directly by users (for example, through car operating costs) are funded initially by governments and recovered from transport users (for example, through petrol duties and road user charges). Governments' road transportation system and their use also give rise to some external costs(externalities). These include global environmental impacts (greenhouse gas emissions) and local environmental and health impacts (for example, noise partial pollution and road accident costs). The direct effects of transportation investments are to reduce road transportation time and costs through reducing travel time, decreasing the operating costs of transportation and enhancing access to destinations within the road network. A good road transportation network also needs to reduce any economic disbenefits, for example where projects reduce congestion or the risk of injury. These incremental benefits of transportation investments may be measured through commercial cost benefit analysis. Other indirect consequences of road transportation network should also be considered when evaluating effects on productivity and the spatial pattern of economic development. Good road transportation design network benefits can include lower costs and enhanced accessibility, due to better transportation links and services expand markets for individual transportation using business and improved access to input.

The economic contribution of road transportation policy can be assessed from various perspectives. These include:

● Effects on aggregate economic welfare (e.g. the sum of consumer and which is the times of cost benefit analysis, as linking to transportation productivity effect.

● Micro economic, for example, enterprise or household level productivity effects.

● Macro economics, for example, contributions to GDP investment or employment and the spatial patterns of economic activity.

One key characteristics of road transportation is split between infrastructure and operations. Infrastructure refers to the right of way on which vehicles operate, which may include ancillary facilities to ensure efficient and effective operations (for example, traffic signals, railway stations). In developed countries, are in most transportation is operated by the private cars, road trucks, the majority of bus and coach services. In long term , overall purpose, to ensure transportation system helps to develop that maximizes the economic and social benefits and minimizes harm. Hence, governments need to concern who are their main target users to use every road. Such as the road is used to near to park and leisure, or local and national economic conditions, keep clean natural environment etc. facilities to provide different benefits to different target users to enjoy to use. It seems that good transportation networks designing can influence economic activities, shopping convenience or business convenience etc. activities to cause whether the country's economic behavior to achieve close relationship successfully. Possible relationship between road networks, location attribute, demand and supply and accessibility and commercial property values of these factors which will influence different countries' concerning to choose where to build main roads and sub minor roads in different cities and rural locations. However, I shall suppose hypotheses how governments to find the most suitable places to build main roads and sub minor roads to whose cities and rural. There is no significant relationship between commercial property values and individual contributions of explanatory variables to variability in commercial property values in whose countries.

In conclusion, I suggest methods how to design suitable transportation networks to governments to build, such as it is essential to establish a technique that may be useful for determining relative accessibility of locations in the network of main roads and sub minor roads. Even, when relative advantages are determined, there is need to develop models that will be useful for predicting commercial properly values. The model may become tool for professional estate surveyors and values to change their practice of using intuition to determine relative access of locations in a road network. Similarly, there is the need to predict the supply of, demand for, and fair market values of commercial properties by developers. Hence if the cities or rural locations can attract many businesses to build commercial properties, governments can build the main roads in the locations. Otherwise, if the cities or rural locations can not attract many businesses to build commercial properties, governments can build the sub minor roads in these locations. Hence, the main roads must have high transportation valuation to let big lorries to drive and park in these main roads easily and conveniently. It seems capital cities may not influence to build the main road factors. Natural environment, commercial properties values, the lands areas size and shape and pedestrian walking numbers on the streets and lorries available numbers on the areas will be other factors to influence where to build main roads in any cities or rural in the country.

In road concept, the route network consists of primary and secondary roads, known as main roads and minor roads respectively. Main roads are usually moderate or high capacity roads that are below highway level of service, carrying large volumes of traffic between areas in urban centers and designed for traffic between neighbors. They have intersections with collector and local streets and commercial areas, such as shopping centers, petrol stations and other businesses are located along such roads. In additions, main roads link up to expressways and freeways with inter-changes in cities or rural. Road network constitutes an important element in urban development , due to urban areas have many farms, gardens, forests , so roads and building needed to provide accessibility required by different land uses and the proper functioning of such urban areas depends an efficient transport network existence. In computing des, the network indicator are used to partition road network into different parts in reasonable way. The results in number of connection to describe density differences in road networks. The parameter records how many roads connect to each road in a network. For two roads with the same length, the ones in the dense area will connect to more roads than that in a sparse area and the connection differences will indicate the density differences to some extent, so road density can also be calculated as the total length of all known roads divided by the total land area in a road divided by the total land area in a road network. Hence, governments need to consider road length to decide how to build main or minor roads to design its transportation systems for businesses activities , such as driving lorries and parking lorries and products are been moving on the streets from roads easily and conveniently. As Wikipedia Contributors (2008) indicate that "transport networks are spatial structures designed to channel flows from the points of demand to points of supply and to link the points together in a transportation system. They are useful for transport network analysis to determine the flow of people, products, services and vehicles." Hence, governments need to research whether where the shopping centers, cinemas, houses, hospitals, schools, offices, factories etc. are located, then, which need to follow these location datas to predict the cars, lorries, taxies, buses etc. of the demand numbers of transportation users to design the lengths, width and distances and the construction of main and minor roads locations and their supply numbers in different capital cities or country roads. It aims to reduce traffic jams and shorten time and air pollution as well as increasing the available spaces to let the lorry drivers to move their logistc on the road easily and reducing the accidents occurrence when the pedestrians are walking on the streets. If the vehicles can be moved on the roads easily. It will also increase time efficiency and productivity to any businessmen. Hence, how to design of the main roads and/or minor roads in any capital or country cities. It will influence any country's economic growth long time in the future.

● Electronic vehicle invention causes future underground train transportation needs to know passenger behaviour reasons
Understanding individual passenger behaviour is essential for the design MTR transportation, because who can choose to catch bus, taxi, tram, train ferry etc. different kinds of public transportation tools. Individual traveler who decides to catch which kinds of public transportation tools, it depends on whether the public transportation tool can provide real time travel information, liking link travel time schedule. So, MTR underground train needs to understand where it has terminal to give convenience to the local living areas of time travelers to choose to catch MTR easily. Although, MTR ticket fare is one factor to influence any passengers choice. But, those other factors can also influence them to choice. e.g. MTR any terminal location of convenience, short time travelling, none crowding in busy (peak) time, MTR platform waiting arrival time, none sudden MTR engineering machines broken accident events occurrence frequently etc. different factors, any one of these factors which can influence passengers who choose to catch MTR or other kinds of transportation tools.

Why route choice can influence passenger behavioural choice ? Usually, the busy time passengers will regard the route choice as a coordination problem to influence them to choose to catch which kinds of transportation tools. The route choice is as an opportunity costs to influence any busy time passengers to decide to choose to catch which kind of transportation tool which is the best right choice in the right time among of them. In the short time, for example, it seems any busy time passengers will choose to catch bus to substitute MTR underground train transportation tool, due to who feels the bus can arrive any destinations to compare other kinds of transportation tools in the most short time. However even if the MTR can either charge cheaper ticket fare to sell full day or charge discount ticket fare to sell in the busy (peak) time to compare to bus fare. It is possible that the busy time passengers will still choose to catch bus, if between the bus terminal and the another bus terminal that distance is the shorter time route to spend time to arrive destination to compare between the MTR terminal to the another MTR terminal arrival time . Also, although the busy time passengers will feel to enounter traffic jam to influence sitting or waiting bus time to be longer time in possible and who also feel MTR can avoid traffic jam problem. However, usually any busy (peak) time passengers will feel the chance of traffic jam occurrence will be less. So, the short bus route choice is more potential factor to influence the busy (peak) time passengers still to choose bus to catch.

However, if anyone wants to investigate results of day-to-day route choice which can be transferred to more realistic environment. It is necessary to explore individual behaviour in an interactive experimental set up to ensure busy (peak) time passenger transportation behavioural choice. For example, a passenger has a choice between a main road (M) and a side road (S) for travelling from (A) to (B). (M) is faster if (M) and (S) are chose by the same number of passengers. So, this method can be researched whether MTR terminal station is located at the main road (M) or the side road (S) where is more suitable to accept to passengers generally.

Why trip time reliability and crowding factors can influence MTR passenger choice? Other problem is MTR busy (peak) time's crowding in public transportation occurrence of MTR underground train transportation tool is becoming a growth to concern as MTR demand growth at a busy (peak) time. To capture the MTR passengers benefits with reduced crowding from improved MTR public transport service and image. It is necessary a identify the relevant dimensions of crowding that are meaningful measures of what crowding means to MTR passengers. Two main influences on MTR model choice that are growing in relevance are trip time reliability and crowding. It represents a benefit-cost framework. In fact, MTR passengers can be willing to pay more expensive ticket fare, it MTR can avoid crowding and short and the accurate arrival trip time between terminals is reliable to occur. How to measure of MTR crowding, e.g. weighting the gap between the busy time, the standard (i.e. objective) and the perceived (i.e. subjective) metrics. We are not in a position to definitely map the two dimensions, which is a crucial requirement for translating objective improvements into equivalent subjective gains that then can be applied, willingness to pay estimates MTR ticket fares to obtain the additional MTR passenger benefits of MTR public transportation investment to any terminal stations. Because MTR crowding has a negative impact on passengers in terms of psychological on emotional distress. MTR passengers are willing to stand for up to 20 minutes of the service is fast and reliable. However crowding outweighed these benefits from a MTR passenger's perpective, experienced crowding leads a increased dissatisfaction. e.g. stress and less privacy during who needs to stand up in MTR. Due to there are no enough places to supply to them to stand up in MTR. If the MTR trip time was longer time between the passenger's terminals, who will feel more dissatisfaction and it will cause who feels whether who ought need to choose to catch other transportation tools to substitute MTR next time. e.g. bus, train, tram, ferry, taxi etc. So, from an operator's perspective, the MTR service frequency or MTR size is significantly influenced by the level of ridership, which sends a signal to respond if the monitored crowding level exceeds the benchmark standard in the busy time. e.g. in the morning time or at the night time, the students or employment people who need to go to schools or offices (working places). The locations of different places between MTR terminals and crowding are regarded as a key service attribute for MTR pubic transportation along with other factors, such as travelling time and reliability, e.g. service quality, none engineering machines are broken to cause MTR stops suddenly.

Given the increasing importance of crowding on both the disutility to existing MTR public transportation users and the influence to it. MTR passenger can choose to use either the MTR public public transportation or other public transportation. It is timely to review the MTR current measures of crowding defined by transportation authorities. MTR operators ought evaluate whether they apporpriately reflect MTR each traveler experiences and perceptions of crowding in busy (peak) time. I suggest that MTR needs to buy other underground trains to supply to the busy (peak) time passengers to let them have enough seats to sit down, so who do not need to stand up in any MTR underground trains when they catch MTR underground trains in busy time. It aims to let who are willingness to pay the estimation of reasonable ticket fares to compare the other kinds of transportation tools in the busy (peak) time.

What is the crowding difference between train and MTR underground train? In fact, crowding won't be happened to brother these transportation tools easily in the busy time and non busy time both. e.g. bus, taxi, train, tram, ferry. Because passengers can not choose to stand up in these transportation tools easily, due to these transportation tools have no enough areas (spaces) to let them to stand up easily . So, the crowding will be avoided to occur in these tranportation tools usually. Otherwise, MTR will have many passengers who can choose to stand up because MTR design of length is very long and it has enough areas (places) to let passengers to choose to stand up, even there have none any seats are provided to let them to sit down. So, MTR passengers will feel more dissatisfaction and crowding easily, especial in any peak (busy) time every day.

Comparing to bus, much more diverse crowding measures are defined in the passenger rail industry. For passenger, different specifications for measuring crowding are found across countries and even within a country. For example, rail crowding measures in the UK, the passengers in excess of capacity is crowding measure that applies to all London and South east operators weekday train services at a London terminus during the morning peak from 0700 to 09: 59 , and those departing during the afternoon peak from 16:00 to 18:59 (office of rail regulation 2011 year). The overall PIXC figure is considered the planned standard class capacity of each train service as well as the actual number of standard class passengers on the service at the critical point. i.e. the location on a trains of standard class passengers that surpass the planned capacity as the difference between the number of actual passengers and the capacity of the train divided by the number of passenger is within the capacity . So, it seems train and MTR underground public transportaton tools had been encountering the crowding problems in peak time, the difference in train passengers need to wait next train or more train arrival is who doesn't plan to enter the train, when who discovers the current train has no seats to provide to them to sit down in whose trip. Otherwise, MTR passengers can choose either to stand up within the large areas (places) if who discovered there are no any seats to provide to them to sit down or who can wait the next MTR arrival in order to who can sit down. It seems MTR transportation tool crowding environment includes in waiting platform and inside of the MTR underground train. Otherwise, train transportation tool crowding environment only includes the waiting platform and the passengers will not have crowding feeling inside of the train, due to none of passengers choose to stand up inside any trains because any train inside has no enough places to let them to stand up. How MTR can attract many passengers. On the commuter departure time choice of any reference point researching hand, the departure time decisions of communters are of fundamental importance of peak period MTR traffic congestion. However, whether on the demand side, MTR underground train congestion relief measures, such as MTR ticket fare to every terminal station needs to be charged cheaper fare or discount fare in the peak (busy) time every day. To aim to attract many passengers to choose to catch MTR Underground train public transportation tools, substitute to choose other public transportation tools in the peak time.

Over the past decades, there have been very active research efforts in the departure time problem, both in econometric modeling and dynamic user equilibrium fields. Although, these works provide valuable insights into dynamic commuter decision making, they do not identify the commuters' response to gains and losses related to whole actual arrival time to reference points who may have relative. The appliability of the reference point hypothesis of prospect theory to the commuter's departure time decision making to obtain a better understanding of how departure time choice in MTR platform during their waiting underground train arrival time. However, every MTR underground train actual arrival time and deviation variables related to reference points (gains and losses) are the key factors in the departure time choice model. How the MTR underground train of every communter's daily departure time decision can be modelled when the reference point hypothesis of prospect theory. The MTR underground train's schedule delay is defined as the difference between the preferred arrival time (PAT) and the actual arrival time (AT) for a given MTR commuter. In a daily MTR commute, a commuter in the indifference band actual arrival time is an essential feature of MTR schedule study. Two reference points are the earliest acceptable arrival time and the work starting time for a given MTR platform waiting passengers. In psychological view point, prospect theory proposes that the displeasure of a loss is perceived or greater than the pleasure of a gain of the same attitude and therefore, the value function is stronger for losses than gains.

To conclude, it seems that if MTR waiting passengers need not spend long time to wait underground train arrival in platform and it can provide seats to let them to sit down in the busy (peak) crowding time. It will make them to feel pleasure, even the MTR ticket fare is not fair and reasonable to charge higher fare to compare other kinds of public transportation tools fares. So the peak waiting time factor can influence the passengers to choose other kind of transportation tools to catch easily. Moreover, MTR's two reference points are the earliest role. Similarly a loss is observed when the MTR platform waiting commuter experiences or actual arrival time which is beyond that the MTR schedule time. Due to that a MTR waiting commuter is as an early side arrival of whose actual arrival time is earlier than whose preferred arrival time.

Reference
Bailey, L., Mokhtarian, P.L. Little, A. (2008). The broader Connection Between Public Transportation, Energy Conservation And Greenhouse Gas Reduction, Report Prepared As Part Of TCRP Project J-11/Tasks Transit Cooperative Research Program, Transportation Research Board Submitted To American Public Transportation Association in http://www.apta.com/research/into/online/land_use.cfmi, accessed 17 April 2008.

The UK Standing Advisory Committee On Trunk Road Assessment (SACTRA) (1999). Transport And The Economy (Report To UK DETR). Retrieved From: http://webarchive.nationalarchives.gov.uk/20050301192906 ; http://dft.gov.uk/stellent/groups/dft-econappr/documents/pdf/dft_econappr_pdf_022512.pdf

Wikipedia Contributors (2008). Arterial Roads In Wikipedia, The Free Encyclopeda, http://en.wikipedia.org/w/index.php?title=Arterial_road&oldid=212832640(accessed May30,2008).

● Electronic vehicle invention casues passengers feel impact of undergrouund train transport to their working time efficiency

Any countries must need road, sea and air transport to assist businessmen to transport products in local or overseas. If the country's road , sea or air transport system service quality is poor. It will influence any products transport time, speed, inefficient transport to anywhere.

How to raise the country's transport system in order to improve efficiencies to let any businessmen can deliver their products to anywhere easily,e.g. warehouses, client homes, supermarkets destination in the most short time to avoid delay occurrence to let clients feel unsatisfactory or complaint their perform their delivery services poorly. I shall discuss the factors how to improve any countrues' transport systems to achieve the most efficient way as below:

Any countries' transport systems will create economic value, e.g. demonstrate value for money, economic worth, viable commercial worth, financial affordable worth, achieveable worth. Any countries' transport systems can bring welfare value by economics. It has direct relationship to take the form of measured economic activity, i.e. GDP. The form of measured economic activity can impact on any countries' economic economic geography, locally , regionally and nationally's local GDP impacts.

The welfare impacts may include: leisure time savings, e.g. the local people drive cars or catch any public transportation tools to go to any geogrpahical location's shopping centers, big gardens, swimming pools, cinemas etc. places to carry on any kinds of leisure activities.

Environmental impacts may include avoiding noise, air pollution on road transportation aspect , when the main road is only on on focus on the main city,
but the city lacks other roads to let any drivers can choose them to drive, instead of the main road in the city. Then, when many cars are driven on the busy transport
time, e.g. morning working time or night busy time between 6:00 and 9:00 AM, between 6:00 and 9:00 PM. When either many working people need to catch public transport or drive themselves cars to go to offices to work or they need to catch pubic transport tools or drive themselves cars to home. Then, the only one main road problem will need them to stay themselves cars on roads, due to traffic jam or traffic accidence occurrence problem causes when many cars are driven on the road in the busy transport time. It will influence they can not go to offices or homes easily daily, even in the busy transport time, their cars' gas need to be used much to cause air pollution and traffic noise is easily caused easily in the busy transport time on the road. When the city has only one main road for drivers in the busy transport time. So, poor road transport system can bring poor impact on economic welfare benefits arising from proved labour supply from commuting, time savings, including exchequer benefits. Consequently, the county's GDP will be fallen down, due to labour market effects which do not add to welfare value.

Whether can poor transport system impact indirectly on GDP or not on local, regional , or national economic geography impacts? Does transport lead to greater economic activity i.e. higher GDP? DO they lead to change in economic activity location? Does transport impact the existence of business location and new economic activity opportunities? The measurement on every country's transport how impacts on economic change, facilitating geographic division of labour and specialization. It can be analyzed on these general aspects:

Costs and speed of travel time (Economic value of travel time savings) . Travel time savings to users from improved transport is a key of economic value, but it has only less influence,journey time reliability is more important to business frieght as well as business travellers, network connectivity enhancements as well as business travellers, network connectivity enhancement can help people and goods travel more quickly (i.e. linked to jounrey time and journey time reliability, as well as opening new destinations and new journeys, comfort and quality service provision is relevant to public transport, e.g. detering jounreys at particular times or by certain modes (e.g. overcrowding), impact on productivity at work for commuters, safety and security , due to loss of output from workers, transport accidents occur easily. All of these issues will impact any countries' standard of living to local people (geography) , even GDP income.

Why does the direct and indirect effects of transportation have a positive impact on the economic growth and development of a country? Does it influence acccess to goods, services and
employment opportunities in any regions? Underdeveloped countries must need to consider how transport system influences their economic growth. For example, the costs of transportation and production are reduced through timely delivery and enhancing the economies of scale in the production process, when the road is often traffic joam, gas cost, time waste , air pollution cost, noise has many roads, but if one lorry drivers needs drive more than one day to day to deliver goods to another city's warehouse every day. It will bring psychological pressure in terrible, when they need long time to drive on the road. They can not sleep easily because road accident will occur easily when they need to spend long time to drive lorries on the road.

So, how to solve the long driving time on road transport problem will be one issue concerns human life welfare benefit aspect, instead of economic benefit aspect. The transport system welfare worth needs to include human life worth. It is a valuable insight into the causality (ot lack of causality) between transport and economic growth and will serve to compare to any countries' national level and local geographical location level both.

In special, underdeveloped countries' public transport time whether it is long or short factor, it will influence workers their going to offices to work time. If they often need spend long time to catch buses, due to traffic jam,then it will influence their efficiences to be reduced, productive number is influenced to reduce also, because traffic jam causes they often go to offices too lately.It can influence workers' bad emotion to work every day. So, traffic jam will bring negative relationship between low efficiency and bad emotion to the workers, because they need to spend long time to wait, public transportation tools and traffic jam also influence their working emotion. Consequently, service and working performance will be influenced to poor, because long time traffic jam problem causes their bad emotion to work. It is one critical factor in the path of more widely spread economic growth and urbanization for traffic jam problem to underdeveloped countries.

However, transport system can also influence developed countries' economy. How does it influence on environmental impacts aspect from mature stage. Its business activities must raise, dramastic expansion during this period, such as underdeveloped country, US, UK. In order to acheive long term sustainable development , new demands are being placed on transport sector, such as underground mass transit rail transport , ferry, local air frieght transport, train , e.g. Japan, Fance, US high speed prior rail. Because their developed countries , business and entertainment activities needs increase, it influences high time efficient and rapid speed public transportation tools needs are also needed in societies. These new technological public transport tools invention will impact on climate, noise, human health, land use and damage to ozene layer, acidification aspects, instead of economic beneficial aspect.

For long -term sustainable development to be achieved, the various activities within developed and underdeveloped societies must be adapted to what can be tolerated by humans and by the natural environment. Transport is an activity which affects humans and the natural environment for both the development of society as a whole as well as for the mobility for the individual. For Swedish underdeveloped country example, air pollution in Swedish urban areas has beed reduced, but in many places concentrations of certain substances deiving from transport activities are still at unacceptable levels and much more has to be done. Carbon dioxide emissions and noise are examples of environmental problems demanding further efforts. Measures to limit the exploitation of valuable natural and cultural environments to protect biological diviersity are also needed. So, if Swedish still hopes to develop its tourism industry to attract many travellers to choose to travel itself country. It needs to solve environmental problems from different modes of transport are of different dimensions, such as improving its air transport to avoid cause different problems and rail transport differs in turn from road transport.

The transport problem to Swedish may include poor technological communication information to its public and purchasers of transportation and communication services as to the environmental effects of different solutions is significant in creating the demand for environmentally sound public transport service concepts. It is therefore important that such lacking high technological communication and information system is presented in as completem accurate and clear way as a method for non-monetary comparison of the environmental public transport service system aspect.

In real, it's public tranport service system is needed to be improved and upgraded in order to let travellers feel Swedish's any rail, underground train, ferry, bus , taxi etc. different public transport travelling service can provide excellent performance to serve their travelling passengers, when they need to catch any kinds of public transport tools to go to travel. They can feel convenient and comfortable to attract them to visit Swedish to travel again. Then, its tourism industry GDP income will be raised, if Swedish government can innovate any new kinds of purchase ticket equipment to install in and public transport stations to let travelling passengers feel that they do not need to spend long time to queue to buy tickets to catch ferry, train, underground mass transit rail on stations conveniently. Because long time purchase ticket queue waiting will cause travellers feel its public service performance dissatisfaction and they will complain , even they won't choose to catch the kind of public transport, even the travellers won't choose to travel Swedish again, if they feel Swedish is one developed country, but it neglects to take care about travellers' catching public transport travelling service needs.

It is one poor or bad feeing to let travellers choose to Swedish again. Hence, Swedish needs to improve its public transport service performance in order to achieve to raise their comfortable and satisfactory catching public transport tools needs to let travellers to feel. They may include efficient land use for transportation tools, comprising issues concerning natural and cultural environment, natural resources, biological diversity and aesthetics, noise reducing, public transportation energy consumption and time consumption reducing, raising public transport service facilities performance functions and other issues concerning the model. For example, Swedish government can facilitate the public transport price conparison and journey time spending comparison information gathering enquiring machines public transportation selection method of public transportation services to let every travellers can evaluate different modes of public transport when they are staying in ferry, bus, train, underground mass transit rail, taxi stations.

A travelling family can seek its sustainable transport selection system for passenger transport tool. When they touch the enquiry machine, they can compare busm ferry, train, underground train, taxi price and journey spending time from their transportation stations to another destinations. Then, travelling passengers can compare these public transport tools ticket prices, journey spending time immediately when they touch the public transport enquiring machines in stations any time. Then, they can make the most righ choice to decide whether they ought catch which kind of public transport tool to arrive the another journey destination. It is one every attractive high technological enquiry method to help any travelling passegners to choose which kind of public transport tool, it can be the most cheap transport tool at the moment in any public transport stations. So , for developed countries innovative its public transport service performance will need future passengers' journey needs daily. Hence, they can not neglect how to improve public transport service needs to satisfy passengers to fccl satisfaction, if Sweden government hopes its tourism industry can raise GDP income in long time.

● Electronic vehicle invention causes underground train MTR passengers to feel catching time reducing .

It has close relationship between globalization and global tranport development. How globalisation impacts on the environment via changes taking place in the transport sectors. In fact, it is not clear how the relative price changes that result from openness will affect the environental composition of economic activity. For example, some countries will produce more environmentally intensive goods, others will produce fewer. On the other hand, liberalisation will raise incomes, perhaps increasing the willingness to pay for environmental improvement. These potential income effects increased outweigh the negative scale effects with increased economic activities. When combined with the positive effects with technology transfer, the net effect on local pollutants could be positive . Hence, we need to find methods to solve the problem of raising transport economic activities and serious environmental pollution creating as the same time occurrence.

Globalisation helps to facilitate greater division of labor, and to exploit its comparative advantage more completely. In longer term, globalization also stimilates technology an dlabour transfers, and allows the dynamism that accompanies economic activities to stimulate the development of new transport technologies and short time transport processes that lead to global welfare improvement.

On shipping transport industry aspect, shipping will increase ocean pollution, when international shipping activities are increasing. Trade and shipping encourages energy use in shipping is coupled with the movement of waterborne commerce. The estimates depending on the transport goods number of at-sea or in port days much increase globally every day. The energy demand of international shipping fuel sale number and domestically assigned fuel sales number also increases for global fuel usage. Estimates of ocean going ships now consume about 2% to 3% and perhaps even as much as 4% of world fossil fuels.Hence, when global shipping energy fuel usage number increases, because global shipping trading activities number increases. It will bring the environmental pollution to ocean level increases. On air transport industry aspect, their travellers' catching air plans travelling needs and businesses' goods transport air delivery service needs are increasing from the requirements for high quality , fast and reliable international transport. Moreover, the networks that airline companies operate have changed often to hub-and spoke networks, many new often low -cost companies have entered the air freight market, any long time air journey is needed, e.g. Australia airline expands its one new air journey flies to UK, it needs two days flying time. It means that every flight to UK from Australia , it needs to use more fuel to fly. Then , air pollution will increase also.

On road transport industry aspect, global road transport cost and transit times, traffic jam occurrence chances also increase because when the road building number is increasing globally. So, it will cause traffic jam and long journey time spending , even fuel usage spending number is also increased. Then, accident occurrence chance is raised. Hence, global business or entertainment transport activities number increasing , it will bring much negative impact on environmental pollution, traffic jams number increases, long journey spending time increases, fuel usage number increases. Although , frequent transport activities may bring GDP income.

On transport service industy aspect, but is also brings negative influence to standard of living. It means that when transport fuel demand increases, transport activities number increases, GDP income on relative any transport activities needs industy , e.g. logistic demand needs, when lorry drivers need to drive lorries to deliver goods from one warehouse to another warehouse or supermarket or office etc. different business places on the road driving activities increase. But, it also bring air pollution , traffic noise and traffic jam etc. transport problems to road and natural environment and raises worse standard of living , bad emotion to working people or learning emotion to students , due to frequent traffic jam causes , low efficiency and productivity to workers, even student individual learning time can be reduced if they need to spend long time to wait bus, ferry, rail, underground train to go to schools , due to frequent long time traffic jam occurs on the roads to influence they can not go to schools on time often when they are catching buses to go to schools absolutely in busy transport time.

Thus, although any countries need to consider how to design their transport system, e.g. how to e.g. how to choose the right locations to build roads to let many cars can be driven available easily when the morning and evening (office and school transport busy time, e.g. 6:00 to 9:00 AM morning, 6:00 to 9:00 PM in the evening transport time usually because these two transport periods are usually , there are many students and working people need to catch any public transportation or drive cars tools to go back homes. So, enough roads number and long and not narrow road area must be needed to design in order to let enough cars be driven on the roads in the transport busy times to the countries have many big cities or have high population , such as UK, US, China, India, Hong Kong. They have many people , but drivers and cars numbers both are increasing. So, efficient road design and road number are also needed to increase in order to let drivers can transport goods to deliver, students and working people can catch any public transport tools to arrive any destinations on reads in the short time rapidly in order to avoid to spend long time transportation time and late to arrive any destinations in possible occurrence. So, any sudden traffic jam is not hoped to be caused by easy traffic accidents occurrence any time.

Hence, global efficient road transport system is needed, when global transport activities are increased, because any road logistic transport activities are increasing, they will also influence the students and working people when they also need to catch any public transport tools or drive themselves cars to go to working places or schools on the roads at the same busy transport time between 6:00 to 9:00 AM morning busy transport time and between 6:00 to 9:00 PM evening busy transport time. Because these both times will be have many students, working people , they need either go to offices or schools or go to homes. Hence, if the country had many lorry drivers need to drive their lorries to deliver goods on the roads in the transport busy morning or evening time in the same driving time on the roads. It will increase the risk to cause frequent traffic jam or traffic accident occurrence easily in possible in the country. So, any countries' governments can not neglect how to design roads and choose anywhere are the roads suitable locations to be built as well as anywhere land useful number to build road location choices in order to solve geographical traffic jams occurrence chance.

Hence, globalization of transport activities may bring geographical GDP growth, but it also bring traffic jams and traffic accidents occurrences, hearing impairment due to traffic noise, air pollution, traffic crashed, bad working emotions to workers and bad learning emotions to students, due to spending long transport time when traffic jam or traffic accidence occurs more easily.

However, transportation is an important tool if a country's progress. Rapid economic growth and increasing level of urbanization enhances a person's living standard have, it leads to a greater travel demands. Hence, governments ought not neglect have to design its roads , measure every road's length or width whether it has how many cars need to drive in morning or evening transport busy time for students, working people and delivery goods drivers of public transportation tools or private transportation tools easy driving needs in order to avoid frequent traffic jams or traffic accidents occurrences in possible.

Moreover, any governments also need to solve these issues, if they hope to develop their transport system successfully. These issues include : What mode of transportation to cost-effective in meeting a region's transportation needs to the country? How should a state department of transportation prioritize its highway delivers to maximize economic growth? What is the trade-off between additional growth in urban area and the cost of expanding transportation systems to accommodate greater growth? What effect does the expansion of transportation systems have on the need to invest in other types of transport modes? For example , the transport expansion may include the construction of additional highway segments, rail lines, runways, or additional sea, air, rail or bus terminal capacity using traditional technology; highway may include the additional of lanes to an interstate highway system; the conversion of an existing two-lane road to a four lane limited access highway, replacement or widening of bridges, and the extension of an existing road. Airport examples, include runway lengthening, apron expansion, and additional terminal gates.

On the other hand, enhancement to new transport technologies may bring efficiency of the existing highway system, examples may include intelligent highway systems, congestion pricing, intermodal freight facilities, geographic positioning systems, and instrument landing systems to mention of a few major transport innovations. So, transport policy makers need to understand the effects of these new transport mode innovations on economic development or GDP growth on transport activities growth transportation services and a more efficient use of limited land supplying scarce resources , air quality ,and noise pollution, traffic jams, long spending transport time to students, working people, entertaining people, even deliver goods lorry drivers their every day essential driving activities or catching public transportation tools needs problems. For example, the concept of intelligent highway systems needs increase trend. In simply , vehicles are being linked to each other and to traffic control devices to improve the efficiency of the total highway system. Similar types of innovations in intelligent traffic management are increasing needs for air, sea, and rail systems. The question is that whether intelligent highway systems can attribute of highways on economic development, raising on productivity of reducing highway congestion or improving pavement condition.

In fact, many developed countries' transportation system is mature. The nation has gone beyond the frontier of building, the interstate highway system and connecting most cities (markets). Tweaking the system with additional lanes and the new intelligent highway systems are useful in China, US, UK, because they have many cities. SO, road efficient traffic congestion control is needed when many students, working people, delivery goods transport people need to drive cars or catch cars on every city's roads in the transport busy time between 6:00 to 9:00 AM morning transport busy time as well as between 6:00 to 9:00 PM evening transport busy time.

However, transportation investment must be needed, if the country hoped to have good economic productivity, efficient transport service can bring good effects on the flows goods and people on roads every day when they use the country's transport system. So, any countries need to collect data, they can not be lack of enough transport information in any time that links anywhere locations of any drivers to the locations of the transport system that provide them with services in any time, e.g. every day morning and evening transport busy time, radio can report the real transport time of any roads traffic jam or traffic accident message to let drivers to listen to know whether anywhere roads are occurring traffic accidents or traffic jams or when the road traffic accident or traffic jam is solved to let the drivers can know whether when the roads can be opened to drive again. So, real time road transport message information is needed to report by radio, in order to let any drivers to know whether they ought choose to drive themselves cars on the road when they need to choose anywhere road to drive to the destination if they can know when the road has traffic accident or traffic jam occurs. They won't drive their cars on the road in the moment immediately.

On conclusion, globalization can being frequent transport economic activities. So, road , air, sea, transport service users' transport service needs are also increased. Every country ought not neglect how to innovate their transport service in order to satisfy their transport needs to achieve economic growth, efficient and short transport time spending, productivities increase, reducing air pollution, traffic noise , raisins standard of living on transport influence aspect to satisfy working people, students, entertaining people, delivery goods transport users' efficient road transport time behavioral spending aspect.

Artificial Intelligent In Road Transportation Strategy
● How artificial intelligent vehicle may interact intelligent transportation tools

Can artificial intelligence (AI) and machine learning (ML) be used in the search for new " consumption" behavioral type variables that affect consumer individual or transportation service organization individual different transportation tools choices, such as road or sea or sky transportation tools? Can artificial intelligent vehicle may interact intelligent transportation tools market development?
Consumers usually have bargaining and on risk choice when they are already shopping, such as who need to accept to use any (AI) new technological products to replace human traditional behaviors, such as intelligent non-manual driving transportation market, e.g. cars are needed to be driven by human drivers on road, but it has bargaining and on risky choice, when non-manual (AI) vehicle buyers who need to depend on non-manual artificial intelligent (ML) system assists them to drive their cars on the roads.
So, any non-manual driving auto car buyers must need to believe (AI) non-manual driving vehicles (ML) systems can make accurate driving judgement

to reduce or avoid any traffic accident occurrences more than human drivers' driving judgement when the (ML) systems are driving their cars on the roads. Then the intelligent vehicle manufacturers will have possible to sell their non-manual driving vehicles success.

This is the first reason or idea influences consumer individual choice to buy any kinds of (AI) non-manual driving vehicles, when consumers believe (ML) systems are more safe and make more accurate judgement to compare human or computer systems, when they are sitting in one non-manual auto driving vehicle on the road.

The another second reason or idea is that some common limits on driving consumer prediction might be understood as the kinds of errors made by poor implementation of machine learning.

Supposing driving consumers believe (AI) machine learning ability is worse to compare to human learning ability. It will also influence driving consumers do not accept to use any (AI) non-manual auto driving vehicles to replace every driver is essential on driving by himself/herself on the road. The third idea or reason is that it is important to influence driving customers believe how (AI) non-manual auto driving technology is used in them can both overcome and exploit human driving skill and safe limits and raise more auto driving safe judgement to compare human driving safe judgement.

However, how to predict any kinds of (AI) non-manual driving vehicles future consumption effort, due to different kinds of (AI) non-manual driving transportation vehicles which have different unique functions and designs to be used by different kinds of road transportation or driving demand of consumers. For example, lorry drivers need non-manual intelligent system can help them to drive fast, but safe to assist them to transport cargo to arrive destinations from their factories or offices. Otherwise, private car driver expects whose (AI) non-manual driving vehicle can auto drive to send to whom to arrive destination in safe way and non-too fast and non-too slow speed in order to avoid accident occurrences.

So, a different road intelligent consumer demand is to define whose individual driving behavior and driving habit and driving attitude and driving judgement and driving speed demand to decide how to design whose intelligent vehicle to satisfy those driving demand more generally, as simply being open-minded about what variables are likely to influence every consumer economic choice, when who decide either to buy any kinds of (AI) products or not to buy any kinds of (AI) products to replace the different demand of consumers their different (AI) useful demand.

Hence, for these three (AI) products group of stakeholders, such as home (AI) consumer group, firm (AI) consumer group and government (AI) consumer group . These consumer groups may consider whether different kinds of (AI) products can give what is special beneficial interest to them to use. These variables can be measurable properties of choices to influence them to choose to buy any (AI) kinds of (AI) products to use, e.g. psychophysiological, biological, social influences, consumer's wealth, moods and personality, (AI) product price etc. variable factors which will influence them to decide to attempt to buy any kinds of (AI) products to use.

If behavioral economics is as open-mindedness about what variables might predict. Then , (AI) machine learning system is a way to do behavioral economics because it can make use of a wide set of variables and select- which ones predict.

In behavioral economic view point, when general consumer overall demand to the product is much than the other similar (AI) non auto driving vehicle products, such as any kinds of (AI) non-manual auto driving vehicles and any kinds of manual driving vehicles case, then any kinds of (AI) non-manual auto driving vehicles will be more attractive to cause many manual driving vehicle buyers choose to buy (AI) non-manual auto driving vehicles. Hence, it seems if any kinds of (AI) non-manual auto driving vehicle products can make more attractive variable efforts to influence overall driving consumers to feel that they have more needs to drive non-manual auto vehicles to compare more than driving manual driving vehicle.

What is the main variable effort to intelligent vehicles to attract driving consumers to choose to accept to drive them ? However, I believe that (AI) machine learning system is a main factor to raise overall driving consumers' acceptances to drive it to replace manual driving vehicle. If it can persuade or prove (AI) machine learning system ability and judgement effort is more accurate than human or computer learning effort or judgement effort, then it is possible that any kinds of (AI) non-manual driving vehicle products will be accepted to drive on the road in popular.

Machine learning system is able to find prediction value in details of how the bargaining occurs. This discovery is the beginning of the next step for driving consumer individual driving behaviors or driving habits. It raises questions that include: What variables predict to influence driving consumers to change whose driving habits or driving attitudes? How can driving consumer individual emotion, face-to-face talking with whose friends when they are sitting in the non-manual driving vehicle to influence whom driving habit or driving attitude to be changed ? Do driving consumers consciously understand why those habit driving attitudes variables are important when they are sitting in one intelligent vehicle? Can (AI) driving machine learning methods capture the effects of motivated cognition to influence driving consumers decide to buy any kinds of (AI) non-manual auto vehicle products more attractively. So, it seems (AI) driving machine learning method is a main variable factor to influence driving consumers to feel who have more confidence to drive them more than any other kinds of similar manual driving vehicles on the road.

Consequently, (AI) driving machine learning system will be one important psychological method to influence driving consumers to choose to buy (AI) auto driving vehicle products to replace manual driving vehicles. The reason is because human and driving machine learning system both which will have limited variable factors to influence general different countries (AI) driving consumers' need desire to be raised.

● Why can (AI) driving machine learning system main factor influence driving consumer individual desires ?

Driving consumer expectations are hard to measure or predict driving attitudes and driving behaviors in (AI) non-manual driving vehicles market. Artificial intelligence is another kind of computer science development to apply intelligent vehicle market. Why do driving consumers feel need to buy any kinds of (AI) auto driving vehicles to drive to replace manual driving vehicles on the roads? What are (AI) auto driving features different to manual driving features?

(AI) is the recreation of cognitive functions in computers; it enables machines to perform tasks like humans and perhaps even better than human. In the real world, scientists develop the technological singularity, in which a superintelligence emerges with unfold human consequences.

Professionals in many industries are intensely interested in the specifics of what (AI) can do today, and how can it helps. They are considering the impact of applied (AI), in which computers are used to address a particular problem, extracting and utilizing patterns found in large volumes of data. Of all (AI)'s subfields, machine learning is attracting the most attention. I shall explain why (AI) machine learning system is the main factor to lead consumers feel need to buy any (AI) products to use. Such as below:

For smartphone, fraud detection to medical diagnosis etc. applied (AI) technological products examples. (AI) machine learning systems can help any one of these products to do any exceed general computer learning systems which (AI) learning systems can do any skills to supply (AI) users to use to compare computer learning systems can not do any skills to supply compute users to use. It seems that (AI) machine learning system is the unique feature to attract consumer consideration in technological product market.

An term for different types of learning, and can be accomplished using different techniques. This has led to a perception that all marketing teams should have (AI) to bring a unified personalized customer experience, when consumers choose to buy any (AI) products to feel what are the different or unique characteristics to compare general computer products. Such as (AI) product has this unique machine learning characteristics, we can predict (AI) and machine learning is connected to influence consumers to feel needs.

Furthermore, over the same time period, and in contrast to predictions for roles in many industries. (AI) won't take the place of marketers and merchandisers themselves although it is already a new value to analytical and strategic marketing skills to persuade consumers to buy any (AI) products. It means different kinds of (AI) products will have different machine learning effort and unique characteristics to attract consumers to choose to buy them to use. Such as, when intelligent vehicles need have unique road driving or sea transportation or flying machine learning system when they are applied on these three kinds of transportation tool aspects. They need have good response safety driving and immediate response learning systems to avoid any boats or air planes or vehicles to crash to them to reduce accident occurrences immediately on any one of either road or sky or sea journey environment.

What is the reason why (AI) driving machine learning system can influence good at making sense to driving consumer desire? Only humans (drivers) , preferably experienced, well informed humans can understand their driving customer needs and decide how to design or reengineer any (AI) intelligent vehicle product functions. (AI) intelligent vehicle can give these professionals the means to do this better to compare manual driving immediate response control function when any vehicles are driving or they will stop immediately to close / near to them in order to reduce crash occurrence on the road, and then maximize relevance through real-time customization of the non-manual auto vehicle driving user experience.

For example, as ever, senior decision makers need to be informed, decisive and results-oriented or risk losing out. Harvard Business Review indicated : Over the next decade, (AI) won't replace managers, but managers who use (AI) will replace those who don't. Such as intelligent vehicle won't replace drivers, but drivers who use intelligent vehicles will replace those who can not control how to drive their vehicles in the most safe way. So, (AI) driving machine learning system will have possible to do any drivers' (human's) driving judgement, driving analytical mind and driving effort to be more accurate than manual driving skills. Such as how to control to drive the intelligent vehicle in the most safe way. It is general manual driving skill can not achieve to drive in the safe way.

For another (AI) digital commerce example, (AI) and machine learning are the most exciting developments in marketing and merchandising to be applied to digital commerce, such as making better decisions through trend and cluster analysis, deploying product and content in mutually reinforcing combinations, increasing customer engagement and satisfaction in real time.

Hence, the key attraction in digital commerce circles is that machine learning is designed to be self-optimizing. Optimizing for revenue example will surface are increasingly profitably selection of products (within the brand parameters selected).

When to apply (AI) capabilities and what value (AI) is delivering for customer and company like. Unlike any technology before it, (AI) is analytical and predictive capabilities offers the prospect for each and every individual. It can maximize real time and engagement. Effective tailored (AI) technology, such as digital experience cloud technology is available now. And once integrated, (AI) starts learning and delivering incremental value from day one. So (AI) could transform the digital experience to any business organizations.

Hence, (AI) driving machine learning system can be applied to road driving skill aspect. When intelligent vehicles are invented to own the most safe driving judgement skill and they can know when either they may auto drive fast speed, when they are feeling to know when there are not many vehicles are moving close/near to them or when they need auto drive slow speed, when they are feeling to know when there are many vehicles are moving close/ near to them. Then driving consumers will have more confidence to choose to buy any kinds of intelligent vehicles to replace manual driving vehicles to drive on the roads.

● Non-manual driving transportation tool market development

If Non-manual driving vehicle manufacturers expect their (AI) automatic vehicles can attract drivers to buy. I feel them to need to consider how (AI) driving machine learning system can achieve these requirements in order to satisfy manual driving vehicle drivers' requirement to change their traditional driving habit to choose non-manual driving needs. It means (AI) driving machine learning systems can help them to drive vehicles to replace manual driving vehicles on the road. This is the main factor to influence car buyers choose to buy intelligence driving vehicles replace to manual driving vehicles. I believe (AI) non-manual driving vehicle machine learning systems, need to be designed as below:

(1) Improving driving safety by preventing accidents from happening.
Every year, drivers are facing a large number of casualties, due to traffic accidents. The amount of killed and injured road traffic related accidents is increasing every year. The real cost of an accident can go well beyond the limits of immediate material destruction, and is impossible to evaluate.
Hence, researchers and car manufacturers are looking for solutions in order to reduce the amount of accidents. They already developed a considerable set of technologies in order to decrease the amount of casualties. Most of them (like airbags, seat-belts, anti-lock systems, shock absorbing car bodies) are efficient in decreasing the impact of an accident, and in protecting the passengers of the cars. The technologies already saved a lot of lives, but they are rarely able to avoid accidents because they do not anticipate them. Moreover, if they are protecting in many cases, the passengers of the car, they do not prevent most traffic participants, like pedestrians on bicyclists from getting injured. it causes (AI) non-manual automatic car manufacturers need to consider how to design machine learning safety system is to prevent accident from happening instead of just reducing their impact.
This can only be possible using intelligent systems that can observe the driving environment, reason and decide if there is a danger, determine how to avoid it and act if necessary

(2) Reducing energy consumption by optimizing the driving.
Nowadays, global air pollution is serious. (AI) non-manual driving car manufacturers need to concern how to design (AI) machine learning system

can reduce degree of air pollution to be the most minimum level to compare to traditional manual driving vehicles.

The reduction of energy consumption if certainly one of the main challenges. Transportation is one of the major factors in fossil energy consumption, and it is also responsible for a large amount of CO2 pollution. It is difficult to ask individuals to voluntarily limit the use of their vehicle of they do not have a strong incentive to do so. Specially in regions where vehicles are needed to drive to go to work every day. It stands to reason that if it is difficult to decrease the amount of vehicles, part of the solution is to make them more energy efficient.

Hence, non-manual driving car manufacturers need to design how to improve engines, which are more optimized and need less fuel to operate, and hybrid and electric cars have been developed and are continuously being improved. But we can go beyond these solutions that do not take into account the environment in which a vehicle is driving. A growing number of scientific contributions presented intelligent systems used in order to improve energy efficiency and reduce fuel consumption, based on the optimization of the way (AI) non-manual driving (AI) vehicles are performing. Such as recharge batteries and electric engine will be predicted the popular fuel in order to limit fuel consumption to future (AI) non-manual driving vehicles. They can reduce air pollution, consume less fuel for (AI) non-manual driving vehicles.

(3) Improving comfort by anticipating (AI) non- manual driving vehicle drivers.

Finally, another application for intelligent vehicle is the improvement of driving comfort. Car industry is very competitive market. Many potentials (AI) intelligent vehicle customers need to enjoy to sit more comfortable intelligent vehicles, who will be attracted by (AI) comfortable systems improving when driving, so part of the research in intelligent systems from cars focuses on how to improve the driving experience, i.e. make it easier and more enjoyable, more comfortable to compare to traditional manual driving vehicles.

As an example, lane keeping assistant systems are technologies that actively keep the vehicle in the lane in highways of the driven drifts out of it. Automatic speed regulation keeps the car at a certain speed without requiring to touch the gas pedal. This can be really interesting for, e.g. (AI) non-manual driving truck drivers that spend a lot of time on highways. But these technologies have a limitation in the case of automatic speed regulation, this technology can not copy of a vehicle ahead drives slower than the desired speed, or if another vehicle cuts into the lane.

This case requires the driver to have a constant focus on the road. In order to achieve more comfort, it is better of the system can adapt to changes in its dynamic environment: let the (AI) intelligent vehicle adapt to the speed of the man-manual vehicle, or autonomously change lane when requires. Again, this requires knowledge about the environment, detection capabilities, reasoning and action planning. Intelligent systems can be used in order to create more attractive and more comfortable and more safe, less energy consumption and less fuel expenditure by intelligent vehicles.

Factors influence public transport service industry reaches life cycle decline stage

In our future road public transport service development. Does underground train improvement bring another new public transport service experience to let passengers to experiece another new road public transport service replace traditional bus, tram, train, taxi , rapid speed train etc. public transport tool service by this kind new " exceed sound speed" underground train public transport tool? Can this kind of " exceed sound speed" underground train public service transport tool replace traditional bus, train, tram, taxi, road piblic transport tools ? Will traditional road public transport tools experience to reach decline life cycle service stage from maturity life cycle service stage in soon future possible, if this kind of " new exceed sound speed innovation underground train is invented ?

What is exceed sound speed underground train ? It can run exceed sound speed to catch above four to eight passengers to sit in the small size circle shape underground train from one distination to another destination in short time. For example, it can run at exceed sound speed at underground from US Washington city to New York city, in the future, it will be possible one kind of small circle size underground train, it may only catch about one to eight passengers every journey, when this kind of new exceed sound speed underground train was really invented. Can it replace traditional slow speed underground train and road public transport tools to be accepted by many passengers?

In this US future new exceed sound speed small size underground train public transport tool case, it only needs spend half hour to transport passengers from US Washington to New York city rapidly. In general, underground train speed needs about three hours from Washington to New York city distance. So, it can shorten time to let passengers to avoid any delay. The question is that : Can it influences future global public transport service life cycle stage to reach decline life service cycle life in short time, if this kind of new exceed sound speed small size underground train public transport tool is invented in success? I shall attempt to answer whether future new sound speed rapid small size underground public tranport service train invention, it will influence other traditional public transport tools to reach the decline life service cycle stage rapidly in short time as below:

In our traditional public transport development history, since 1900, human had been beginning to consider every country ought own themselves public transport fools, e.g. for passengers service. So, passengers can pay cheap ticket to catch either bus, or tram, or train ot ferry, or taxi, or underground train from one destination to another destination in short time conveniently. So, public transport tool needs had been popular increasing, because there were not many people like to buy cars to drive when any kinds of public tranport tools are invented in 1900 beginning. The reason may be that they feel expensive gas expenditure and cars will need to repair or become old etc. different reasons. So, from 1900, public transport tool service tools may be whole public transport service industry's birth life cycle service stage. In this stage, global any passengers had been attempting to choose to catch either bus, trains, trams, taxi, underground trains etc. public transport tools to go to anywhere conveniently. They would compare whether public transport service can provide comfortable feeling and rapid transport service quality to be better than purchase one car to drive.

Hence, in this global public transport service birth life cycle stage, global human had been attempting any kinds of public transport tools catching feeling whether which one kind could bring more comfortable service feeling , e.g. bus service is better or tram service is better or train service is better or underground train service is bettr or ferry service is better. Hence, in global whole public transport industry tools will be compared by all passengers . Passengers will choose the best kind of public transport tool to catch in any time when they feel need. Hence, bus, taxi, train, tram, underground train, ferry transport service performance level must bee very high to avoid their passengers to make decision to choose another kind of public transport service to replace them.

From 1900 to 1950, global public transport service had been experiencing fair or birth stage competition because any one passenger had been attempting to choose which kind of public transport tool to replace purchase car need. After 1950, global public transport service had been experiencing growth life cycle service stage. Because many people began to feel different kinds of public transport tools prices are cheap and reasonable . So global had had many different transport tools to replace purchase cars needs to anyone. Also, bus, taxi, ferry, train, tram , underground train number and transport service frequent time will need to increase in order to satisfy increasing passengers transport service needs in transport service market.

After 1990, global transport service industry had been experiencing mature life cycle service stage, instead of non owning car people must need to catch any kinds of public transport tools to go to aywhere, even owning car people, when they feel that they often drive cars, frequent driving car behavior may bring high gas expenditure in long time. So, when they feel any one kind of transport tool can transport them to go to anywhere conveniently in short time. On the day, they will not drive themselves cars to go to anywhere, they will choose any one kind of public transport tools to go to the destination on that day, because they do not want to spend much gas expenditure or avoid traffic jam or accident occurrence when they need to go to the destination in shor time.

So, in this mature public transport service life cycle stage, global any one includes owning car person and non owning car person, we had been accepted to choose any one kind of public transport tool to replace cars to go to any destinations conveniently. Because bus stations number increased, bus number increases, bus can arrive in short time, taxi, train, tram , ferry , underground train public transport tools services can follow bus service to provide accurate shorten arrival time, comfortable catching environment, reasonable price, none delay arrival time, high passengers transport service quality to let global any one passenger to feel satisfactory. Hence, after 1980, global public transport service had been experiencing mature life cycle service stage.

Global public tranport service needs had been increasing. At the same time, when any one kind of public transport tool is popular to be accepted to choose to catch by any one passenger. In this suitation, if one kind of public transport tool is improved, e.g. shorten transport distance, arrival destination time can be decreased, price is reasonable cheap, such as Japan rapid speed train, China, prior rapid speed train etc. These rapid speed electric trains can transport many passengers from one station to another station in short time. So, in road train service industry, nowadays, it is experiencing mature life cycle service stage. It means that any passengers will be influenced to catch this kind of rapid speed train in prefer to compare tram, traditional old speed train, bus, ferry to catch.

However, in the future, it is possible that one kind of underground train may be invented successfully. It is short circle size underground train, it can catch one to maximum eight passengers only for every journey in underground. Nowadays, US scientists had been attempting to manufacture this kind of " exceed sound speed‘" underground train, if it can be invented in success, it may catch maxium eight passengers from Washington to New York city within half hour time . In general, traditional US underground train needs two to three hours to catch passengers from Washington underground train station to New York underground train station. So, if this kind of " exceed sound speed" underground train is invented in success, it will be possible to influence global public transport train, tram, bus, ferry, taxi, public transport tool passengers number may be influenced to reduce, duc to its fee is reasonable cheap, more comfortable, rapid destination arrival and on time arrival transport service etc. factors.

The question is that: How this kind of " exceed sound speed underground train tool" bring positive or negative changes to influence global public transport service life cycle stage?

Nowadays, rapid speed train or underground train public service transport tool had changed traditional gas energ train or electric train transport service need to mature life cycle stage. Since electric train or rapid speed train invention. This kind of public transport had provided one kind of more comfortable and rapid transport service choice to any passengers. So, train or underground train transport tool compares to general bus, tram , ferry to experience rapid mature life service cycle stage. Many passengers many feel to catch underground train or train in preference because their ticket prices are reasonable cheap and they are provided rapid short time journey to arrive any destinations any any countries. For London underground is a rapid transit system serving greater histry . These two ran electric trains in circular tunnels having diameters.

In 1933, most of London's underground railways, tramway and bus services are accepted in popular . Hence, UK, LOndon railway public transport tool has developed long time. The average speed on the London underground is 20.5 miles per hour, including station stops. On Metropolitan line, trains can reach over 60 mph. The shortest distance between teo adjacent stations on the network is only 260 metres and the longest is 6.3 kilometres.

Nowadays, the fastest underground train is the Victoria line, it can reach speeds up tp 50 mph because the stations are further apart. The metropolitan line has the fastest train speeds, sometimes reaching over 60 mph. IS light rail faster than buses? IN fact the data is from the National trainsit database website and it shows that it costs almost twice as much, one average to move one light rail vehicle per hour versus onw bus. Hence, light rail must be faster than buses, comparing rail versus bus trainsit transport service life cycle stages, rail versus may reach mature transport service life cycle stage. Otherwise, bus transit transport service life cycle stage will be possible to be influenced to experience decline life service cycle stage from nowadays mature stage. The reason is that future " sound speed underground rail transport will be possibe to invent successfully. Then, this kind improved exceed sound speed underground train transport tool may replace to traditional electric train or underground electric rail, when any countries passengers can accept to choose to catch this kind of developed " exceed sound speed" underground rail tranport tool in habit.

In fact, underground rail versus bus tranit focus primary on vehicle travel speeds and operating, per capita vehicle travel grew rapidly between 1970 and 2000. If one day, US " exceed sound speed" underground short size rail is invented successfully., it will change the whole traditional public tranport service industry mode to persuade passengers to enjoy this kind " exceed sound speed feeling" and choose to catch this kind public transport service in preference, due to they can enjoy rapid short time destination arrival journey, and it can bring benefit to transport providers for lifecycle saving energy and emission carbon pollutants reduces. It may reach the rail public transport tool invention to the topest mature life cycle service stage, if this kind of exceed sond speed underground train can be invented successfully. It means that rail transport service industry only needs to spend less developing time to reach the mature life cycle service stage from birth and growth life cycle service stages .

In global whole public transport service life cycle development stage, underground rail transport tool is the most rapid experiencing the topest mature life cycle service stage of only one kind public transport tool to compare bus, ferry, tram , train . Although, transport infrastructure has long operational life, there are too many urban public transport networks, including light rail (metro and tram), but if the kind of new " exceed sound speed" underground rail can be real invented. Then, in underground rail public transport tool development history, it will help underground electric rail development to let any passengers to feel more comfortable, most rapid, reasonable ticket price and convenient underground journeys in every day. Hence, if it can be invented successfully, it will not only help whole rail transport service to reach mature life service cycle stage or it will be future the best or the most comfortable one kind of using public transport tool choice to global any passengers by 2041. Because when it could real be invented in success, it proved that it may fight physical barriers and fast moving or elevated sound speed levels can cause that any passengers can feel more comfortable and none long time distance to arrive destination anywhere. For example, if this kind of exceed sound speed underground short size rail transport tool can transport US passengers from tunnel to go through ocean to another countries stations. Then, any one does not need to catch airplane transport or ship to go to another country easily. They can catch it to go through ocean underground tunnels to any country from ocean in short time also. So, instead of this kind of sound speed underground rail can replace traditional tram, train, transport service on the road, even it can also replace airplanes and ships, ocean and air transport service by 2041 in the future. So, its transport inventio may change global traditional transport mode, it can provide underground ocean tunnel and underground and tunnel transport channels to arrive any underground road tunnel transport channels to arrive any destinations conveniently. Then, it can bring shop and airplane transport service changes to let wholc passengers to have more one kind of new transport tool choice, such as underground exceed sound speed rail feeling need. So, ship and airplane transport service life cycle may also be influenced to experience decline life cycle service cycle stage after 2041, if this kind of exceed sound speed short circle size underground rail could be invented in success to catch any countries passengers spend short time to catch it to go to another countries' underground rail stations from himself/herself country's underground rail station by ocean tunnel conveniently.

Consequently, future exceed sound speed underground short circle size rail public transport tool invention may influence other kinds of public transport tools to experience and reach decline life cycle service stage early after 2041, if it can real invent successfully by 204. Hence, it explains that why bus, tram, train, ferry, airplane transport tools need to continue to invent or improve rapid flying speed or rapid flight speed and comfortable feeling quality in order to fight this kind of future new exceed sound speed underground rail transport tool to avoid rapid decline life cycle service stage easily after 2041. So, " this kind of exceed sound speed small circle size underground rail" transport tool invention " it will bring global other different kinds of road and sea and air transport tool will face decline life service cycle stage early after 2041 in possible.

Economic recession or boom how influences consumer behavior when the business had been experiencing decline life cycle stage

COVID -19 disease how influence businesses may experience either growing life cycle stage or decline life cycle stage.

Nowadays, we are facing global economic recession period, since COVID 19 human mouth disease effect can bring economic crisis. Can it influence businesses feel difficult to adapt how global economic recession change after their decline life cycle stage? However, the effects of COVID 19 spreading will have wider implication , not just on how economies function, but also on how consumers behave, across china, Asia-pacific and around the world. Another effect of China;s economic rise is its influence in the adoption and adaption to new technological invention to manufacture , e.g. manufacturing robotic products had sold to China factories to replace workers to manufacturer products. It also will influence many China manufacturing workers lose jobs, when many China factories apply manufacture robotics to replace them in nowadays economic recession period.

Considering the adoption of online-offline shopping and home online office tasks, they are influenced by COVID-19 human disease influence, it also influences on regional travel in China, even global travel income is also reducing, because many travelers feel afraid to catch air planes to avoid to get COVID 19 human disease when they are sitting in close window airplanes by air . HOwever, COVID 19 also influences global consumer behavior changes to online shopping, because many people are afraid to enter crowd shops to avoid get COVID 19 human disease easily. So global shops will lose many visiting shop consumers, if they do not decide to attempt to open online stores to let customers to apply internet to buy their products. So, COVID 19 human mouth disease induced changes in consumer behavior. Shop online will be one new trend to influence young and old consumers make shopping from online stores. They will enquire whether the kind of product is worth to choose to buy by social media, e.g. facebook, online post . Hence, COVID19 human mouth disease may influence global economic recession, but it also brings e-commerce boom chance, when many consumers are fear to enter any crowd shops , when they need to stay long time in any shops. Then, they get COVID 19 human mouth disease chance will increase. Hence, it will influence many customers reduce to visit shops times, but it also creates online-shopping new business model . For example, China families are renewing their joy in home cooking. Onlns cooking videos are helping with the discovery od new recipes, new ways to create dishes , and new influences. So, opportunities are opening for more cleaning products, new ways to clean and new home hacks from online videos will bring global home consumers spend more time on their wellness or beauty routines ? So, COVID-19 disease also influences many families choose to cook dinner at homes at nght. Restaurants will lose many eating clients, because they are fear to enter restaurants to eat together to avoid to get COVID19 human mouth disease. But, it also creates home cooking products sale chance, e.g. rice cookers, dishes or any cooking tools because many families choose to cool at home. Hence, in some situation, economic recession will create new business chance , such as online store or rice cooker sale increases, they may be influenced in this COVID 19 human mouth disease occurrence environment.

Economic recession also influences business strategy changes. Many companies seem to be applying many aspects of a retrenchment approach , e.g. reduced fixed costs, narrower product offering, reduced staffs, but also there are some aspects of an investment approach which can be observed , because customers number will be influenced to reduce in economic recession environment. Companies have felt the robustness and quality of the approaches being applied had been allowed to decline. As a consequence of the challenges of a recession, urgent improvement have needed to be made because factories will reduce workers number to avoid salary expenditure spending more , but customers umber reduced in recession environment .

Hence, they will choose to buy manufacturing robotics to replace workers. If robotics can be improved to be proficient manufacture. Then, they won't need to buy many robotics to help them to replace to replace many workers to manufacture any products efficiently. So, manufacturing and improvement to robotics number demand may increase to any factories , e.g. vehicle manufacture, electronic products, e.g. computer hime cooking electronic products , e.g. rice cookers, heaters etc. products may be manufactured by manufacturing robotics. It creates the manufacturing robotic sale improvement quality chance in recession environment. It may impact on medium, or long term, it depends on how long time of recession. So, economic recession may bring robotic manufacture industry boom , when electronic products manufacturers need many improved robotics to replace workers in factries in order to reduce spending too much salaries expenditure in recession.

It is one external environmental factor to influence sudden manufacture robotic industry boom absolutely ,because electronic manufacturer's manufacturing robotic needs increases in recession environment. So, robotic manufacturers' strategy need to change , such as how to improve any manufacturers' needs in recession, e.g. manufacturing robotic product categories, market segments, geographic areas, core technologies, reliability , price, customisation, robotic manufacturing efficiency how to be improved of business.Change strategy to any manufacturing robotics manufacturers. So, recession may influence some kinds of manufacturing robotics' needs raise in robotic manufacturing market.

● How recession influences the role of advertising changes?

Advertising plays a key role in a dynamic economy. It may provide valuable information about products and services in an efficient manner, communicates client value, builds brand awareness and creates demand. However, when one country is experiencing recession, how it influences the country's businessmen spending on advertisement behaviors? Due to clients number reduces, a company usualy cuts come from the advertising budget than companies begin to cut back on advertiseing during an economic recession, they become less visible to the public because they predict clients number ought reduce next three months, even half year or one year. It depends on how long economt recession occurs. So, economic recession many impact any companies' advertising budget expenditure to be reduce . How much on the reduction on advertising budget expenditure, it depends on the company predicts how many clients number will reduce.However, due to advertising number reduces, it can influence consumer behavior changes indirectly.

In economic boom environment, consumers can watch to different kinds advertisement from television. Advertisement may bring positive alternative evaluation phase of biying decision-making process is bring exposed to buy several communication messages. In such an economic boom environment, any organizations may be clearly heard by the consumers, after any advertisement programs are broadcasted on television. Therefore, advertisemtn can persuade clients to choose to buy the kind of product after the kind of product advertisement is broadcasted from television absolutely.

However, when recession occurs, any companies; advertisement time is shortened , even number is reduced . Hence, they can not receive any client's positive or negative feedback immediately in short time afer advertisements are broadcasted from television . So, recession may influence advertisement time is shortened and number is rediced . On consequence, companies can not have any repsonse to know whether how market or customers' demand is changing to themselves products in shor time.

However, recession may bring worse advertisement effect to influence any businesses . On one hand, there is a negative economic recession environment because of the negative media reporting, these would be a decline in demand for the products and services and eventually companies would want to save more than they spend , But in the other hand, when the companies cut back advertiseing expenditures, they become less visible to public. Hence recession may influence many companies brand image will be lost, due to spending on advertisement expenditure wil reduce. Then, clients number may be influenced to reduce, because they can not watch the kind of product advertisment from television home often.

When one country is encountering recession, how are the various components of household consumption affected ? How is the impact of the recesion distributed across socio-demografic group? How does the recession compare to previous recessions? When book will boom? In fact, any country's recession may impact consumer behavior changes, it depends on these factors: age, race, education and wealth groups resulted in a decline in consumption inequality. The rich group is the " wealth effect influence group" when recession comes, it may influence their wealth reduces, so their enjoyment dsires will be influenced to reduce, e.g. purchase expensive cars driving enjoyment desires, purchase expensive house living enjoyment desires. If one rich person loses jobs , it may influence him to spend less time to drive themselves cars, so consumption of gasline will be influenced to reduce.

Economic theory (e.g. consumer behavioral economic theory) predicts that when economic recession occurs, it will cause many businesses may experience decline cycle life stage rapidly, that link between income shocks and consumption has close relationship, such as rich person consumer group, if his income reduces, then he will buy less gas to drive himself car, even if he loses his job in recession environment, he will choose to sell his car to exchange cash. Hence, consumption may fall as a direct consequence of a fall in income induced by job loss, reduced hours or productivity and negative returns from assets, if there are long term changes to a household's econmic resource in recession environment. Hence, in recession environment, job loss or income reduction factors that may affect consumers and their shopping attitudes in the recession period. Otherwise, for low income group, recession may influence food consumption to low income consumer behavior changes to worse. Because low income person may reduce income ot lose job, then cheap food consumption will be influenced to worse to low income consumer group.

In recession period, if the food price is raised , due to the cost increase of food, it will lead to change in the reductin on quantity and type of food being purchase to low income food buyers. This may lead to a reduction in the quantity of food consumed and/or the substitution of high-priced food for cheaper food, which is often less nutritous and of worse quality. Hence in recession perios, low income food consumers will consider whether the kind of food price has how much increase or decrease. They won't consider the quantity of food consumed for maintaining energy balance and the quality of food consumed for maintaining ample intakes of protains, fats and micronutrients, such as vitamins, minerals and trace elements on food issue. So, if the kind of food price reduced in recession period, it ought may attract many low income food consumers number, even its food nutritious is worse. Hence, if the kind of meat price can be reduced in recession , the cheap types of meat consumption to low income consumer may be increased, even its nutritious is worse to compare the recession occurs before period.

On conclusion, in either economic recession or boom period, in general, consumer behavior will be influenced to change. Some products may be influenced to have higher sale in recession period, e.g. home electronic rice cookers , due to COVID 19 human mouth disease influenced many households choose to cook dinner at home at ight. Otherwise, some products may be influenced to have lowr sale., e.g. expensive cars sale in recession period, many high income people may lose jobs or reduce salaries , then it will influence their car purchase desires to be reduced. But if COVID 19 human mouth disease has medicine to kill this kind of disease. Then, economy will boom, many households will choose to go to restaurants to eat dinner. The, the electronic rice cookers sale number may reduce, when they reduce time to cook at home at night. Hence, it explains why economic recession or boom period may have impact to influence consumer behavior in behavioral economic view.

Applying business development strategy to raise the educational robotic manufacturer sale number in recession period

● What does business development strategy ?

An effecting business development strategy ought have these five steps: The first step is market analysis. Who are your clients , knowledge of your market? Second step is how to adopt for each penetration, your business needs to learn how to adopt for each group of clients, your first need to review your own capacbility. It is important that you are realistic and honest with yourselves over where clients truly sit, learn how to classify your clients into similar groups relative is the scale of the opportunity. Third step learns how to review your performance , market matrix to plot your results to help you determine your market penerstion. In addition, it will help you then discuss and consider various strategies for growth. By potting your clients you will get a sense of where your strengths and weaknesses are against the opportunity that total market offer.Fourth step learns how to consider alternative growth strategies on the market matrix. The final step , you need to consider these questions in order to decide whic is the most effective strategy for your business. For example, which model is the most (least effective? Why? which model work best for line managers, HR are finance, why? How might we most effectively progress from one model to the most reasonable questions?) Then, you will need to decide how to launch new services, new products, opening new markets, how accessing new geographic territories.

● How to apply business development strategy to help educational robotic manufacturers to enter traditional education market ?

Many thinkers concern robots that are used in manufacturing workplaces, homes, roads, hospitals and care centre aspect, but they don't feel robotics may be possible to apply on social service aspect, e.g. educational service aspect . In fact, robotic may have both functions. Industrial robotics, e.g. manufacturing function as well as service robotics, e.g. professional robotcs, medical robotics, entertainment robotics, e.g. toy and education robotics and service robotics , e.g. personal and domestic robotics.

Educational robotic is on the birth stage in its industry life cycle. So, any educational robotic products will need time to persuade schools or any educational institutions to buy their products to assist teachers to teach students in classrooms. The question is how to apply business development strategy to help the educational robotic manufacturer to develop its educational robotic products to persuade educational clients to choose to buy ? I shall attempt to explain as below:

Due to educational robotic product is one new educational tool to assist any schools to buy to assist teachers to improve teaching service performance to let students to feel more learning satisfaction, so any educational robotic products must need time to introduce whether what it can bring schools benefits to let students and teachers to feel. When robotic can be popular to use on manufacturing, educational service industries aspect, e.g. warehouse , factory, shopping center, even restaurant's kitchen cooking robotics, office environment's accounting, law draft etc. clerical robotics may be invented to replace human 's general simple tasks. However, if future robots can be applied to educational aspect, e.g. classroom, school teaching students. Can educational robotic may assist or replace teachers to teach students in clasrooms? Will future teachers be replaced by teaching robotics . I shall attempt to explain whether it is possible that educational robotic can be developed to global educational organizations successfully as below:

Robotic technology has been invented to own " mind " ability, e.g. writing words, writing song, simple calculation tasks reading tasks . So, future robotics can be invented to own " mind " ability, when robotics' mind ability can be improved to own how to " communication" ability and " analytical" ability. Then can it be possible to apply robotics to do teaching tasks in classrooms, e.g. learning any books , the it applies the book's contents to analyze any "knowledge" in order to follow the logic mind to teach students in classroom. It is one major factor to influence any schools to explain why they need to buy any educational robotic in schools in any educational robotic product business development strategy. So, they need to find whether what their educational robotic strengths , any competitors won't own or their product weaknesses, they need to improve their educational robotic products in order to attract educational organizations to choose to buy.

Can future teaching robotics learn to do teacher individual same education tasks? It will be absolute competitive point to any educational robotic product manufactures. If it is true, can teaching robotics may be trained to exceed teacher individual teaching skill? It is another competitive point to any educational robotic product manfacturers. Is it ethic to apply robotic to teach students to replace teachers if teaching robotic can perform better teaching service to compare teachers? If the eduational robotic manufactuer can persude the school can accept eduational robotic ethic issue to assist or replace teachers to do teaching tasks, then it's sale chance will raise. So, ethic to educational robotic will be another factor to develop the educational robotic business. Can teachers be teaching robotic's teaching assistant role if teaching robotics can have teaching ability to teacher in the school? So, if the educational robotic manufacturer can persuade the school to feel that its products can be teacher's assistant to improve their performance to let students learn more easily. The educational robotics manufacturer may develop its product to sell in this educational market more easily, in business development strategy view.

All of these will be future any one educational robotic development challenges if they hope their products can sell more easily. They also need to know to let schools to know these disadvatages to their products to become advatanges in order to attract they to choose to buy their producte more easily. Such as what potential harmful consequences may come from the inventing of teaching robotics? What happends to important education moral, such as teacher or school privacy then robotic are starting to become an teaching tool to the school? Do such robotics hace any roght and responsibilities if the class has many students learning ability are influenced to poor or examination results are poor when the educational robotic has been bought to assist the school teachers to teach their students? Why does the school need to buy educational robotic to do teaching tasks? Any school organizations must need any one educational robotic product seller to answer any one of above questions, before they decide to buy their products. So, they must need to ensure teaching robotics will be used to help the school to teach students to learn more understanding to compare teachers only.

● Future educational robotic are applied on development teaching maths market

In the future, business development to educational robotic market may be teaching maths. I shall explain as below:

It is possible that students can use mobile robotic to learn mathematics subject to compare teachers more easily. Why? For example, young age from 4 to 14 age, they may apply mobile robotics to learn add, multiple, divided, simple math equation more understanding than math teaches. Robotic kints and apps is currently available on the maket for teacher of 4 to 14 age students,due to mobile , kits app price is cheap. So, they can be popular to be accepted by any primary schools , even in secondary schools, robotics may be applied to teach computer science, statistical methods subjects of one robotic kit for teach team of 2 to 3 students, short theory lessons , and tutorials to link theory and practice, realistic but affordable tasks linked with curricular subjects, teachers at ease with the robotic etc. So, future primary and secondary , even university teachers may need to choose the more suitable robot kit for their students,and carefully design where and how to use it and with which role.In fact, children will be possible to raise interest to learn when they can contact for any kind of teaching robotic to learn maths in classrooms together. So, teaching robotics may help 4 to 14 children students to raise learning interest instead of learning about ability.

In the future, robotic role is school may be one tool to engage the students as teachers role may be transfer base knowledge when teachers teach maths, geography, statistics, computer science subjects to promary , secondary even university students. This is one good example , whether what subjects robotic may be applied when it is invented to own human mind and anlaytical skill and communication ability. Robotics can perform more better to be applied to teach these subjects. It can let students to understand easily, e.g. understanding how to create equations that describe numbers a relationship understanding solving equations as a process of reasoning and explain the equations and inequalities in one variable, helping students to find different solutions, then best solves the problem , given the criteria and the constraints, helping students have more understanding how science knowledge is based upon logical and conceptual connections between evidence and explanations, even robotc can ask questions that can be investigated within the scope of the classroom, outdoor environment, and museums and other public faciltities with available resources and when appropriate frame a hypothesis based on observation and scientific principles. Even, robotics may help students to learn how construct, use and present oral and written arguments supported by evidence and scientific reasoning to support or refute an explanation or a model for a phenomenon, or robot can hep students to learn how obtain, evaluate and communicate information in 6-8 builds on k-5 and progresses to evaluating the merit and validity of ideas and methods, integiate qualitative scientific and technical information in written text with that contained in media and visual displays to clarify cliams and findings, helping students to anlyze data from texts to determine similarities and differences among several design solutions to identify the best characteristics of each that can be combined into a new solution to better meet the criteria for success, even helping students to learn how analyze data in 9-12 builds on k-8 and progresses to introducing more detailed statistical anslysis, the comparision of data sets for consistency and the use of models to generate and analyze data, analyze data using tools, technologies , and/or models e.g. computational, mathematical in order to make valid and variable scientific claims or determine and optinal design solution more easily than human teacher. So, there are human-made educaton machine advantage to students more than human teacher.

Educational robotic has been introduced as a powerful, in fact, flexible teaching / learning tool stimulating learns to control the behavior of tangible model using specific programming languages (graphical, or textual and involving them actively in authentic problem -solving activities. Howeverm in future educational robotic development, it may be divided two separate categories as below:

Robotics as learning object: This first category includes educational activities where robotics is being studied as a subject on its own. It includes educational activities aimed at configuring a learning environment that will actively involve learners in the solution of authentic problems, facing on robotics -related subjects, such as robot construction, robot programming and artificial intelligence as well as robotic as learning tool: In the frame of this second category, robotics is proposed as a tool for teaching and learning other school subjects at different school levels. Robotics as learning tool is usually, seen as an interdisciplinary, project -based learning activity drawing mostly on science, maths, informatics and technology and offering major new benefits to education in genera at all levels. However, I believe the role of teacher is crucial for the successful industry of technological and innovations in classrooms, when robotics are been particiapted to any education tasks in classrooms. Schools can focuse on the training of prospective and in-service teachers in the use of robotics technologies through courses.

In future electronic learning environment, robotics can be participated, such as recognised their active participation in all sessions of the course and their creative involvement even in the theoretical parts introducing principles and methodology for designing robotic-enhanced projects, very much liked the activity-orientation of the educational content, acknowledged the central role of the e-workspace during the face-to-face meetings and beyond ehem in enhancing sense of community, acknowledged the potential of educational robotics as a teaching tool but also as a subject, in different displines , such as technology, informatics and engineerinfg, highly appreciated the opportunity to create their projects.

How to develop robotic in technological subjects on teaching, learning and educational aspect? Learners can be encouaged hen robotics participate actively in the learning process. Through robotic learners build something on their own, preferably a tangible object, that they can both touch and find meaningful. In robotic learners are invited to work experiments or problem-solving with selective use of available resources, according to their own interest, search and learning strategies. Robotics can help them to seek solutions to real world problems, based on a technological framework meant to engage students' movitation. So, when students can have control of specific robotc in a rich learning environment, the construction of robots and programs to control them the emphasis might move on interesting learning actiities in the frame of specific learning areas , such as science and technology. Thus, the design of robotic construction activities is associated with the fulfillment of a project aimed at solving a problem. In such a learning environment, learning is driven by the problem to be solved. To engage students in activities requiring to design and manufacture real objects, i.e. robotic structures that make sense for themselves and should devise activities that will encourage students to support in order experiment. So, robotic participation any science experiments, they may encourage students to create problem solving and combining interdisiplinary concepts from different knowledge areas,: science, mathematics , technology and research educational tasks, the role of students will change, when preparing a work with a programmable robotics studies experiment with simple programmable sobotics devices , e.g. a car-robot, motors, sensor etc. Students are asked to synthesize their finds and reach conclusions and solutions to the problem uner investigation. SO, robotic is educaional participation to any scientfic technological or research experiments, they may help students to work with creativity , imagination and independence and finally organize the evaluation of the activity in collaboration ith studens. Also robotic participation to any technological or scientific research experiemtn, it also change teacher role . The teacher is such a constructist theoretical framework, like that teacher 's role that does not transfer ready knowledge to students, but rather acts as a organizer, coordinator and facilitator of learning for students. when educational robotics participate to any science or technological any research experiments, students may be organize the learning environment, raise the question , problem to be solved by students allow students to work with creativity, imagination and independence and finally organize the evaluation of the activity in collaboration with students. So, any educational robotic manufacturers must let their school clients to feel all these benefits which can bring to let students to raise learning abilty and learning interest to compare that are only taught by teachers, if they hope their educational robotics can be sold successfully in business development strategy view.

Learning behavioral economy to solve social challenges

● Why do some social challenges may influence customers number ?

In our societies , we shall have different challenges to our every day. However, in general , the challanges seem that they do not have relate to influence businessmen profit, but in fact, these social challenges have relationship to influence business profit and clients number. I shall indicate some social challenges to explain why these social challenges may influence any business profit indirectly as below:

In investment or raving individual preference decision aspect, for some people , it may be interesting or fun to think cbout the best investments or the right health care plan. But, for other people, these choices are unpleasant, they may be persuaded to buy anythings, e.g. car, computer. So, if car seller can have persuasive methods to influence many people feel the health care plan or investment plan is not prefereable choices, driving car enjoyable feeling or material enjoyment is the most preference choice. Then I believe that the car seller's car selling number may increase, because some people greatly enjoy thinking about their pension and the best investment or health care insurance preferable decision, their decision had been influenced to choose to buy the car seller's cars. When they feel driving car enjoyable feeling is more important than future benefit.

Hence, in behavioral economy view, they had felt the driving car benefit is much to compare pension investment or health care insurance future benefit. The question is how to car seller can persuade these investment ot pension plan or health care preference decision individual to change purchase car driving decision>

I suggest that the car seller may have discount or cash coupon or installment payment method to attract them to consider , instead of advertisement promotion method. because this preference investment or pension saving or health care plan decision individual customer group will be more difficult to persuade them to choose to buy car immediately at this moment. Hence, if the car seller can not implement cheap car discount strategy, it will be difficult to attract this prefeence long term future benefit consumer to make purchase ca r decision easily. Because they think pension or investment or health care plan ce help them to bring long term future benefit, also it means that purchase car may only bring short term present benefit. It is general social behavioral consumption model to influence their purchase choice. Hence, I assume that general social long term future benefit product or service, e.g. insurance, investment , pension may influence th scocial shor tterm present benefit product , e.g. car consumer. It is the main reason, it can explain why car sellers can not persuade this long term future benefit consumers to make decision to buy their cars easily, when they have no enough money to spend to buy car and make investment, saving , medical care insurance , pension plan in the same time. They must need to make either purchase car or insurance etc. decision in our nowadays societies.

So, in behavioral economic view, it explains why consumer individual purchase choice behavior has relationship to himself/herself spending budget. I assume that it has two kinds of behavioral economic consumers. One kind if long term future economic benefit in preference more than short term present economic benefit, such as purchase car and investment or health care plan insurace saving term present benefit consumer, he / she considers to earn driving enjoyment at this moment is not preference than purchase insurance or investment future benefit decision . So, our society, any business will encounter these two kinds of behavioral consumer. They persuade either long term futuer benefit consumers or short term present benefit consumer to change himself/herself products or services more easily. Otherwise, such as if car seller can not implement coupon or cash reward or discount or installment cash payment strategy to attracr the long term future benefit consumer. Then, it will lose this group car customers number absolutely. So, it explains why businessmen need to learn consumer behavioral consumption model in order to increase client number more easily.

" Social welfare" usually measured by people's prefences, and it also focuses for the conventional economists, on how to maximize social welfare. What then is the task of behavior law and economics? Such as, this cate seller case example, whether what social welfare the car seller can bring to society when the individual decides to buy its car to drive or when the individual chooses to buy health care insurance or pension plan or investment . When he/she chooses to buy health care insurance or make pension plan or buys any companies' shares. Then, these investment service companies will bring what benefits to our society? So, instead of consumer benefit, we also need to consider whether the kind of product or service will bring what long term social benefit . However, I think that when global many people own cars, then many cars are driven on the roads, it will bring serious air pollution to influence our health. Then, when many people are got lung diseases by air pollution. Then, many people will need to pay more medical expense. It will be long term negative medical cost increasing expense to future us, but it also bring possible income for insurance firms, when many people plan to buy medical care plans when they feel air pollution will influence them to need to pay future medical expense. So, it seems that the effect on many people own cars and their driving behaviors will bring serious air pollution, but it will also create the health care medical insurance need to be increased due to many people feel air polluton will bring lung disease and they need to pay long time medical expensein the future long time in possible. So, many people driving behavior may bring air pollution, but it also bring medical insurance need increases in our society in possible. It means that air pollution may create medical insurance market develops in possible, such as most smokers say they would prefer not to smoke, and many pay money to join a program or obtain a drug that will help them quit.If many smokers forgive to smoke, then the medical care insurance need for smokers number may be influenced to reduce.

In social benefit view, medical insurance for smokers insurance will be influenced to reduce, due to many smokers forgive to smoke. Although, many smokers may get health, when they do not smoke, they do not pay to buy any cigeratte often, they can save more money, but cigeratte sellers and medical insurance service providers , their income must be influenced to reduce. Hence, when our society government's advertisement concerns smokers often smoke cigeratte, it may bring poor drug health or many cars air pollution, these two messages may influence or dissuade many smokers forgive to smoke or many people do not buy cars. They choose to catch public transportation, or owning car people who do not often drive cares, then car gas or fuel suppliers income will be influenced to reduce, due to many car owning people do not often drive cars or many people do not choose to buy cars. Then, car sellers' income wil be influenced to reduced. Moreover, in long term social influence, when many people do not feel lung disease . Then, the medical care insurance need will also influenced to reduce.

It may bring insurance industry develops in difficulty for lung dissease medical care insurance. So, it explains why consumer behavior may also influence our social economic development in long term . They have cause and effect close relationship. When many consumers individual forgive or dislike to do the behavior in habit, e.g. driving car behavior or smoking behavior. Then, it will influence car seller market and cigeratte seller market to be poor in any countries , even global market.

Hence, in our society, when one individual feels that he.she has individual challenge, it may be economic or emotion or health problem, such as smoking influences health case, driving influences air pollution case. These both kinds of individual behavior may influence the individual may need to spend money for lung disease if he/she has continue smoking habit every day or he/she often drives car . Then, the individual will seek methods to solve these possible occurrence of problems before they do not occur. As it occurs in the natural environment, e.g. air pollution or lung disease is caused by cars or smoking. When individual begins feel these negative effect may case, if he/she continues to do smoking or dirving car behavior. He/she will begins to find methods to solve problem, problem solving is defined as the self-directed cognitive -behavioral process by which an individual , couple or group, such as smokers and drivers group in our society, they attempt to identify or disciver effective solutions for specific problem encountered in everyday living. More specifically, this cognitive -behavioral process (a) makes available a variety of potentially effective solutions for a particular problem and (b) increases the probability of selecting the most effective solution from among the various alternatives (D'Zurilla & Gold field 1971).

reference

D' Zurilla, T. J. & Goldfield, M.R, (1991). Problem solving and behavior modification, Journal of abnormal psychology, 78, 107-126.

As this definition implies social problem solving is conceived as a conscious, rational, effortful, and purposeful activity. Depending on the problem solcing goals, this process may be aimed at changing the problematic situation for the better, reducing the emotional distress that it produces or both.

Hence, it implies that when any one feels he/she will have individual problem, e.g. health problem , economuc problem,emotion problem. He/she will avoid to continue to do the kind of behavior often every day ,e.g. smoking behavior or driving car behavior .When our society has many people make to forgive to do above themselves behaviors, such as smoking or driving habit. Then, it will influence cigeratte sale number and car sale numner to be reduced. So, when our society has any consumer groups, they forgive to do themselves behaviors in habit. Consequently, the kind of product seller or service provider may lose man customers. So, in our society , when one kind of product or service consumers , their habital behaviors are changed to reduce, then it may influence the kind of product sellers or service providers their income or clients number to be either decrease or increase. On conclusion, it explains that why social behavior has close relationship to influence business income or clients number in our societies.

Learning organizational life cycle stage strategies
advantages

Any organizations may experience organizational life cycle stages from birth stage to growth stage to maturity , then it may also experience decline and/or regrow stages. But this two stages, they are not all organizations must may attempt to experience. It depends on whether economic environment how changes, organizational itself SWOT strengths and weaknesses etc. unpredicted factors to influence that when the organization will experience decline life cycle stage. It means that if the organization has very poor performance, then the organization has possible to experience decline life cycle stage in short time or long time. Otherwise, if the organizationhas very good performance, it ought not experience decline life cycle stage in short time, when it can reach mature stage in its the topest level. Even, when the organization has poor performance, so it is experiencing decline stage, but if it may implement effective strategies to help itself organization to develop . Then, if its strategies are very effective , in consequence, the organization ought may experience regrowing stage to re-experience its mature life cycle stage again. So, it seems that if the organization can have very good performance. Client number can increase significant as well as profit can also growth rapidly. Then, the organization ought may experience long time in mature life cycle stage or it means that it will be difficult to reach decline life cycle stage. Unless, some sudden inpredicted economic environment, or strong competitors etc. influence its performance, then they will have chance to cause it experiences to decline life cycle stage from mature stage suddenly. Hence, all organizations must need to experience birht life cycle stage in beginning to this stage.

However, when the business founder starts to set up his/her business. He/ she needs time to deal any difficulties,e.g. how to advertise his/her products to let customers have much knowledge, promote them to sell to market, how to implement strategies to solve organizational challenges. So, in birth stage, any organizations ought feel difficult to improve its whole performance or evaluate whether its future performance can improve to be better or can not improve or worse. Then, when the organization operates one period, it ought experience to growth stage, but it still depends on external factors to influence whether when it may experience growth stage, the factors may include: Whether strategies can be effective, economic environment is good or bad, customers purchase desire level is high or loe, cost expenditure is high or low etc. difficult factor.

So, before any organizatons may experience growth stage, there are many different complex factors to influence whether they can succeed to experience this stage easily. If the organization can not implement any effective strategies to solve its customers purchase emotion challenges, then its business is difficult to continue grow, also it means that the organization can not growor expand its business easily. Due to it can not continue to develop its business easily. It must not reach mature life cycle stage easily. Thus, any organizations can reach mature life cycle stage. It represents that its business has good strategies to solve any challenges in order to its products can attract customers to choose to buy or it can provide good service performance to satisfy clients needs to compare irs competitors in this market successfully.

In fact, it is not all organizations can attempt to experience the mature life cycle stage. This stage is any organization individual the topest stage. In this stage, the organization may have many clients increasing number significantly every year, its market can continue expand, profit can continue increases . All is the best to any organizations, if it can reaches this stage . All many organizations may only experience birth stage or growing stage . They reach this either birth or growth stage, then they have none good strategies to compete their clients number can not increase, but only decreases, profit reduces , even loss. They can not know how to change strategied to improve their performance or competitive effort to fight this competitors. Then, their businesses can not continue grow or expand. So, they have more chance to experience decline stage after either birth or growth stage only. They can not reach mature life cycle stage to attempt the topest level in whole business (organizational) life cycle stage or process. Thus, it brings these questions: Why do organizations need to learn organizational life cycle stages? What advantages to bring if they can attempt to learn how to reach growth or mature life cycle stages easily? I shall explain as below:

● Why do organizations need to spend time to learn how may experience different business life cycle stages?

The business life cycle is the progression of a business in phases over time and is most commonly divided into five stages: Launch or birth, growth, maturity and decline or regrow. Each company begins its operations as a business and usually by launching new products or services. Because any organizations will encounter challenges in every stages . If they know what factos may help them to enter another new stage of business life cycle or what challenges may threaten them can not enter another new business life cycle stage easily. Because businessman need to learn and how adjust their business model to ensure profitability. That is why an awareness of what stage of the business life cycle , you are currently it can be helpful. Hence, how to maximize each stage of the business life cycle, the businessmen might still need to learn how to work in order to improve performance when the businessmen are experiencing any one life cycle stage. Moreover, each business life cycle stage comes still need to learn how to turn a profit and the first outlines of their governance and compliance and this is one big reason why most businesses fail at this stage.

So, I assume that business life cycle stage is similar to school examination, the student needs to spend time to learn in the birth learning stage, then he needs to test in the growth learning stage, next is examination in the mature learning stage, if the student fails, t is decline learning stage to the school. It may be due to the teachers can not teach students to learn easily. So, these are many students fail in tests or examinations. So, if the school teachers can improve teaching methods to let many students may earn high grades in tests or examinations. Then, the school may experience growth, even mature teaching life cycle stage in short time rapidly . Hence, teaching quality can improve or not , it will influence any school organizations ought feel to schools to learn how to improve teaching methods or strategies in order to let students can experience the maturity learning stage or it can also experience the maturity teaching stage. It means that it ought learn how to improve its teachers teaching service performance to satisfy students learning needs if it hopes to reach maturity learning and teaching life cycle stage in short time for itself school organization benefit.For example, the organization founder may ask himself/herself why he/she wants to start this business, learns how to manage exployees strategies? It is the learning needs in the third stage, such as maturity stage. Otherwise, in the first stage of the business entity birth life cycle is sometimes called the seed stage and a matter of iteraing, testing an learning , and trying again, knowing that the businessman is unlikely to have.

What advantages may bring to the organization if it can attempt to learn how to solve different challenges in different business life cycle stages ? What advantages to the organization, if it can know how to experience every business life cycle stage?

In fact, the business life cycle is the progression of a business in phases over time, and is consumer segments by advertising their comparative advantages and vale. For example, when the business is experiencing growth stage , in the growth phase, the business founder needs to spend time to learn how his company can experience rapid sales growth. This learning may assist his business to develop his business to enter next mature how stage easily , for example, he can learn how the rapid growth stage takes advantage from the proven sales model, e.g. online sale or traditional visiting shop sale model which is more suitable to his business, marketing model and operations model, e.g. how to advertise his product or promote his products can affect more audiences concern this will see the businessmen's jounrey from idea to start up, and if successful, how to keep to stay long time in the mature stage. Rememeber, when having a successful business model behind any businessmen is undoubtedly an advantage, it is not a disadvantage when the founder spends more time to learn hoe to run his business. In fact, he won't waste his time to learn how to improve his business in different business life cycle stages. So, a tactical plan will take any business strengths and reduces to avoid weakness cause to influence its development. So, knowing where you small product is in its product life cycle, it is important to continue to develop your business successfully. SO, any impacts of all life cycle stages, any businesses need to be considered comprehensively , for one new technological product firm example, its new technological product life cycle begins with the introduction or birth stage. The high technological product company must succeed at both developing new product and managing them in the face of changing tastes, competitors' technologies similar change. So, it is what it needs to learn in this stage for this new product technological firm preparing development to next growth stage.

On the conclusion, learning how to achieve in every business life cycle stage, it can bring these benefits to any organizations, such as : they can understand and redefine this role from a more, if the organization ony to learn sale frameworks what it could have picked up. It is not enough, because most organizations will only find that a majority of their total sale number which is to use solely supplier-specific data about the life cycle, but they neglect how to set targets to learn how to improve their sale to be better in the future time, it is one important factor explain why many organizations only reach the growth stage, but they can not experience to next mature stage more easily, due to they do not consider how to implement strategies in order to achieve their next targets. They feel often implment targets which will help them to know whether they need to how to do in order to improve their businesses to satisfy clients needs. As with any effort in your organization, communication plays a critical role, craft machine learning to predict and manage human for remote teams to work through the innovation lifecycle, serve them well. Any organizations need to learn how to satisfy any customer individual purchase jounrey (called purchase experience) which the customer has with the organization, because when the organization can learn how to satisfy any client individual real need in any life cycle stage. On consequence, its clients number with have possible to influence increase. Thus, any organizations can bot neglect to learn how to satisfy client individual real purchase experience need in any life cycle stages because improvement to salepeople sale performance, they need spend time to learn in every time sale experience . When the organization can build excellent sale teams, then they may help it to build famous loyalty and good client relationship in order to expand its business more easily. Hence, in any businesses' life cycle stages, they must need to spend time to learn how to improve product quality service performance to bring customers' satisfactory emotion in order to expand their business developmenr more easily. So, i recommend that all small organizations expand to large size, they must need time to learn and attempt to find the best methods to solve any difficulties when they are facing in any one business cycle stage, if they want to expand their businesses successfully.

● The relationship between learning change management and rapid reaching mature life cycle

It is one good question: Can the manager or CEO help whole organization to develop rapidly if he/she attempt to learn how to help his/her organization to implement different strategies to solve different challenges in different business life cycle stages? Does it easy to help the organization to grow up when a learning CEO or learning manager accepts to learn anything to compare a non learning manager in different business life cycle stages? IIas it relationship between learning or non learning manager and rapid experiencing business life cycle stage and rapid developing business growth? I shall attempt to explain as below:

In fact, it is not essential to any managers or CEOs need to spend time to learn how any why what factors may influence their organizations to grow up to next business life cycle stage, but in comparison one learning how to change organizational life cycle stages manager and non-learning how to change organizational life cycle stages manger. Can learn attitude or strategy to help the manager to develop or expand his organization to next life cycle stage more easily or rapidly? I shall attempt to explain as below:

In fact, any organizations expect to change to next life cycle stage in success , can the manager(s) learn how to implement strategies to achieve to change management to their organizations' development in success? How the organizational management learns how to adapt organizational management change, it may be one important factor to influence whether the organization needs to spend how long time to reach growth life cycle stage from birth stage or reach mature life cycle stage from growth stage. So, it seems that how management spends time to learn how to change his/ her organization. It will have relationship to the organization needs to spend long time to reach next life cycle stage successfully.

Hence, learning how to train employees in each life cycle stage, it is the important factor to influence any organizations succeed, the employee lifecycle is an ongoing process that starts and ends with competent employees in any managers' organizations. There are nine elements ofa successful change management process, if the organizational management expects whole organization can real reach to next life cycle stage in success. The nine elements of a successful change management process, any management needs to spend time to learn. They may include: readiness assessments, communication planning implementation, sponsor activities and sponsor roadmaps organizing, organizatons need to provide change management training for managers to learn how to achieve effectiveness as well as providing training development and delivery learning methods to them, resistance management learning and learning employee feedback and corrective action. Moreover, managements also need to spend time to learn change management steps in order solve any challenges in order to reach next life cycle stage easily.

The change management learning steps may include: Step 1: Urgency creation , step 2: Building every team serves to every department efficiently, learning how to create avision, how to communication of division, how to remove obstacles, going for quick wins, let the change mature, integrate the change. These elements are incorporated into change management phases process. For example, some elements of communication planning occur early in the lifecyle. At this stage, change management is not fully achieved effectively, so management needs to spend more time to learn how to achieve effective communication planning in order to achieve effective communication planning in order to keep whose organization employees can communicate to work efficiently. Also, it will help client service employees to know how to build good communication management method to deal or answer or satisfy their clients' sale service and improving service performance absolutely.

Because organizations are nor statis, they change , if one organization still stays long time in birth stage, it represents that the organization feels difficulties to continue develop . So, the management needs to find whether what challenges threaten its organization can not reach growth stage more easily. One failure changing management organization, it has these characteristics: failure to change, inexperienced management, not enough revenue, inadequate leadership. Hence, it has close relationship between employee life cycle and organizational life cycle . If the organizational management expects its organization can continue develop or reaches next life cycle stage in success, it needs to learn how to let employees to adapt when its organization is changing in order to keep efficiency and improving service performance absolutely . So, I believe that it has relationship between learning change management and reaching to mature business cycle stage rapid and achieving long time staying in business cycle mature stage .

The question concerns that how management can learn to implement change management strategy in order to let his organization can reach mature cycle stage in short time as well as keep to stay in this mature life cycle stage in long time?

Firstly, we need to know what change management life cycle means ? For information technological industry example, it may be explained that the change management process is designed to help control of the life cycle of strategies, tactical and operational changes to IT services through standardized procedures. The goal of change managent is to control risk and minimize disruption to IT service and business operations. So, IT industry, the process change management maturity model presents five levels of organizational maturity in change management: The five level may include: from the lowest level 1 to the highest level 5, level 1: Absent or Ad hoc, level 2: Isolated projects , level 3: Multiple projects, level 4: Organizatinal standards and level 5: organizational competency. So, for IT , software manufacturing industry, if the management knows how to manage and change software manufacturing quality in order to satisfy manufacturing organization can follow software users' needs to change old function to new function and improve their qualities to achieve the highest level 5 organizational competency level.

Then, I believe that due to this organization's software management can learn how software user needs change and change its any kinds of software functions (software life cycle), when its all softwares can be often changed to more new functions to create many different kinds of new software functions to satisfy software users needs and fight its software competitors in this often changing needs market. Due to software product may experience often changing life cycle stages. So, for often one learning software manager example, I believe that he can help this software organization to reach growth life cycle stage, even mature life cycle stage more easily in short time as well as he can also help his software organization to stay in mature life cycle stage long time if this software organizational manager can keep learning attitude to continue to create any new kinds of different functions software to satisfy software clients' changing needs for long time . Then, I believe that this software organization may experience or reach growth life cycle stage, even mature life cycle stage as well as continue staying long time on mature life cycle stage or avoid to encounter decline life cycle stage occurrence chance, if this software organization's softeare management can learn how to change software organization operation and software manufacture and sale strategy in order to satisfy this software users' needs in this software users' need often changing market . So, it is one example to explain why it has close relationship between learning organizational management method and business life cycle stages. As this software organization case, the software management needs often to create and change any new kinds of software functions in order to satisfy software users' needs . So, the software managers need to spend time to learn software life cycle stage , it can help the software organization may reach products life cycle stage, even mature life cycle stage in short time,even the software product organization may also stay long time in mature life cycle stage , when it can reach this stage. Hence, learning how to change organizational management or strategy, which is one important factor to help any organization can reach growth or mature life cycle stage eadily in short time.

As Lewin describes that the change as a three stage process of unfreezing, change and freezing . In this phases of change model, Lewin emphasizes that change is that a series of individual processes, but rather one that flows from one process to the next . So, in general, services mature firms pace greater emphasis on more bureaucratic form, control systems might need to change throughout the life cycle to fit in with. He explains they have relationship between both organizational life cycle stage and management control.

Effective management control may help the organization to reach mature life cycle in short time rapidly. So, leadership managment and the way of thinking are required to balance control and through several stages of growth, maturity , decline or re-grow changes in the external environment influence. Hence, managers position in each of the stages of life cycle and providing practical solutions are, however world where environment changes have proven a rapid growth, the management of varios , they also need to implement how to change their organizational cultures, strategies in order to let their organizations to reach mature stage with a distinction-oriented rapidly. Hence, to successfully implement change initiatives, for each phase of life cycle. Any organizations need to produce resistance to change (the old model wins out over management boils down to improving the relationship) learning the relationship between leadership style and the organization life cycle were important. The change from one organizational life cycle phase to another, it depends on how the manager'c capacity to learn and change.

However, organizations at any stage of the life cycle are impacted by external environment, for example, threats in the start up stage differ from those in the maturity stage. So, managers must need often to learn when the right time is to be needed to change the goals, instead he also needs to learn types of changes in the maturity stage, comparisons with other, having strong personal and professional relationships in the organizaton's maturity stage. Hence, I believe that it has close relationship between learning change management and reaching maturity life cycle and staying long time in this stage.

● How to achieve the experience of mature life cycle reaching stage rapidly for product and service ?

Any businesses expect they can have chance or possibility to attempt to experience this nature life cycle stage, but it is not guarantee any kinds of businesses must may experience this the topest stage, the question is that: Have any methods may help any kinds of businesses to reach this the topest level of business life cycle, when their businesses had been developing or expanding in a period, e.g. after five years? So, it has no absolute to guarantee any kinds of businesses must may experience this the topest stage in one fixed time. How businesses can adapt to birth and growth life cycle stages in order to reach this the topest mature stage in their business life cycle stages? I shall attempt to explain whether it is possible that achieving what strategies may help businesses bring high successful chance to reach the business life cycle mature stage as below:

Product life cycle with maturity stage, it foucs as an important strategic inflection point. A number of techniques can help their businesses to attempt to reach this stage more easily. In fact, the product life cycle contains four distinct stages: introduction, growth, maturity, and decline. Each stage is associated with changes in the product's marketing position . Any firms can use various marketing strategies in each stage to try to proplong the life cycle of their products.

How do the firm extend the maturity stage of a product? I shall recommend change price , place or promotion extension strategy , what does change price extension strategies mean? Change prices mean proces can be lowered to allow ew customers to buy it as well as change place means that products can be sold in different countries or territories to gain more sales, change promotion means different advertising or sales promotion techniques can proplong the life of the product, giving it a new image. So, any organizations can attempt to achieve this extension strategies in order to adapt in different birth, growth and maturity stages for ther product sale easily. This extension strategies' characteristics is at the product;s price, sold places and promotin methods can be changed in order to adapt clients needs when their products are selling in birth, growth and maturity three stages in order to achieve the most effective sale effort and clients growth increasing for long time.

In fact, any product is like human beings, products also have a limited life-cycle and they pass through several stages in their life cycle. A typical product moves through five stages, namely, introduction or birth, growth, maturity or saturation and decline stages. So, when the product needs the maturity life cycle stage, in this maturity stage, it has these characteristics: The maturity stage of the product life cycle shows that sales will eventually peak and then slow down. During this stage, sales growth has started to slow down, and the product has already reached widespread acceptance in the market, in relative terms, utimately, during this stage, sales will peak . Hence, any businesses ought need to consider what key strategies can be implement to achieve the best sale performance throughout the different product life cycle stages and how to make the most of each stage. For example, when the product is selling in the birth stage, e.g. one author's book , his book is selling to the publisher in the first year, there are not many readers knew this book existence, so this book is not popular, its price ought not change high to compare similar topic book, e.g. story book in this year, but after this year, if there are many readers know this book and readers number can grow up rapidly. This author's this topic story book does not change, either increases or decreases , but its sale number has been significant increasing after the first year . So, this author's this story book ought be raised book price to attempt to sell easily. It is one good example of extension strategy to this author's this story book in its life cycle stages. So, such as ths publisher book sale case, it may attempt to achieve extension strategies to every author's book sale, it can follow every author's book prices, publishing places and promotion methods to help every author to sell in the most competitive book sale price, sale place choice and promotin methods in order to earn their readers growth aim . So, any book , it is as product to book shop, it will experience introduction, growth, and maturity life cycle stages. Some books may attract many readers to consider or some books may not attract many readers to consider to read . So, it causes their reading life cycle stages staying time will be different. So, extension strategies can help any books to be sold easily.

In fact, instead of product has life cycle stage, any service also has life cycle stage. There are five stages in service lifecycle. Thay may include: Service strategy, service design, service transition, service operation and continual servce improvement five stages. The service strategy phase of the service lifecycle provides guidance on how to design , develop and implement service management. Because any service business needs to manage to any employee service performance in order to provide excellent service quality, e.g. property management service to building tenants or property owners , if the peoperty management furm can train employees to provide excellent property management service to let their managing building clients to feel satisfactory. Then, the property management firm ought may keep long time property management service to this building. So, service provider will also experience service performance different stages.

In different service performance life cycle stages, such as this property management service case, they ought implement dfferent strategies in order to let their employees to know how to achieve service performance improvement to let their servicing building clients (tenants or builgin owners) can feel their property management service can be continue improved to avoid to choose any property management service provider to replace it easily.

The purpose of the service strategy stage of the service life cycle is to define the perspective, position plans and pattern that a service provider needs to be able to execute to meet an organization business outomes. The objective of service strategy may include: An understandng of work strategy is thus either the concept of the product life cycle or the concept of the service life cycle is today at about to give a propsed new product or service , how and to what extent. This generally requires important changes in marketing strategies and methods, because any learning kinds of service or product lif cycle stage why and how to change to any organizational management, it may be an important tool for marketers, managers, and product and service providing designers alike, If specifies four individuals stages of a product's or service's life and offers guidance for developing strategies to make the best use of these stages and promote the overall success of the product or service in the marketplace.

Reasons managment needs to spend time to learn how to manage his/her product or service life cycle development stage? They may include: The product or service life cycle is determined by how long its marketable . Product or service life cycle also plays a critical role in marketing strategy . So, learning how to adapt your product or service to meet the coming trends , this is the stage what will occue in which differentiation when the kind of the product or service will have possible to reach the another new experience life cycle stage in order to adapt its business development more easily.

Hence, each stage is associated with changes in the product's or service's marketing postion . The organizational management can use various markting strategies in each stage to try to prolong the life cycle of your products or services . Any product or service reaches the marketplace, it enters the service or product life cycle . This product cycle typically has for stages: Introduction or birth, growth, maturity and decline (and possibly deaths stages for product as well as service strategy stages includes service strategy. service design, servic transition, service operation, and continual service stages four service stages. So, the organization management can spend time to learn how to develop its business product or service needs to change in order to adapt marketing change in its product or service different life cycle stages. It can bring these benefits, such as: true benefits of product or srvice life cycle management may include, reduced time to makret, reduced market entry costs, more efficient and profitable distribution challen, higher return on investment from promotional cappaigns in possible, extending the lifetime of your product or service by adapting your approach as it moves through the lifecycle , for example, any management needs to learn what can make its products or services move from growth to maturity. After the introduction and growth stages, a product or service passes into the maturity stage. IN the first two stages , companies try to establish a market and then grow sales of their product or service to achieve as large , a share of that market as possible. Hence, marketers must be sure that a product or service has moved from one stage to the next before changing its marketing strategy. At each stage, marketing strategy varies. Strategy for the different stages of the product or service life cycle strategies may include: such as more benefits may be provided to the customers, e.g. extending the warranty period, guarantee period etc. However, company's market strategy depends on which stages the product or service is in its life cycle, for example, when one software manufacture company expects to expand its software sale market to overseas from local in growth stage. If it expects that it can reaches maturity stage in short time rapidly. It needs to implement technology innovation strategy for competition advantage reasons in global software sale markets development. Thus, the software organizational manager needs to spend time to learn what its present organizational characteristics are what resources and skills it owns or lacks, that gives it to comparative advantages over different countries to the operating changes that result in the learning curve to prepare this software product sale organizational maturity life cycle stage development more successfully. So, it needs to look at the advantages of focusing on what kinds of software manufacture and sale services in this software development industry whole life cycle stages and find the best or the most suitable competitive straregy, e.g. a discountinuous change to the software product development marketplace, what the global software product development industrial stage is and the tertiary or sale services sector durig the maturity life cycle stage to this softare manufacturer and sale organization strategy to this software firm during this growth stage may include example of it how changed its software product sales channels to which countries will be its another expanding sale market choice.

On conclusion, any organization management ought spend time to learn whether which strategies are the most suitable or the best to implement as well as how to implement when it is experiencing in the prodiuct or life cycle stage in order to spend less time to reach the maturity life cycle stage and proplong its maturity life cycle stage more success.

Organizational life cycle stage decision making strategy
Every company must have strategy to make any important or not important decision. Any decisions must be very important because they may influence any companies' future development. So, our company management can not neglect to cosider whether all strategies are reasonable to influence any organizations success. However, we need to consider how to achieve effective decisions to avoid wrong decisions to cause our companies' development in long term.

The question is how to implement effective decision making to achieve every consequence to gain the best benefits to any organizations? Any organization managers ought need to follow these steps in order to make effective decisions. Acknowledge and compensate for your biases, use positive and negative lists, experiment by reversing your live of thinkin, create a scoring system. Any organizational decisions have four decision making styles. They may include these four basic categories for decion making, these being: Directive, conceptual, consultative, and consensue. So, strategic decisions usually mean managers must plan for change and risk.

Many factors are unknown, since managers are planning for future changes. Another example for a major change is the decision to modify the company's culture. For instance, the firm may be having trouble with increased employee turnover. It may be the company's culture needs to be changed in order to employees can adapt to work together. Hence, when one company's working environment and employees attidude is poor, because they feel unhappy to work, so working environment will be caused poor. It may be influenced whole organizational culture to be more poor. Hence, the organizational ought need to change its organizational culture to be more happy in order to let whole organization's employees can feel happy to work in this enjoyable working environment . Hence, any entrepreneurs or managers ought need to consider employees' emotion issue how to let they have good working emotion to do their tasks every day, e.g. get comfortable with the cost of deciding , teaching employees hoe to control themselves emotion, understand that logical decisions have a secret emotional intuitive is one of the simplest, and arguably one of the most common ways to make a decision, rational decision making is the type of decision making many people want to believe what they do.

The first stage model to any making strategic decisions, they may include: defining the problem, consider these questions, gathering information, seeking information on how any why the problem occurred, developing and evaluating options, generating a wide range of options, choosing the best action, selecting the option that best meets the decision objective. Hence, decision including strategies are the ways, we use information to make a choice, in this case, managers need to make strategic choices as muually exclusive options, start with the most apparent options, generate alteratives, specify the conditions under which each option is attractive, identify barriers to each option, design and run tests to prove or disprove each of the conditions, finally using the data, make a decision. Hence, business leaders use strategic decision-making when they plan the company's future strategic management involves definingl long term goals, responding to market forces and carrying out the firm's mission, so making strategic decisions managers look at the big picture.

In psychology view, decision making is regarded as the cognitive process , knowledge necessary to know when to use any strategies. They do posses to change their approach to decision making. Rather, think of it is a decision making process that keeps you from making the same mistakes year after year. Making-judgement-based decisions among a variety of variable options is made easier when a systematic process is utilized. So, decision making strategies are the structured method and operational guidelines followed by decision makers. So, any strategic decision making process is needed in the procedural rationality stage, if the organization expects to do the most reasonable decision making to solve any challenges. So, strategic decision making is essential on how top managers use process and tools to implement long-term goals. Also, decision making is a process that reduces uncertainty to a considerable level.

In most decisions, uncertainty will be reduced, when the manager had prepared one good strategic decision making method, the most difficult decison making suitation is that when the manager needs to implement a multi-perspective strategic decision making. It is the process of making long-term decision's that helps or helps the organization t build long term benefits. However, any organization's managers ought need to spend time to learn a large variety of decision making techniques, it can help improve decisions of different types.

It can be useful in decision between strategies or investment opportunities with constrained resources. This is called strategic decision making, where decisions are made according to a company's goals or mission. At many organizations, it is up to managers to make the key decisions that influence business strategy. So, managers must need to learn how to implement any kinds of strategic decision making method in order to help their organizations to achieve the most reasonable long term benefits. However, with any strategic planning process, any organization will be able to know. What it wants to achieve in the long term vision is on ongoing process that involves crafting strategies to achieve goals.

● Why do managers feel difficult to make decisions?

Usually these factors may cause managers feel difficult to make decision for their organizations: Making decisions will always be difficult because it takes time and energy to weigh their options. Things like second-guessing the manager himself/herself and feeling indecisive and just a part of the process. However, decision-making is important to achieve the organizational goals/objectives within given time and budget. It searches the best alternative, utilizes the resources properly and satisfies the employees at the workplace. As a result, organizational goals or objectives can be achieved as per the desired result. Moreover, decision-making is an integral part of modern management.

Decisions play important roles as they determine both organizational and mangerial activities. A decision can be defined as a consequence of action purposely chosen from a set of alternatives to achieve organizational or managerial objectives or goals. The first step to making those decision is understanding what makes managers themselves so hard, the decisions that may include senior leaders, middle managers, frontline staffs , they many face short time or long time decision making challenge , when they need to find solution methods to solve any organizational challenges. For example, one manager needs to make decision to resolve organizational challenge before tomorrow morning time. Then, time pressure can lead to poor decision making to influence the manager feels physically, mentally ad personally pressure. He will have much chance to make poor decisions when he feels he is in a position of power. IF he can not make any decisions to help his organization to solve challenge before tomorrow morning, he will not achieve any satisfactory management effort to the company's senior management, even CEO . So, time pressure may be one main factor to cause the manager to do poor decision making to help his organization to solve the challenge.

So, if the manager hopes to make better decision making , he needs likely feel comfortable and confident making decisions, e.g. learning how to manage his senior manager or CEO expectations. However, some decisions carry enough weight that the prospect of simply making a choice can be made in short time. SO, the manager ought need to learn how to weight whether which choices may bring more benefits or advantages ro make any decision in short time frequently every day. It can train that when the manager encounter difficult problem to be solved in short time. He can be trained to judge whether which is the most suitable choice easily to do any decision more easily. So, daily learning how to solve any short time or long time decision making skill frequently, this learning behavior must help any managers to raise short time critical thinking decision making skilful effort. Hence, learning managing uncertainty and making the most reasonable choices , strategic decision making skill, it will be any organizational managers ought need to consider issue if they want to be the best strategic decision maker in themselves organizations.

Hence, any organizational managers need to know that decision making is difficult to taugh, particularly when there may not be one right answer. It's common for managers and leaders to feel alone. Being alone as a decision maker comes with the job. However, decision making is absolute one of the toughest parts of running a business. They will feel responsible for it, compared to the management announcing the change in policy without listening to what. Hence, self confidence, time management factor, is a important part to influence any managers to do any important decision making more success. So, they can not neglect how to train themselves to attempt to find the most reasonable decision making to solve any chalenges for themselves organizations in order to achieve one strategic decision maker for their organizations.

On conclusion, managers' attitudes toward work and incentives may influence his decision making whether it can be more accurate, when reviewing upon motivation, incentives, the social psychology of work and behavior at work, it is tempting to conclude that managers are motivated when manual workers need bonus payment, between ideas , beliefs attitudes. So, any managers individual personal attitudes will influence their behaviors, also his behaviors will motivate how he can make resonable decision making. So, manager's working attitude can be one factor to influence whether his/her decision making can be made more reasonable for his/her organization.

Computer technologic firm merger cooperational strategy

● IBM and Apple merger strategic advantages and disadvantages

IBM and Apple computer firms, they merger to cooperate together, whether merger will help them to bring what advantages and disadvantages ? What is the life cycle stage to these two big computer organizations? These two computer companies IBM and Apple , they had set up abut forty years. From 1970 year, when Apple founders, they had invented new computer machine to bring human playing electronic game to entertain at home. Then, IBM founder also invented micro softword clerical software to let any office workers or students or home users can type on computers to replace typing machines . So, Micro soft word software invention also help office workers or students or home users to choose to apply computer to do typing tasks to replace traditional typing machines. So, these two firms' borth stage, is that when Apple desktop computer products are innovated as well as Microsoft IBM micro soft word softwares are also innovated to this traditional typing market.

When, 1980, there are not that Microsoft word softare functions are, so these two founders will spend long time to promote desktop computers and microsoft word software new products to let many people know what their real functions are, e.g. playing electronic entertainment game activities and clerical tasks , these two main functions to let them to know, when they may be known whether what microsoft word software and Apple brand desktop computer can help any students or clerical office workers or home users to do any clerical tasks or play electronic playing game leisure activites at homes or offices. Then , many people begin to accept these both new products to use for their daily clerical tasks or electronic playing game lesiures activies .

However, in their birth life cycle stage time needs about two years short time only, because their advesrtisement strategies are effective to let global many people feel computer product can belp us to fo any clerical tasks or bring exciting electronic playing game leisure feeling when students feel bore, they may spend some times to apply computer to play any games at homes. Even they may turn on computers to apply Microsoft word sofware to help them to do any homeworks or assignments. Students can use computers to replace typing machines to type any clerical documents at homes or schools conveniently.

After1982 year, global IBM computer and Microsoft word software buyers number had been increasing rapidly. So, from 1982 year, these two firms are experiencing life style growing stage period. Till to 1988 year, these two firms may ensure global computer and software products main suppliers their computer and software technological products had high market share. So, in global computer and software technological market, these are not many competitors to win them. So, they do not need long time to enter life cycle growing stage. They only need four ro five years time to attract many global computer and software buyers begun to accept their products and also choose to buy their IBM and Microsoft computers and softwares to use. Hence, then 1988 year, these two high technolgical computer and software product firms had been experiencing life cycle mature stage till to 2000. Although, in this forty , IBM and Apple computer firms number had been increasing rapidly globally. But, other computer and software competitors number is also increasing, e.g. Dell computer brand had be familiar to global computer buyers. Dell's market share is also high. So, their computer and software buyers may have many kinds of computers and softwares brands of product choices in global students and office clerical workers and home users computer and software product market.

In fact, IBM and Apple began to enter life cycle decline stage , due to laptop products need increase and many different brands of laptop computers may be supplied to let computer users to choose to buy in global computer market. So, after 2000 , these two computer firms began to change to new technologial product or service market, e.g. apply also invented Smart mobile products because it felt desktop and laptop products competitors number had been decreasing , due to they had many laptops and desktops competitors' products to choose to buy. So, Apple brand computer begun to invent smart mobile phone and small flat laptop , it has or has none phone function products in order to earn high market share to smart mobile and flat laptop product user market ratio in order to avoid life cycle decline stage reachs rapidly.

In fact, IBM smart mobile strategy may be effective to absord global some smart mobile customers. But IBM is skill desktop same smart mobile competitors. Also, IBM laptop and desktop products may also face different similar computer function products to choose from competitors.So, IBM will may enter life cycle decline stage rapidly. Also, Microsoft brand computer may be its main competitor, Microsoft can attempt to apply interest technology to help it to sell electronic book, because it felt desktop and laptop product market has reached mature stage.

It is common that global every family had own at least one laptop or desktop or both computer product. So, it means that product needers number begins to decrease, when global every family own at least one computer product to use at home, even global every office also wn at least one computer in offices. Unless, their computers are broken , thwy ill feel need to buy another new. Otherwise, they use computers about three to five years when they feel too old,then they will choose to change another new. So, Microsoft applies internet to help it to sell electronic book, it can bring another electconic publish business chance, instead of selling laptop, desktop, Microsoft software products only, because it also feel that when computer market had reached mature period. Global many people had owned computers, their needs will also decrease. Since internet invention, it creates e-commerce chance, electronic publishing is also popular to let global readers to read any books from desktop or laptop computers or mobile computers tools anywhere. So, Microsoft is attempting to enter this electronic publish market . this electronid publishing reading service market does not need readers to buy paper books to read, they won't need feel heavy if they need to bring bags to carry many heavy books to go to schools, libraries , students only need to bring laptops to read any

Microsoft publish electonic books from computers anywhere conveniently. So, Microsoft electronic book pubishing new market help it to avoid to experience the life cycle decline stage rapidly. But, these two firms are still main competitors , if they choose not to merger or coopeerate to do technologic product, e.g. laptop, desktop , software or electronic book publish online reading service together. They may influence their clients number to reduce. Otherwise, if they can merger or cooperate , then it is possible that their clients nu,ber may increase or profit increase, even fight other computer and software companies competitors easily. Then, their computer and softare market share may raise when other competitors number reduces, e.g. Dell may be their main computer competitor, but if they cooperate or merger , then Dell's clients may be influenced to choose to buy their any desktops, laptops, softwares products. They can help themselves invention high technological products , if they can attribute their unique computer technology to help to invent any new kinds of more advanced computers or softwares , e.g. even high technological electronic reading platform to be improved to publish high reading quality of electronic books to attract many readers to read their electronic books from their publishing webstores.

IBM and Microsoft merger or cooperation can help them to raise market share or fight competitors in this often changing high technological computer product market. What are the disadvantages and advantges when they choose to merger or cooperate together? I shall explain as below:

Can IBM and Microsoft merger can keep their computer , software , even electronic book publish market in the mature life cycle stage in long time in order to avoid decline life cycle stage occurs. IBM's global strategy is based on three aspects: cloud , data and engagement . IBM's strategy imperatives may is business growth on cloud, analytics, mobile, social and society . So, it has changed its old strategy only concentrates on computer sold aspect. Since internet technology had been invented. However, IBM's primary generic strategy is cost leadership.

In Michael Porter's model, the generic strategies are what companies use to ensure competitive advantages . The cost leadership generic competitive strategy supports IBM's competitive advantages through cost-effectiveness of its operaton. However, if IBM can operate or merger to Microsoft, then Microsoft ought may help it to reduce more cost , when their technology can assist to develop their products, e.g. IBM's clouds , data technologic strengths can be brought to Microsoft 's product or Microsoft's electronic book publishing technology or software manufacturing technology strengths can bring to IBM' s products to assist themselves to raise computer, smartphone phoe, electronic publishing reading technological service business competitive effort in global computer , smartphone and electronic book publish markets. Then, when IBM can own Microoft 's technology , it may help it to reduce manufacturing cost in possible.

In fact, instead of IBM may merger to microsoft to reduce its cost to be more. It may also merger to Amazon, Amazon is us one online electronic book sale provider, it help global different businesses to apply itself online platform to sell their products. It is middleman role, it helps any sellers to sell their products from its online store platform. Any one can turn on computer and click to Amazon website to buy any products . Amazon will help any buyers to deliver their products to their homes by flight , after they pay visa card, because Amazon is global the topest online product sale service middleman provider. It's cloud technology is very proficient. If Amazon and IBM can merger to cooperate to do themselvers cloud service high technological business. IBM can apply Amazon's cloud high technological platform to help itself to grow its business and increase its cloud service clients number more easily. So, IBM ought choose Amazon's cloud platform to assist itself to continue to develop its future cloud service business, e.g. electronic book publish, because Amazon's electronic book publish market has have high reading market share.

Hence, IBM needs to find, e.g. Amazon or Microsoft to expand its high technological product or cloud strategy or cloud technology may be IBM's main competitors. If Amazon and IBM and Microsoft can merger or cooperate to expand themselves unique computers or softwares ot smart mobiles or electronic book platform sale markets to be merger together, then global computer buyers , smart mobiles buyers , electronic book readers, electronic platform product buyers must may enjoy the most benefits, because they can attribute their unique computers, smart mobiles manufacture, cloud service platform technology to be applied to themselves unique computers, smart mobiles, electronic book reading flatform and ebooks ale mix together, t means to improve these products or services unique function or improve themselves technology in order to let global computer , smart mobile or electronic book readers or electron platform product buyers feel that their these products or cloud platform products sale or reading service performance can br improved. Hence, their merger ought bring advandages more than disadvantages.

However , I shall also indicate some possible disadvantages to IBM merger strategy. Higher prices to IBM products, A merger can reduce competition and give the IBM more monopoly power with less competition and greater market share to IBM, but when IBM chooses to merger to Micrsoft and / or IBM chooses to merger to MIcrosoft and/or Amazon , they may influence IBM's computer or smartmobile phone products can usually increase prices for consumers. Then, consumers may also compare IBM's products to other computer and smart mobile phone sellers. If they feel its price is not reasonable, they may choose to buy other smart mobiles or choose to buy other brands of laptops, desktops to replace IBM's product. Because IBM's any products prices may be controlled or dominated by Microsoft or Amazon after they merger. So, IBM can not change itself products prices more easily. It is its weaknesses . Another risk's associated with mergers and acquisitions to IBM, it may be differences in culture between Amazon and Microsoft and IBM. It may bring inefficient communication and lack of transparency to IBM organization when Amazon and Microsoft staffs may participate to IBM any important decisions. It may bring miscalculations in the evaluation of assets to IBM. For example, merger may bring disadvantages when the main drivers behind the Lenovo and IBM merger. The drivers behind the merger between China's Lenovo and US IBM was inspired by several moves. The main one being the loss that the latter incurred to IBM itself pc division after a change of business strategy.

On conclusion , before IBM decides to implement merger strategy to any technological firms, it needs to consider whether what risks they may bring and what benefit they may bring after IBM itself chooses to merger to the firm in order to avoid miscalculation consequence to influence IBM's business continues to develop or reachs life cycle decline stage rapidly.

CHAPTER THREE

How airport service strategy influence future tourism industry development

Our global tourism development had been developed from birth cycle stage to decline life cycle stage nowadays. From 1960 beginning, when airplanes were popular to be increased need to global travelers. Hence, from 1960 to 1970 is whole global tourism industry birth cycle stage. Till to 1971 beginning, many Asia, e.g. Singapore, Japan, China and Western, e.g. UK, UK etc. countries people, they have jobs to do ,and they have more extra money to prepare to choose any leisure activities. From 1971 to 1980, it is growth life cycle stage to global tourism industry. Many airplane manufacturers had been beginning to manufacturer many airplanes because they felt global traveler number would increase. In fact, in this ten years, global traveler number had been increasing every year. Then, from 1981 to 2019 this fourty years, it is global tourism industry nature life cycle stage. It means that every year travel number had been increasing more significantly to compare past. Also, many travelers feel need to travel every year. So, global travel tourism industry may reach the most top travel clients level in this fourty years. However, till to 2020 , due to COVD19 human mouth and discase occurrence, it influences global travelers feel fear to catch air planes to travel because this kind COVD 19 human mouth disease may cause lung disease from air. When many travelers are sitting in the close window air plane, if one person has ths kind COVD19 human mouth disease. The sick person may contact air to let the persons to breath to cause lung disease in possible in airplane. So, global travelers number is decreasing after 2019 . Also, it implies that tourism industry is facing decline life cysle stage.

It brings these questions: IS it right time to develop space tourism? Can space tourism help future tourism industry to re-grow its life cycle stage from nowadays decline life cycle stage? Can space tourism develop to nature stage from birth life cycle stage ? I shall attempt to give evidence to explain whether space tourism may be developed to let human has more one kind tourism . It may be future leisure new trend for travelers, instead of earth travel. Because one day earth tourism destination may not bring leisure interesting to global traveler, then space tourism may be attempted to replace this kind of travelling activity . So, space tourism is birth life cycle stage. However, our earth tourism may define moral tourism, nature tourism, green tourism, responsible tourism in future new travelling leisure trend.

It bring these questions: Can our future tourism industry meet the expectations with the terms " ecological tourist"? Which factors affect the product life cycle of eco tourism? Nature and green tourism may be our earth new kind of travel activities, when many young and old age travelers like to climb mountains, they feel life nature scene more than non-man made) nature scene in their journeys, they do not like to visit cities to travel. It is possible that they often work in offices, this office working factor may influence many travelers like green tourism in the future. So, green or nature tourism will be our future popular tourism leisure activities. It may influence nowadays our tourism decline life stage to re-grown to nature life cycle stage in possible in this COVD19 people mouth disease influential environment.

New economic development in Tourism and oil industries

● How to develop new economic tourism industry

How to develop tourism industry in new economic environment? Any examination of the new economic development of travel and tourism requires definitions of the subject and its components, which are suitable for economic analysis. However, in new economic development to tourism industry, it is also important to look at tourism conceptually, in order to set the scene for a deeper understanding of the future new tourism industry development.

Tourism is neither a phenomenon nor a simple set if industries, however, in new or old economic development environment. It is a human activity which encompasses human behavior, use of resources, and interaction with other people, economies and leisure enjoyment environment. It is also involved physical movement of tourists to locales other than their normal living places.

In future new economic environment, traditional travel needs to include these element in order to satisfy traveler enjoyment and leisure feeling: They may include: Tourist needs and motivations, tourism selection and behavior and constraints , travel away from home , market interactions between tourists and those supplying products to satisfy tourist needs and impacts on tourists , hosts, economies and environments.

In new economic environment, the tourism products may include: carriers, in any forms of transport for tourist travel accommodation, man-made attractions, which could also include the managed areas of natural attractions, private sector and public sector support services, middlemen, such as tour wholesalers and travel agents.

The tourism resources may also include: Natural resources, lands , minerals, water and biological; labor resources, human work, and enterprise; capital resources, manmade enhancement and other resources. The travel and tourism resources problems may include: As there is frequently a mismatch between producer and consumer perception of what constitutes the tourism product , there may be conflict in ideas of which resources are properly involved as well as many of the resources likely to be in demand for tourism are public goods , or even free resources.

In new economic development to tourism industry view, we need to consider that tourism and travel has the reputation of being a relatively clean and pleasant industry in which to work or invest in order to attract a greater number of resource suppliers than as less well-perceived industry, which therefore keeps rewards prices down by competition, how to attract those retiring from or travel business for example, if their finances are already sound, income from travel is not expected to be optimal , travel and tourism is frequently highly seasonal , offering rewards that are competitive with other industries only some of the time, destination products are often in locations which are of little use to other industries, so that competition for resource use if minimal and hence rewards are low.

In general, tourist purpose may include: recreational purpose : holiday, health and sport and religion as well as business purpose: company business , e.g. conventions and sales trips. So, in new economic tourism development aim, tourism industry need consider hoe to achieve incentive trips to let these both tourists to feel. For example, the overall type of tourism required, destination arrangement, travel mode, accommodation and attraction visiting and purchasing method or distribution channel. The purchasing method choices may include: whether to buy an inclusive package or separate service, whether to buy direct from suppliers, such as airlines or hotels or use an agent , which tour wholesaler or operate or agent to use.

I predict the tourism development in new economic view, it may have these characteristics: Few enterprises in travel and tourism are large, highly cashed-up and have a large asset base, enterprises within travel and tourism that are not in a financial position to diversify, and those do well success to the above –average growth obtainable in travel and tourism compared with many other industries, they would therefore tend to expand within the sector. The result of individual enterprise growth and integration within travel and tourism is an increase in the concentration of that industry. The degree to which output is produced of fewer and fewer enterprises. This can be only be accounted for realistically with the context of an individual economy, Levels of concentration in any part of travel and tourism in the future are likely to depend on two opposing factors: The constant demand by many tourist market segments for new experiences and products, which encourages the development and survival of more and diverse enterprises, and therefore leads to the reduction of concentration as well as technology, which in travel and tourism frequently calls for large capital outlays and requires mass markets for efficient use, promotes integrations and large scale enterprise, especially in air travel and non-personal services (marketing and information communication, travel insurance , tourism payment methods). IN these areas, concentration will undoubtedly increase in future new economic development environment.

HOW TO PROLONG TOURISM LEISURE MATURE LIFE CYCLE STAGE AS WELL AS AVOID DECLINE AND DEATH LIFE CYCLE STAGE OCCURENCE FROM COVID 19 HUMAN DISEASE

Any businesses expect to reach the mature life service cycle stage and they also hope to prolong to stay in this stage and avoid to have chance experience decline life service cycle stage, even death stage in future whole business life cycle stages. However, in fact, there are many businesses need to spend long time to have effort to reach mature life cycle stage from birth and growth both stages, even when they have effort to experience this the topest level stage, many can not stay to prolong time in this stage, then they will reach next stage, such as decline life cycle stage, even final death life cycle stage possibly. Hence , research whether how can reach the mature life cycle stage in short time and prolong to say in this stage. It is one common researching value question to any businesses. Such as COVID 19 human disease had been occurrence in 2019 end , it bring global tourism industry traveller number began to reduce. I shall attempt to explain how airline organizations implement strategies to avoid to enter decline service life cycle stage as below:

● How to avoid to reach the decline service life stage rapidly to global airlines tourism service industry due to COVID 19 human disease occurred Strategies for growing and maturity a product or raise service performance, and increasing profit margins and prolonging to stay on the mature service life stage. I believe that it is any service businesses final aim. However, in any service life cycle stages, when the service , e.g. airline tourism leisure service industry will experience the decline service life stage , due to the COVID19 human disease influences to global travelers began to feel fear to catch airplanes to avoid air contact to give this kind of disease from 2020. So, nowadays, airlines ought have the suitable or right strategies to help them to solve travelers reducing number to influence their profit growth to encounter decline life service cycle stage later.

Life cycle strategy is based on product or service life cycle thinking from marketing, the factors may influence when the business can reach the mature life cycle stage, but some unpredicted factors may influence their clients number reduce, such as this airlines organizations traveler number reduces is due to COVID 19 human disease influences they feel fear to catch airplanes to travel case, their strategies may include: market growth rate, market growth potential, breach of service lines, number of competitor, distribution of market, share among competitors, customer loyalty , barriers to entry and technology improvement etc. factors to influence the global airlines tourism service industry can continue develop or expand to future overseas tourism market, when COVID 19 human disease may be killed by new medicine later.

Such as this COVID 19 human disease influences travelers feel fear to catch airplanes to avoid get this kind of disease and it influences global travelers number is decreasing in 2020 case, when the airline organization reaches the growth life service cycle stage from the birth stage, if it expects to spend short time to reach the mature life service cycle stage. Before COVID 19 human disease had not been killed by new medicine, if they hope to attract many travelers to choose to catch their airplanes to fly , the extension strategies that any airline organization can attempt to achieve, they may include, rebranding, establishing airline service in order to differentiate the other airline competitors tourism service , ticket price discounting and seeking new marketers, rebranding is the creation od a new look and feel for an established airline tourism service from the airline's competitors.

The airline service life cycle extension strategies also may include these methods to help the airline organization to grow or grow up or develop its airline tourism market rapidly, e.g. repackaging and new sizes, the appearance of airline tourism service can be crucial gaining a passenger's attention and developing tourism interest , new formulas or additional airline tourism features to the tourism country, lower ticket prices to maintain interest or liquidate surplus stock new airline tourism service advertising campaign, altering the new airline channel of destination, such as online ticket purchase.

Hence, after COVID 19 human disease had been skilled by new medicine , any airline organizations need to consider how to choose the most suitable strategy from different kinds of key strategies to expand their airline new tourism channels throughout the different airline tourism service life stages, in these four distinct stages: introduction, growth, maturity and decline or possible death stage, when this COVID 19 human disease had occurred from 2019 end, it may influence global travelers number had significant been reducing to bring any airline organizations may enter the decline life service cycle stage rapidly, even death life service cycle stage comes consequently.

Any airline organizations can use various marketing strategies in each stage to try to prolong the life cycle or attempt to reach the mature life cycle stage in short time. Avoiding to experience decline life service cycle stage, such as the COVID 19 human disease occurrence causes global travelers number began to reduce. It is ensure that any airline organizations do not expect to experience or reach the decline service life stage due to this COVID 19 human disease influences. The question is that how the airline organizations can maintain a strategy in the decline stage , such as COVID19 human disease influences global travelers number reduced and it brings many airlines income began to reduce, for example, reducing the airline promotional expenditure in this COVID 19 human disease occurrence period, reducing the number of airline distribution outlets , e.g. Hong Kong to New York airline flight channel reduces implementing ticket price cuts to get passengers to but the maintaining the airline tourism service and waiting for airline competitors to withdraw from the global airline tourism market.

Thus, following the initial growth, in this COVID human disease occurrence period, when the new airline organization enterprise enters the expansion stage during which the routing operation succeeds. The new airline organization can either reach the mature life service cycle stage either it can prolong to stay in this stage or it can not prolong to stay and enters to decline service life cycle stage , even death service life cycle stage. So , how to avoid the decline service life cycle stage comes to the new airline organization in this COVID 19 human disease occurrence period. It is any airline organizations concerning question when they are experiencing in the mature life cycle stage, but when COVID 19 human disease occurs to influence global travelers number began to reduce. May the airline organization experience the decline service life cycle stage rapidly when the COVID 19 human disease occurs ? It depends on whether it's strategies implementation are effective , its' strategies are effective, it may avoid to reach the decline life service cycle stage in short time easily due to COVID 19 human disease influences.

For this COVID 19 human mouth disease case , since 2019 had occurred, it brought serious tourism industry economic loss to any countries, many people loss jobs, many people feel fear to enter any shops when they are in crowd shop environment, e.g. restaurants can not permit to allow many people to sit closely, because when one person has COVID 19 human mouth disease, he can bring this disease to another person from air. So, many restaurants lose many clients in morning, lunch and night busy eating time, even ships also can not permit many people to enter their ships, because they avoid many people may contact, if one or some people has/have COVID 19 mouth disease, when he/she talks to the salespeople in the shop. It has high chance to cause many people get COVID human disease by mouth. So, any shops can not allow crowd in themselves shops to avoid any people have COVID 19 human disease occurrence. So, this COVID 19 human mouth disease may influence many businesses are experiencing decline life cycle stage, because clients number is continue decreasing, unless drug invention succeeds to fill this kind human mouth disease. Otherwise, on the consequence, many businesses will face death life cycle stage in short time possible. So, it is good example to explain unpredicted external environmental factor to bring global businesses will face decline life cycle in 2020 or next year, even after two years latter. So, COVID -19 human mouth disease may also influence any businesses had been experiencing long time in the mature life cycle to change to decline life cycle stage in possible.

Instead of the businesses are experiencing in either birth or growth life cycle stage. for example, UK Cathay airline had been experiencing long time in the mature life cycle stage from 2000, when its clients number had been increasing, but when the end of 2019, COVID-19 human mouth and air contact disease had occurred in global to influence any people feel fear to catch airplanes to travel or business travel frequently, due to airplanes have none windows, its none window environment will bring COVID-19 disease to any passengers when the airplane has many passengers are sitting together closely, if anyone has COVID-19 disease, he will cause any one airplane service waiter, passenger , even pilot to have COVID-19 disease easily.

So, global airline industry is experiencing decline life cycle stage. even Cathay airline is one big UK developed airline , it's passengers number is large in the past, but when COVID-19 disease occurs to cause travelers number had been decreasing. Hence, Cathay airline is experiencing decline life cycle stage from mature life cycle stage. It needs to implement dismissing staffs to keep salaries expenditure reducing strategy in global, e.g. HK will have 4,000 front line airline service staffs or airport check in service staffs , they will be dismisses in HK Cathay airline market. Although, HK government had given money to support it to continue to alive in order to avoid dismissing employees decision . But, Cathay airline had made decision that it will dismiss many airline service staffs in different countries. In fact, if Cathay airline expects it would not reach to the decline life cycle stage later, this dismissing employees strategy aims to avoid spending much salaries expenditure , it may be one good method to avoid decline , even death life cycle stage occurs in this year or latter.

On conclusion, it is difficult to predict what factors may cause the business itself will face decline life cycle stage occurrence in any time. Hence, any businesses ought to spend time to research whether which methods or strategies can help them to continue to expand their market or fight any kinds of threats in those four identified business life cycle stages. To avoid business can not continue develop or die, when the business is experiencing in the decline life cycle stage, the strategy is that , the organization needs to spend time to observe or learn how and why its market environment is changing in order to make the most accurate or effective strategies decisions to solve any challenges in any one of these four life cycle stages successfully.

● How new economic development in oil industry

The future global economic growth, it will influence personal incomes and GDP rise. They would carry different weight in different countries at different times. Starting from low levels of incomer and economic development. Household consumption will change from being dominated by basic heat to rapidly rising energy use for higher levels of comfort in space heating and cooling (and large dwellings), and greater use of electrical appliances, finally to a degree of saturation influenced by the income distribution patterns of the country concerned. Income distribution typically changes very slowly, so that the technical market for heart will never be saturated because there will always be a proportion of poor people living in small spaces less comfortably than the average. Industrial energy consumption will be influenced by technical efficiency within each sector, and by changes in the structures of the economy, e.g. changing proportions of agriculture, heavy and light industry, and services. One may eventually see evidence of diminishing marginal returns to additional energy inputs compared to other inputs. Energy consumption in the energy transformation sector may be influenced by income, which drives the demand for electricity to influenced by income, which drives the demand for electricity to grow faster than the demand for heat, but is also subject to the chosen technology of transformation, which is influenced by the cost and availability of primary energy inputs (fuels) in new economic development environment.

IN new economic development environment, it will influences that fuels do not compete in all sectors; for example, the transport sector is dominated by oil. Nuclear and hydroelectric power (and most renewables) reach the user through electricity; electricity itself competes with the direct burning of fossil fuels. Electricity provides the means by which other fuels can compete with oil and gas in sectors, such as space heating and process heat. It also is the only means of powering applications such as motors, computers and lighting: these subsectors are difficult to analyze. However, there is strong evidence that higher incomes do not weaken the demand for electricity so much as the demand for energy in total (in contrast to the effect on the demand for non-electric energy forms).

Econometricians look at the historical record of change in fuel prices and quantities to distinguish several factors between the new economic development and old economic development to oil industry in the future. An income effect. Increasing (reducing) fuel prices reduces (increases) the purchasing power of consumers' income: higher incomes caused by lower prices will increase energy consumption; the consumers' allocation of the increased income to energy purchases may reduce as income rises. Thus income may be heading in a different direction from fuel prices that the effect of fuel price changes when incomes are rising means simply that rising incomes have increased demand. Reducing the cost of using energy through win-win efficiency measures causes a similar problem . On the consequence, in future new economic development environment, it may influence in both cases demand will be less than if the future oil price or efficiency has not changed. The other effect is that an efficiency or substitution effect. An increase in fuel prices may cause consumers to spend more on new equipment, building materials and management operations, which will reduce the amount of fuel required to give the same energy result to the user. The extent of the efficiency effect depends on what happens to the price of the new equipment or building: if those price s rise in line with the fuel price, changes in the balances between fuel and capital or management will not occur. A new user technology , such as the development of the combined cycle gas turbine generator may increase efficiency and thus greatly reduce the quantity of primary fuel needed to produce the required output in this case electricity. If electricity prices had remained sticky, and the electricity and gas markets were not competitive, some of this advantages could have accrued to the gas suppliers in the form of an increase in price, because th4 unit of gas produces more output of electricity, it would have a higher value. In reality, the development of new economic competitive environment in both gas and electricity has tended to ensure that the benefits of such technical advanced accrue to the consumer through lower final prices. The same many apply in the case of improved efficiency in future non-manual driving auto vehicle development: the consumer's cost of motoring is reduced in new economic non-manual driven auto vehicle (Artificial intelligent vehicle) can replace manual driven vehicle , even electricity battery can replace oil energy to be used in vehicles. So, oil price may be influenced to reduce in future new economic development environment.

New and old economic theories explain oil is not main factor to influence tourism income

● Can economic theory explain old price change to influence tourism income?

I shall attempt to apply old and new economic theory to explain whether oil changing price has direct relationship to influence global tourism indusry development or tourism income as below:

Is oil changing price the main to influence tourism income or tourism development or economic growth ? If oil price rises ar falls, it will or won't cause tourism income decreases or increases? If they have cause and effect relationship, what are the main factors to influence tourism income changes by oil price rises or falls ?

I aim to investigate how any why among oil price shocks will influence tourism income variables. We may distinguish between these oil price shocks: Supply-side , aggregate demand and oil specific demand shocks. I assume that oil specific demand shocks affect inflation and the tourism sector equity index. By constrast, I also believe that aggregate demand oil price shock exercisr an effect, either directly and indirectly tourism generated income and economic growth. So, in old economic theory, supply-side , aggregate demand view to oil specific demand shocks will influence tourism income varies. So, governments ought implement strategies against future oil price movements or plan for economic policy development.

In fact, instead of oil price changes will influence tourism income, it could also harm economic growth and tourism activities, due to the effect they expert on transporation, production cost, economic uncertainty.Because tourism activities is one important sector to influence any country's leisure consumption GDP income source. So, sudden fluctations in oil prices may also influence economic growth. It is based a hyphthesis known as the tourism led economic growth. So, it seems that they have direct or indirect relationship to case effect between oil price and tourism activities and development. So, increase on tourism income, the called " economic-driven tourism growth". In addition, high oil prices are affecting certain tourism industry segments , e.g. airlines, cruises lines, hotel, rent travelling car services etc. for oil, importing countries example, with reference to macro economic effects, higher oil prices generally lead to higher inflation, when they negatively influence to country's income.

Hence, from a micro-economic perspective, positive oil price shocks lead to a decline in disposable income. for low income people, it will bring an immediate and negative impact on tourism, mainly due to they feel tourism leisure is regarded as a luxury good, when oil price shocks to rise suddenly . It influences any airline or cruise entertainment service providers' costs are influenced to raise. Then, they need to increase air ticket or cruise ticket price. It will bring on negative tourism leisure demands-side the oil price increases low income group, potential tourism leisure consumers. Hence, it seems that oil price may have indirect relationship to influence tourism leisure consumers' needs.

● How the price of oil changes influences global tourism industry growth or recession?

In macro-economic view, sudden mid and long term oil price shock can influence global torusim industry growth or recession. For example, a oil price of US$180 per barrel was considered only a few years ago, now this has a realistic scenario to which all plaers in the T&T sector have to adapt. At such a high level, the price of oil will become even more critical to almost every part of the tourism value chain. Although, weak global demand, caused by global economic recesson, resulted in a steep oil price decline to US$45 per barrel by the fourth quarter of 2008 in the past low oil price occurrence history, this won't change the mid to long -term oil forecast.

In fact, the past oil price occurrence history of the dramatic structural had changed a high price imposed on airlines, travelers, and destination countries, all of which will have to navigate through times of shifting or even declining travel demand. I assume that a high oil price scenario is assumed in the long term in order to highlight the changes , such a senario would mean for consumer behavior and the competitiveness of several destinations.

Low oil price in the 1970 and early 1980 did not bring significant growth of international air travel, but its growth has been strongest between 1980 and 2004, a period with stable and relatively moderate oil prices. Also, the rapid development of the low-cost carrier business model in the 1990s further fueled air travel growth by capturing tourism leisure demand , such as weekend leisure travel to cities using mostly secondary airports in any big area countries, such as UK, US . However, the tourism growth is whole influenced by high oil prices, due to oil price had been continue rising in possible.

Basis of oil is shortage supply product, oil is assumed to be the main energy source for the aviation sector for the nest 30 years. Although, second-generation biofuels seem to be on the horizon, the economics as well as the production scalability and aviation biofuel shortage will be a main challenge to airline industry. So, I assume that oil price will continue rise up, if there have none any aviation biofuel can be reflected to oil to use for air plane energy.

Until 2004, the only factors to have affected air travel growth, negatively were in external shocks , such as 9/11, causes catching air plane crisis or US regional geopolitical conflicts. It brings some travelers feel fear to go to US travel, as well as until recently 2019, human mouth disease can influence air to have disease to anyone from mouth. So, global travelers number had been continue decreasing, because they are fear to get disease by air when many themselves every stranger travelers are sitting on the without windows air planes. Although, mouth human and air disease and US 9/11 air attack both matters may influence oil price falls effect, because air planes flying times will reduce. They won't need frequent to fly, to cause aviation oil energy need reduce. Consequently, oil price will decrease, due to travelers number reduces and air planes flying times are also influenced to reduce. (oil demand decreases cause oil price decrease). Although, air lines ' cost will also be influenced reduce, but oil price decrease can not bring travelers number increase , when air ticket price reduce because global many leisure and business trip travelers feel fear to catch air planes frequently when human mouth air disease occured in 2019. So, oil price decreases can not grow up tourism industry growth or rise tourism income.

However, the obvious impact of a high oil price is an increase in the operating costs of airline. Moreover, fuel cost as a percentage of airline operating costs vary significantly based on the length of the flight. The longer the flight, the higher the fuel costs as a percentage of the airline operating cost. So, from an online's perspective, long -hauel flights represent the most criticial challenge to profitable operation because the share of fuel on these flights, compared with other cost items, is largest, because of the unfacorable fuel economics, due to fuel costs even at high-load factors. For example, Thai airways dropped its non-stop Bongkok to US flights in the summer of 2008 for commercial reasons, because fuel reached operating cost levels of 55 percent on this route, a cost burden that could not be passed on to their customers. So, the estimated price elacticity of passengers demand at this Bongkok to US flights route is high, if Thai Airways rises less air ticket price, it will influence many travelers to choose other airlines to catch air plan to fly. Hence, due to Thai Airways can not make decision to rise air ticket price, because it believes that it will lose many travelers, so it only chooses to drop this non-stop Bongkok to US flights to avoid fuel cost rising economic loss.

However, although micro and macro economic theories may also that oil price variable or change, it may influence global tourism income. But, recently, on 2019, human mouth and air diseases, it can influence global individual leisure and business trip travelers feel fear to catch air plans to avoid their bodies get this kind of death sickness when they sit in the no fresh air supplying air planes. They feel that they reduce leisure travelling flying times or business trip flying times with strange travelers to sit in crowd air planes together. Then, they must many avoid human moth and air disease to avoid death crisis. Hence, in this global human mouth and air diseases threat environment occurrence, even oil price sudden reduces to low price, it brings airline's cost reduces and air ticke price reduces. However, when air ticket price reduce to be very cheaper, it can not still attract global many leisure or business trip travelers to buy air tickets to fly frequently. Why does air ticket reduction, it can not attract many leisure or businee trip travelers to buy air ticket to fly ? The main reason is because human mouth and air disease influences global many travelers feel fear to catch air planes frequently. In psychological view, this kind of human mouth and air sickness will bring long time negative influence to global traveles do not want to catch air planes for business trips or travelling leisure frequently. So, it implies that oil price changing to influence air ticket price reduction factor ought not main factor to influence tourism income. It may include traveler individual negative emotion psychological factor, such as human mouth and air disease or 2019 9/11 attack both cases, they can influence global travelers feel fear to catch air planes to fly to avoid death threat. So, oil changing price ought not be only one absolute main factor to influence global tourism income significantly.

On conclusion, in economic view, it seems that oil chang price may have indirect or direct relationship to influence tourism income, instead of some unpredicted external environment factors influence, such as US 9/11 attack crisis and human mouth and air disease factors, they may be main factors to influence travellers number to reduce in non-economic external unpredicted environment view.

How can artificial intelligent tools predict travelling consumer behavior in airline and air agent travelling market

I believe that applying (AI) big data tool to predict vehicle buyer consumption choice behavior, it is similar to predict traveler consumption choice behavior. In this chapter, I shall indicate how to apply (AI) big data gathering tool to predict vehicle buyer consumption choice behavior. Then, I shall its what its similar points to be applied to predict traveler consumption choice behavior.

Nowadays, many vehicle manufacturers hope their vehicles can attract to vehicle buyers to choose to buy their vehicles. However, there are many different brands of vehicles to provide to them to choose, so the vehicle market competition is very serious.

How to judge their different kinds of vehicle price which is reasonable acceptance to attract vehicle buyers to choose to buy the brand of vehicle manufacturers' any kinds of vehicles, e.g. fast speed sport style vehicles, comfortable and slow speed common cars, for four passengers common small size or more than four passengers common large car size?

How to evaluate the vehicle prices issue is important factor to influence vehicle buyers' choices. Either if the brand of vehicle price is too high to compare other brands of similar vehicle price, it will influence many vehicle buyers choose to buy other brands' vehicles or if the brand of vehicle price is too low, it will influence vehicle buyers feel this brand's vehicle machine quality or safe driving level or manufacturing steel material or speed or not comfortable sitting etc. different factors is worse to compare to other vehicle brands' similar vehicle products.

Thus, if the brand of vehicle manufacturers can predict how to design vehicles which can attract many vehicle buyers to choose to buy whose any vehicle products. What are future vehicle buyers' favorable vehicle styles? Then, the vehicle manufacturer can concentrate on manufacturing the kind style of vehicle products to sell already. It will reduce its vehicle manufacturing investment risk.

How to apply (AI) tools to predict vehicle buyers' behavioral consumption model? Whether artificial intelligent tools can predict automotive buyers' behavioral consumption model and predict future vehicle design trend. In fact, automotive brands and dealerships are facing an increasingly competition when attempting to manually gathering the vast quantities of data required to create customer focused programs that increase retention, ultimately new sales and service automotive business.

Building a based on that client's intrinsic needs and interests to any kinds of automotive vehicles at any given time. This is especially true in the automotive industry where the time span between purchases is measured in years. Because vehicle buyers would not like often to change their old vehicle to another new one. So, their decisions to buying another new vehicle, the time is usually after one year, even longer time. Hence, it seems any vehicles won't be frequent consumption products to the owned at least one vehicle family consumers (vehicle buyers). It implies that why vehicle manufacturers ought need to spend time to predict future vehicle buyer design choice for whole year vehicle buyer number growth because they won't often change preferable vehicle design to change another new vehicle more easily.

Hence, how to predict vehicle consumers' taste or preferable which styles of vehicle choices issues is very important. If the vehicle manufacturers can not manufacture any attractive vehicles to sell easily in this year. Then, it will lose time, money in this year because it won't know when the owned least one vehicle users or non-owned any vehicle users who will decide to buy one new vehicle or change another new vehicle ensure. The different brand vehicle dealers will possible wait more than one year to attract them to buy their vehicles if their styles are not attractive to compare other brands of vehicle competitors.

However, artificial intelligence and machine learning can help any vehicle manufacturers to find solution to solve patterns in highly to solve patterns in highly complex data-sets that are beyond the capability of a human brain, and then building and automatically acting on the customer insights it generates.

Given the automotive customer need for individualized communications, this technology is positioned to become a critical component of any successful vehicle retailer's domestic or/and overseas vehicle markets. How can vehicle manufacturers and retailers use (AI) to enhance their vehicle marketing campaigns? How will (AI) affect their vehicle sale marketing strategy? What criteria would they use when selecting on (AI) solution?

Vehicle consumers today are able to quickly access different brands of vehicle information, research vehicle products and reviews, negotiate prices and compare one vehicle brand or retailer to another resulting of the brands of vehicle customers. At the same time, the rise of " big -data mining", wearable devices that track user's every move and preference and greater contextualization in advertising and social media has resulted in consumer expectations of individualized. Thus, it seems that (AI) tools can be used to gather " big-data" and then they can make human's mind to analyze how to design kinds of vehicles to satisfy vehicle buyers' needs.

As automotive vehicle marketers can apply (AI) tools to achieve messaging strategies to meet the needs of this new generation of informed vehicle consumers, using data from a variety of sources to move from a variety of sources to move from mass- messaging to more personalized messages aimed at particular vehicle buyer segments, e.g. fast speed sport vehicle buyer segment, slow speed comfortable small size or large size of buyer segment. However, when 90% of vehicle marketers believe having a single vehicle buyer view is important, only 6% have achieved it.

However, one of the main issues vehicle marketers are facing the lack of capacity to efficiently sift through and analyze the massive vehicle buyer amounts of data required to create vehicle buyer individualized vehicle customer experiences easily. This is especially difficult for automotive dealers, the long periods between purchase cycles, and the highly considered nature of the vehicle purchase means that each vehicle dealer needs to not only track a large number of potential vehicle customers for an extremely long period of time, but each of those vehicle customers will generate a huge amount of different kinds of vehicle behavioral consumption data as they research their next vehicle purchase. However, by choosing the right (AI) technological tools and programs , vehicle dealers can solve this big data gathering challenge into a major advantage.

For Forrester vehicle brand example, vehicle consumers have more power over the Forrester vehicle brand's reputation than ever before. Mayne, L. (2014) indicated that Forrester calls this new (AI) tools is the " age of the vehicle customer", a 20 year business cycle in which the most successful vehicle enterprises will reinvent themselves to systematically understand and serve increasingly powerful vehicle consumers. To win in this new age, Forrester declares companies must become vehicle customer obsessed and the only sustainable competitive advantage is knowledge and engagement with customers, such as (AI) gathering data knowledge.

Thus, the biggest challenge vehicle businesses currently face is not the collection of a large quantity of vehicle consumer data, but what to do with that data once they have it. Even at a large vehicle data research firm, the data sets are often too big for a single analyze, or even a team of analysts to sort through and draw conclusion from. However, enter artificial intelligence and machine learning , an efficient technology solution that can continuously find patterns in highly complex data sets that are way beyond the capacity of a human brain and then automatic drive action based on the customer insights is generated.

What is (AI) machine learning tool? Machine learning is a type of (AI) that learns from data and is not explicitly program. Think Amazon, face book. Machine learning serves up relevant content based on an individual vehicle purchase behavior and experiences. More simply, machine learning is a computer program that can learn relationships between data, subject those learnings to errors functions, and then learn from its errors. The program in effect, trains itself.

Lee, T. (2016) explained that "Thus, (AI) tools can learn deep a more advanced branch of machine learning inspired by how our brain's nervous function, has also been found to be especial effective in identifying patterns from data."

When this way sound is complicated from a vehicle dealer perspective, the implementation of a marketing program driven by artificial intelligence can take care of these tasks in an automatic vehicle fashion with little to no manual intervention required from the staff at time vehicle stores.

In practice at a vehicle dealership, the program will continue track vehicle customer behavior online, merging that data with any offline source (like CRM or DMS data) and then analyze this aggregated vehicle buyer data set to predict what vehicle customer may be shopping for and what information they might like to relevance from different kinds style of vehicle design photos.

Why does travelling market seem to similar to vehicle market which can apply (AI) learning tool to predict travellingconsumer behaviors?

Artificial intelligence refers to complex in vehicle market and travelling entertainment market which is very seem to be applied to predict consumer behaviors.

(AI) machine learning that posses the same characteristics of human intelligence and that have all our sense, all our reason and think just like human vehicle buyer who prefer vehicle purchase choice or travelling consumer who prefer travelling package or travelling destination and airline choice. Besides, machine learning is the practice of using algorithms to collect and examine data, learn from it, and then make a determination or prediction about something in the world.

So, it can be attempted to gather data concerns that travelling consumer past travelling destination choice and air ticket price choice and different travelling package, e.g. high, middle, or low class hotel and foods supply and entertainment places choice in their past travelling journeys.

The machine is " trained" using large amounts of data and algorithms that give it the ability to learn how to automatically perform a task with increasing accuracy. Otherwise, deep learning is primarily based on artificial neural networks inspired by our understanding of the biology of human's brains.

Thus, (AI) big data can gather all these past traveler consumption behavioral choice data to make reference to analyze whether how many travelers will choose to go to the specific travelling destination in any time by the past traveler number record to different travelling destinations, then it can gather the past air ticket sale price to different destinations and past travelling package design to different destinations in order to analyze whether it is the cheap airline ticket price factor or attractive travelling package factor or attractive travelling entertainment etc. in order to predict which factor is the most potential influential factor to they choose to go to the destination to travel in different time within one year. Then, traveler agent or airline can collect these big data to judge how to design their package to attract travelers to go to anywhere to travel or what the main factor influence most of them to choose to visit the destination to travel.

For example, travel agents or airlines can apply "Deep learning" breaks down tasks in ways that enables machines to assist them to predict when travelling consumer choice will be changed and why their travelling choice will change and how their travelling choice will change with increasingly complex tasks.

So, such as why (AI) technology can be applied to predict how travelling consumer behavior changes to bring to judge whether anywhere will be many travelling consumers who will prefer to choose travelling hot destinations next year or next month.

Then, travel agents and airlines can gather overall past travelling consumer data to analyze and conclude the more accurate prediction of different travelling destinations to the number of traveler. Then, they can choose how much air ticket price is more reasonable to charge to the travelling destination or how to design the travelling package which can bring more attractive to the prediction number of different travelling destination travelers in order to achieve to raise the different travelling destination number next year.

Thus, (AI) big data machine learning can help airlines or travel agents to solve how to design any attractive travelling package challenge. A travelling package is both one of the most important and carefully considered travelling entertainment consumption the majority of travelling people will ever make in their lifetime at least one travelling time.

It is also a prediction how travelling package will be designed that tends to be fundamentally tied to a travelling person's travelling destination choice identify and travelling package view of themselves. As the same time, travelling consumers' travelling choice changing lifestyles result in changing travelling destination needs, e.g. the country's young travelers can choose to change non-extreme exciting travelling entertainment package from past extreme exciting travelling entertainment package. Due to personal feeling factor in general. However, I believe that (AI) big data can also be attempted to predict when the country's young travelers will choose to change non-extreme exciting travelling behavior.

It is similar to automotive dealers need to remember that vehicle customers and prospects are individual human beings with risk, complex and ever-changing lives factors, these factors will influence every vehicle consumer why who feels has vehicle purchase need, and how who choose to buy the first vehicle if who decided to buy the first vehicle.

It seems that travelling agents or airlines need to remember that travelling consumers and different features or designs are very traveler beings with risk, complex and ever-travelling package attitude personal changing factors in different travel season, these factor will influence every individual traveler why who feels has travel entertainment need, and how who choose to buy different feature or design travelling package if who decide to travel. The (AI) big data technological travelling customer behavioral prediction tool seems to be the best travelling behavioral prediction tool in the world are those that know every one of different country's traveler need. Their likes and dislikes which style of travelling package, preferences and travel destination changing tastes to travelling destination choices.

The capacity of the human brain, however, limits us from achieving these different type of travel package sales. In this competitive travelling destination choice entertainment environment, (AI) big data machine learning enables platforms to assist the air ticket and travel package sales team by tracking the travelling consumer behaviors of each travelling customer, learning and memorizing their preferences and predicting their future travelling destination choice and travelling package design needs.

Finally, I recommend that for a travel agent or airline travelling marketing platform to make their travelling customer engagement efficient and fully-functional, I should be able to: applying (AI) tools to track every travelling customer behavior across the web, connecting to a society of data sources, CRM, DMS, third-party, web travelling brands, social traveler email, click etc., aggregating and accurately cross-reference data from a variety of sources, leveraging this data to drive insights on a mass scale, as well as on an individualized basis, driving actions and automatically direct travelling customer engagement via multiple channels based on where each customer is in their travelling individual lifecycle.

Why is (AI) big data gathering tool better than psychological and survey methods to predict traveler individual travel choice behavior?

Prediction travel behavioral consumption from psychology and survey methods.

How to predict travel consumption? It is one question to any travel agents concern to use what methods which can predict how many numbers of travelers where who will choose to go to travel more accurately. I think that who can consider how to predict travel behavioral consumption from psychology and survey travel choice prediction method, but it is better to apply (AI) big data gathering method to predict travel consumer's destination choice more accurate. The reason is as below:

The first reason is that traveller individual travel psychological desire is difficult to predict accurate more than (AI) big data gathering method, it is due that the data is past traveler's destination choice and travel package and ticket price actual data from (AI) big data gathering method. Otherwise, survey investigation is only traveler psychological thinking method. It lacks enough past actual traveler data gathering.

The second reason is that on the weakness of traveler individual psychological thinking view of survey investigation. It has evidence to support the relationship between self-identify threat and resistance to change travel behavior to any travelers, controlling for whose past travelling behavior, resistance to change if a psychological phenomenon of long standing interest in many applied branches of psychology.

Past travelling behavior has been acknowledged as a predictor of future action. Such as travelling behavior that is experienced as successful is likely to be repeated and may lead to habitual patterns. Some psychologists differentiate habit between two concepts, such as goal oriented and automatic oriented both. Although repeated past travelling behavior is addition goal oriented and automatic oriented. Further non-deliberative nature of habit may make appeals to judge and to predict future individual traveler's behavior accurately.

However, repeated one traveler will choose the destination to repeat to travel without a necessary constraint of goal orientation and automatic oriented both. So, it seems that psychological factor can influence any individual traveler why and how who choose to decide to repeat to choose the destination to travel.

So, survey investigation is only the traveler's thinking to answer the travel firm. It is not sure that the traveler's past travel experience is real answer. Otherwise, (AI) big data gathering method is computer gathering method which gather past traveler consumption actual data to analyze and conclude future traveler possible repeated travel destination choice and travel package choice more accurate.

The third reason is that on the strength of (AI) big data gathering method computer statistic view to predict future traveller consumer's destination and travel package choice. It is structural equation modeling is an extremely flexible linear-in-parameters multivariate statistical modeling technique. It has been used in modeling travel behavior and values since about 1980 year. It is a software method to handle a large number of variables, as well as unobserved variables specified as linear combinations (weighted averages) of the observed variable.

Can (AI) big data gather data to predict when climate will change to influence poor travelling behaviours?

(AI) big data tool can predict the flexibility of human travelling behavioral change is at least the result of one such mechanism, our ability to travel mentally in time and entertain potential future. Understanding of the impacts is holidays, particularly those involving travel.

Using focus groups research to explores tourists' awareness of the impacts of travel own climate change, examines the extent to which climate change features in holiday travel decisions and identifies some of the barriers to the adoption of less carbon intensive tourism practices.

The findings suggest many tourists don't consider climate change when planning their holidays. The failure of tourists to engage with the climate change to impact of holidays, combined with significant barriers to behavioral change, presents a considerable challenge in the tourism industry. In the future, computer (AI) big data tool can attempt to predict when the country's climate change to influence travelers to choose to go to the country to travel, e.g. next month or next half year or next year hot travelling destinations.

Tourism is a highly energy intensive industry and has only recently attracted attention as an important contributions to climate change through greenhouse gas emissions. It has been estimated that tourism contributes 5% of global carbon dioxide emissions. There have been a number of potential changes proposed for reducing the impact of air travel on climate change. These include technological changes, market based changes and behavioral changes.

However, the role that climate change plays in the holiday and travel decisions of global tourists. How the global tourists of the impacts travel has on climate change to establish the extent to which climate change, considerations features in holiday travel decision making processes and to investigate the major barriers to global tourists adopting less carbon intensive travel practices.

It will bring this question: Will tourists aware the impacts that their holidays and travel have on climate changes to influence their travelling decision?

When, it comes to understand individual traveler's behavioral change, wide range of conceptual theories have been developed, utilizing various social, psychological, subjective and objective variables in order to model travel consumption behavior. These theories of travel behavioral change operate at a number of different levels, including the individual level, the interpersonal level and community level. Whether pro-environmental behavior can be used to predict travel consumption behavior in a climate change. However, the question of what determines pro-environmental behavior in such a complex one that it can not be visualized through one single framework or diagram.

Despite the potentially high risk scenario for the tourism industry and the global environment, the tourism and climate change ought have close relationship.

However, (AI) big data tool can be applied to find what factors to influence the time of travelers' travelling choices. What are the important factors and variables which can limit tourism? e.g. money, time, family problem, extreme hot or cold weather change, air ticket price, journey attraction etc. variable factors.

Mention of holidays and travel were deliberately avoided in the recruitment process, so as not to create a connection factor to influence traveler's individual mind. However, the dismissal of alternative transportation modes can be conceived as either a structural barrier, in the sense that flying is perhaps the only realistic option to reach long-haul holiday destination, or a perceived behavioral control barriers in that an individual perceives flying as the only option open to whom.

The transportation tool factor will be depend to extent on the distance to the destination. This can also be interpreted in a social perspective as an intention with the resources available where much international tourism is structured around flying. To increase the availability of different transportation modes, tourists could choose holiday destination closer to home.

Finally, also how to predict future travel behavioral consumption. I feel that travel agents need to predict whether any country's random daily variation of weather factor is also important to influence travel behavior. e.g. in weather, temperature, rainfall and snowfall with traffic accidents factors will have relationship to cause travel demand.

Some scientists estimate suggest that when warmed temperatures and reduced snowfall are associated with a moderate decline in non-fatal accidents, they are also associated with a significant increase in fatal accidents. Thus increase in fatalities and temperature. Half of the estimated effect of temperature on fatalities is due to changes in the exposure to pedestrians, bicyclists and motorcyclists as temperature increase.

So, if any countries have rainfall, snowfall and low temperature to cause traffic accidents, whether this accident occurrence will influence the travelers who liking climb snow hills, riding bicycle, running sports who will avoid to travel to these countries' bad weather after occurs. So, why I feel that this natural climate factor will also be one serious factor to influence travel behavioral consumption. However, (AI) big data tool can predict more accurate than survey method when climate change to influence the country's climate to be poor, then it can predict when which countries are not popular acceptable to global country consumers' travel choice next month.

How can apply (AI) to provide travelling businesses with better-informed decisions ?

I shall explain how (AI) big data gathering technology can provide travelling businesses with better-informed decisions to drive top-line growth, deliver meaningful experience for travelling customers and smooth their path along the travelling consumer journey. The widely understood definition of (AI) involves the ability of machines or computers to learn human thinking, reasoning and decision-making abilities.

So, such as (AI) learning machine system can attempt to learn travelling consumer's travel destination or travel package thinking, judgement of their reasons why they choose to go to the destination to travel or why they choose to buy the travel package and learn how and why they make their past travelling decisions from their past travel big data gathering.

A Narrative science study in 2015 year identified that (AI) was being used primarily in voice recognition, machine learning virtual assistants and decision support. This study also highlighted the many branches of (AI) and that techniques and their definition are used interchangeably. It is possible that (AI) can be used to gather big data , then to analyze to help travel businesses to predict travelling consumer travel destination and travel package choice behaviors. For example, one of the most common techniques is traveler machine learning, where algorithms are used to perform tasks by learning from the airline or travel agent whose past all travelers' travelling destination choice and travel package choice historical data.

However, during 2017 year, search engines will begin to find what additional factors can influence past traveler personal travelling destination and travelling package travelling behavioral data into prediction of future travelling customer behavioral results, such as the online traveler (user's) history of travelling data searches, such as anywhere are the most popular travelling locations or travelling destinations and previously captures conservations.

Artiticial intelligence will use this past travelling destinations and travelling package information to power predictive search results, e.g. predictive future travelling consumer's choice behavioral processing for where will be their preferable travelling destination choice and how to design travelling package to satisfy future travelling clients' needs.

Predictive search will improve the quality of online travelling search results, and provide new insights into travelling consumers' travelling destination and package behavior and the moments which matter to them. Search will give recommendation into tailored how travelling consumer individual travelling destination choice in travelling decision making process. Several of the largest online platforms already use (AI) travelling machine learning to improve predictive travelling consumer behavioral search results.

For example, Google's rank brain technology adds research by understanding the context in which the travelling consumer has entered it. Over time, rank brain will learn further from user behaviors Amazon's DSSTNE (pronouned destiny) learns from shoppers' purchasing habits and consumption behavior to offer better product recommend actions, which Amazon can offer before a consumer has entered anything into the search bar.

Such as (AI) big data can gather past online travelers' e-ticket purchase transactions to conclude that online traveler's travelling choice habits and online traveler consumption behavior to offer better travelling destinations and travelling package opinions to travel agents or airlines. However, this technology is not independent of human input. For example, Google engineers will periodically retain the rank brain system to improve the models it uses.

For another example, in 2016 year , Apple computer revamped its travelling scene photos app to allow travelling consumers to search for specific travelling destinations in the travelling scene phots, they want to find anywhere travelling destination photos, not just dates and locations. Each travelling photo that an intelligent phone or intelligent pad user takes goes through 11 billion computations, so that travelling scene photos can understand exactly where is the travelling destination photography to let online travelling consumer to feel anywhere they plan to go to the location to travel. So, (AI) learning machine can make online travelling photos more attractive to influence potential travelers choose to the destination to travel after they see the travelling destination scene photos from internet.

It seems that in future, (AI) machine learning will allow online travelling search to evolve even further. Search engineers will deliver refined recommendations to airlines' online traveler e-ticket search users and use less human input to predict travelling consumers' needs from internet channel. For IBM computer example, it indicated 90% of the data that exists today has been created in the last two years.

This huge explosion of past traveler's e-ticket consumption data gives the opportunity to quickly spot and react to the latest trends, fashion and fads among its travelling clients and potential clients. This will allow airline or travel agent companies to better engage with younger travelling consumers, who gain influence access to the latest travelling destination and package trends.

They associate with to help define who they are as individuals. Thus, travelling company brands have to identify and make use of them before travelling consumers move on, but the vast quantity of past e-ticket purchase data available makes from internet channel. This a resource-intensive task. For next example, Lesara, a based online clothes store, uses this machine learning to inform its product decision often gathering information from internal and external sources.

When its trends -spotting shoes. Lesara has a range of over 20 styles and sells hundreds of pairs a day. It focus on giving consumers, the very latest trends allow Lesara to develop on average of 50,000 new items each year. It compared to 11,000 old items each year. Thus, travelling agents or airlines can attempt to apply (AI) big data gathering method to gather all past e-ticket purchase data, concerns where they prefer to choose to go to the destinations to travel and what travelling packages are the most attractive to the travelers to choose to buy. It aims to help them to predict where future travelers will prefer to choose to go to travel or what travelling package they will prefer to choose to buy next year.

For another (AI) big data prediction example, Lesara is one online clothes store, uses machine learning decisions after gathering information from internal and external sources. One of its most popular products, shoes with LED started life when its trend spotting software flagged up a blogger wearing similar shoes. Now Lesara has a range of over 20 styles and sells hundreds of pairs a day. Its focus on giving consumers the very latest trends allows Lesara to develop an average of 50,000 new items each year, compared to 11,000 for its competitor Lara.

It seems (AI) big data gathering machine learning can help Lesara business to predict what kinds of shoes design or style that shoe consumers will prefer choose to buy in future shoe market trend. Thus, Lesara can predict shoe consumers' taste successfully and it can manufacture many attractive style of shoes.

(AI) machine learning can gather global past shoe consumer's shoe shopping experiences, then analyzes to make conclusion to give lesara recommendation successfully. This will make the experience more enjoyable for shoe consumers and allow Lesara to advert whose different new style or design of shoes to deliver them move relevant messages by understanding the context of the experience.

So, online travel agents or online airline can also attempt to apply (AI) big data gathering method to predict where travelers will prefer to go to travel and how they ought design travelling packages to attract them to choose to buy next year. Hence, (AI) big data gathering technology can conclude how to design traveler agents' travelling package products to be the most attractive to excite many travelers choose to buy their travelling package, due to it has more accurate to predict travelling consumer destination and travelling package choice behaviors to compare human themselves prediction judgement effort, e.g. travelling survey or marketing research, or telephone enquire. It seems that (AI) machine judgement effort is more accurate to compare to human judgment effort in travelling industry.

Future travel consumption behavior

Can (AI) big data gathering tool predict traveler individual habitual behavior , e.g. renting travel transportation tools ?

Can (AI) big data gathering tool can predict past traveler destination and travelling package choice habit and it can be intended to predict of future traveler behavior to people are creatures of habits judgement of future anywhere travelling destination choice next year or next month or next half year destination prediction ?

Many of human's everyday goal-directed behaviors are performed in a habitual fashion, the transportation made and route one takes to work, one's choice of breakfast. Habits are formed when using the some behavior frequently and a similar consistency in a similar context for the some purpose whether the individual past travel consumption model will be caused a habit to whom. e.g. choosing whom travel agent to buy air ticket or traveling package; choosing the same or similar countries' destinations to go to travel ; choosing the business class or normal (general) class of quality airlines to catch planes.

Does habitual rent traveling car tools use not lead to more resistance to change of travel mode? It has been argued that past behavior is the best predictor of future behavior to travel consumption. If individual traveler's past consumption behavior was always reasoned, then frequency of prior travel consumption behavior should only have an indirect link to the individual traveler's behavior. It seems that renting travel car tools to use is a habit example. So, a strong rent traveling car tools useful habit makes traveling mode choice. People with a strong renting of traveling car tools of habit should have low motivation to attend to gather any information about public transportation in their choice of travelling country for individual or family or friends members during their traveling journeys.

Even when persuasive communication changes the traveler whose attitudes and intention, in the case of individual traveler or family travelers with a strong renting travel car tools habit. It is difficult to change whose travel behaviors to choose to catch public transportation in whose any trips in any countries. However, understanding of travel behavior and the reasons for choosing one mode of transportation over another. The arguments for rent traveling car tools to use, including convenience, speed, comfort and individual freedom and well known.

Increasingly, psychological factors include such as, perceptions, identity, social norms and habit are being used to understand travel mode choice. Whether how many travel consumers will choose to rent traveling car tools during their trips in any countries. It is difficult to estimate the numbers. As the average level of renting travel car tools of dependence or attitudes to certain travel package policies from travel agents. Instead different people must be treated in different ways because who are motivated in different ways and who are motivated by different travel package policies ways from travel agents.

In conclusion, the factors influence whose traveler's individual traveler destination choice behavior The factors include either who chooses to rent traveling car tools or who chooses to catch public transportation when who individual goes to travel in alone trip or family trip. It include influence mode choice factors, such as social psychology factor and marketing on segmentation factor both to influence whose transportation choice of behavior in whose trip. So, (AI) big data can be attempted to gather past traveler transportation tool choice, rent travelling car tools choice or catching public transportation tools choice to predict where destination can provide what kind of transportation tool to attract many travelers to choose to go to the place to travel.

How (AI) big data determine future travel behavior from past travel experience and perceptions of risk and safety for the benefits to travel consumers?

How (AI) big data determine future travel behavior from past travel experience and perceptions of risk and safety for the benefits to travel consumers? Why does individual traveler avoid certain destination(s) is(are) as relevant to tourist decision making as why who chooses to travel to others?

Perceptions of risk and safety and travel experience are likely to influence travel decisions. If travel agents had efforts to predict future travel behavior to guess whether travelers will feel where is(are) risk and unsafe to cause who does not choose to go to the country to travel. Then, the travel agents will avoid to choose to spend much time to design the different traveling package to attract their potential travel consumers to choose to travel. The reason is because in the case of individual traveler's tourism experience, the traveler whose past disappointment travel experience (psychological risk) will be a serious threat to the traveler's health or life (health, physical or terrorism risk). The past safety or unhealthy risk to the country(countries) will influence the traveler decides to choose not to go to the countries(country) to travel again in the future.

What is push and pull factors to influence any traveler who chooses where is whose preferable travelling destination ?

How to apply (AI) big data to predict individual traveler's behavioral intention of choosing a travel destination?

Understanding why people travel and what factors influence their behavioral intention of choosing a travel destination is beneficial to tourism planning and marketing. In general, an individual's choice of a travel destination into two forces.

The first force is the push factor that pushes an individual away from home and attempt to develop a general desire to go somewhere, without specifying where that may be.

The other force is the pull factor that pull an individual toward in destination, due to a region-specific or perceived attractiveness of a destination. The respective push and pull factors illustrate that people travel because who are pushed by whose internal motives and pulled by external forced of a destination. However, the decision making process leading to the choice of a travel destination is a very complex process.

For example, a Taiwanese traveler who might either choose new travel destination of Hong Kong or another old travel Asia destinations again or who also might choose any one of Western country, as a new travel destination. The travel agents can predict where who will have intention to choose to travel from whose past behavior and attitude, subjective and perceived behavioral control model. When (AI) big data gather past every country traveler number who chose to go to which countries to travel in order to judge where destinations will be the country travelers' travelling choice destinations in the future.

The factors influence where is the traveler choice, include personal safety, scenic beauty, cultural interest, climate changing, transportation tools, friendliness of local people, price of trip, trip package service in hotels and restaurants, quality and variety of food and shopping facilities and services etc. needs. So, whose factors will influence where is the individual travel's choice. It seems every traveler whose choice of travel process, will include past behavior. e.g. travelling experience, travelling habit, then to choose the best seasoned travelling action to satisfy whose travel needs. This process is the individual traveler's psychological choice process, who must need time to gather information to compare concerning of different travel packages, destination scene, climate change, transportation tools available to the destination, air ticket price etc. these factors, then to judge where is the best right destination to travel in the right time.

Hence, (AI) big data can gather past different countries' climate changing data, transportation tool changing data, destination scene environment changing etc. different data to give opinions to travelling businesses whether any country's these above factors will influence about how many traveler number will be increase or decrease in the future.

Why can expectation, motivation and attitude factor influence travelling behavior?

Social psychology is concerned with gaining insight into the psychological of socially relevant behaviors and the processes. For instance, on a global level bad influence to global warming, it influences some countries extreme cold or hot bad climate changing occurrence, then it ought influence some travelers' behavioral decision to change their mind to choose some countries to go to travel at the moment which do not occur extreme hot or cold climate (temperature). e.g. above than 40 degree in summer or below than 0 degree in winter. Due to the extreme climate changing environment in the countries, it will cause them to feel uncomfortable to play during their trips. So, the global warming causes to climate changing factor will influence the numbers of travel consumption to be reduced possibly. This is global climate changing environment factor influences to bad or uncomfortable social psychological feeling to global travelers' mind of traveling decision. What is individual traveler expectation, motivation and attitude? Tourism sector includes inbound (domestic) tourism and outbound (overseas) tourism both incomes to any countries. According to recent article, a tourist behavior model has been developed, called the expectation, motivation and attitude (EMA) model (Hsu et al., 2010).

This model focuses on the pre-visit stage of tourists by modeling the behavioral process by incorporating expectation, motivation and attitude. Travel motivation is considered as an essential component of the behavioral process, which has been increasing attention from the travel; industry. The economic approach defines "tourism" is an identifiable nationally important industry. It includes the component activities of transportation, accommodation, recreation, food and related service. So, tourism behavioral consumption is concerned the individual tourist's usual habituate of the industry which responds to whose needs, and of the impacts that both the tourist and the tourism industry have on the socio-cultural, economic and physical environment.

However, travel motivation means how to understand and predict factors that influence travel decision making. According to Backman and others (1995, p.15), motivation is conceptually viewed as " a state of need, a condition that services as a driving force to display different kind of behavior toward certain types of activities, developing preferences, arriving at some expected satisfactory outcome." So, motivation and expectancy which has close relationship to any tourist before who decided to do any tourism of behavior.

Some economists confirmed motivation and expectancy which has relations, such as expectation of visiting an outbound destination has a direct effect on motivation to visit the destination; motivation has a direct effect on attitude toward visiting the destination; expectation of visiting the outbound destination has a direct affection on attitude toward visiting the destination and motivation has a mediating effect on the relationship in between expectation and attitude.

Hence, (AI) big data can gather all the country's climate environment change, transportation tool change, entertainment scene change, hotel price and restaurant price change etc. data to give opinions whether the country will attract how many traveler to choose to go to travel in the year.

What is (AI) deep learning techniques to forecast travelling environment behavioral consumption

Prediction how many travelers will choose to go to the country to travel. It is similar to apply deep-learning technology to predict how to raise the agricultural farming productivity in the agricultural export country.

The (AI) deep-learning technology leads to performance enhancement and generalization of artificial intelligent technology. It influences the global leader in the field of information technology has declared its intention to utilize the deep-learning technology to solve environmental problems, such as climate change.

So, it will help agriculture farming businesses can raise any plant food: vegetable, fruit, rice which grow up very easily if farmers can apply (AI) deep-learning technology to solve environment problems to influence their plant food grow. If the whole year seasonal change is very good and it is suitable for any plant food to grow in farming land easily, e.g. rain is enough and soil is enough for any plant food to grow in the farm lands. Then, fruit, rice, vegetable etc. agriculture businesses will have much beneficial attribution to global farmers.

The question is how to use deep-learning technologies in the environmental field to predict the status of pro-environmental consumption. We predicted the pro-environmental consumption index based on Google search query data, using a recurrent neural network (RNN model). To certify the accuracy of the index, we compared the prediction accuracy of the RNN model with that of the ordinary least square and artificial necessary network models.

For example, the RNN model predicts the pro-environmental consumption index better than any other model. we expect the RNN model to perform still better in a big data environment because the deep-learning technologies would be increasingly as the volume of data grows. So, deep-learning technologies could be useful in environmental forecasting to prevent damage caused by climate change to influence any rice, vegetable, tomato, potato, fruit etc. different plant food grow in any countries' farming land easily.

For South Korea example, over 800 government agencies spent 2.2 trillion Korea won on eco-products in 2014 year. However, green products are rarely purchased outside these agencies. This phenomenon occurs because there is a gap between consumer attitudes and behavior , that is environmental attitude is a major factor in decision making vis-a-vis the consumption of " green" food and services (Jorea Ministry of Environment, 2015).

Therefore, it is necessary to understand those consumer attitude, that will lead to sustainability-conductive behavior and consumption. (AI) Deep learning system can be applied to attempt understand those traveler attitude to environment protection to fly to which country. For example, (AI) deep learning system can attempt to gather data concerns how many Hong Kong people concern air pollution challenge to influence their health, then it can attempt to predict how many Hong Kong travelers do not choose to go China travel, due to the air pollution challenge to influence their health.

Environmental travel consumption prediction

Recently, many researchers have studied pro-environmental consumption and household indexes as well as suicide rate predictions using messages posted by internet users on Google trend, Tweets etc. channel.

Whether can environmental consumption be predicted by (AI) deep-learning technological internet channel to influence how many travelers choose to go to the country to travel?

How can impact the pro-environmental consumption attitudes of green policies to influence how many travelers choose to go to the country to travel?

For example, Korea scientists estimated pro-environmental attitudes using search query data provided by Google trend and confirmed through regression analysis, that pro-environmental attitude has a positive correlation with the pro-environmental attitude index. They also explained that environment-friendly attitude of residents plan an important role in policy making. In the past, most household consumption indexed were calculated through surveys, but (AI) deep-learning technological tool " big data" have recently gained research attention (Lee et al. 2016). So, (AI) deep learning technology can attempt to gather whether how many Korea residents who concern environment pollution to influence their eating green food attitude then to judge whether how many Korea residents hope to leave their country to travel anywhere either high risk environment pollution countries to travel or low risk environment pollution countries to travel in the future.

It seems that (AI) deep-learning technology can help agricultural export countries' farmers , e.g. US, UK, Canada, New Zealand, Australia, Japan, China, India etc. they can predict environmental behavioral consumption to any rice, tomato, potato , fruit, vegetable etc. plant food consumers. The beneficial advantages to them include as below:

(a) Assuming they know their countries' weather, when it has less rain to cause drought or when it has more rain in any seasonal time in the year.

They can choose not to grow any kinds of above these plant food to avoid loss.

(b) They can make any kinds of above these plant food price raising after their prediction of these bad seasonal time to cause their plant food shortage supply challenge. Because these plant food consumers' demand number is more, but the supply of these above plant food supply number is less. However, due to they had predicted when the bad seasonal time can not allow them to grow these above plant food before. So, they have enough time to grow many these above plant food number in predictive good seasonal time to prepare to supply to their plant food import countries' plant food consumers to eat. Thus, these predictive environmental consumption plant food export countries can raise their plant food price to sell to them. When, the other non-pre-predictive environmental consumption plant food export countries can not supply any one of those plant food to them to eat, due to the bad climate to cause them can't grow any one of these plant food to export to sell.

Thus, (AI) deep-learning technology can be applied to predict how to raise the plant food supply number in order to raise price to the import plant food countries consumers to eat, due to they feel difficult to buy these plant food to eat in the bad climate seasonal time in whole year.

(c) (AI) deep-learning technology can help climate scientists to find what reasons cause their countries; rain sudden increases or cause their countries' rain sudden decreases. After its gathering data analysis, it can assist climate scientists to find solution methods to attempt to control the rain level can be right falling down level to let agricultural export farmers who can grow their plant food to sell to agricultural import countries in whole year.

(d) The agricultural export countries' farmers can apply (AI) deep-learning technology to help them to choose whether growing which kinds of plant food in that whether climate time to earn more plant food consumption number more easily.

Due to the agricultural countries climate will often change, for example, tomato, potato, rice, fruit etc. plant food can be adapt to grow in more rain time, but vegetable can not be adapt to grow in more rain time. If farmers can apply this technology to predict when it will have move rain or when it will have less rain to fall down in their countries. Then, they can choose to grow which kinds of plant food number more, in the suitable seasonal climate time in order to raise plant food growing number productivities to supply to sell to satisfy any agricultural food import countries' demand effectively.

(e) (AI) deep-learning technology can help agricultural import countries to solve agricultural food shortage challenge in long term. When this technology can be popular to base applied by the agricultural plant food export countries. It will solve global agricultural food shortage challenge. For example, when one agricultural export countries' farmers can popular accept to apply this technology to predict when to grow which kinds of plant food more to rise number productivities to sell. e.g. vegetable, fruit, rice Besides another agricultural export countries' farmers can also accept to apply this technology to predict when to grow plant food, e.g. potato, tomato to raise number productivities to sell. Then, they can concentrate on growing the specific kinds of plant food in order to raise the specific plant food number productivities in every seasonal change time every month. Then, global agricultural plant food supply must be raised, due to these predictive environmental change farmers can know who ought grow which kinds of plant food to sell to raise number productivities.

Consequently, (AI) deep learning can gather where countries will have high risk environment pollution to influence health food supply. Then, it can give opinions to travelling businesses when these high risk environment pollution countries will encounter the traveler number to be decreased, due to the environment pollution serious challenge will occur.

What methods can predict future travel behavioral consumption ?

How to use qualitative of travel behavioral method to predict future travel consumption from (AI) big data ?

I also suggest to use qualitative of travel behavioral method to predict future travel consumption. Methods such as focus groups interviews and participant observer techniques can be used with quantitative approaches on their own to fill the gaps left by quantitative techniques. These insights have contributed to the development of increasingly sophisticated models to forecast travel behavior and predict changes in behavior in response to change in the transportation system. I shall indicate the weaknesses of human travelling investigation methods as below:

First, survey methods restrict not only the question frame but the answer frame as well, anticipating the important issues and questions and the responses. However, these surveys methods are not well suited to exploratory areas of research where issues remain unidentified and the researched seek to answer the question "why?".

Second, data collection methods using traditional travel diaries or telephone recruitment can under represent certain segments of the population, particularly the older persons with little education, minorities and the poor. Before the survey, focus group for example can be used to identify what socio-demographic variables to include in the survey, how best to structure the diary, even what incentives will be most effective in increasing the response rate.

After the survey, focus, focus groups can be used to build explanations for the survey results to identify the "why" of the results as well as the implications. One Asia Pacific survey research result was made by tourism market investigation before. It indicated the travel in Asia Pacific market in the past, had often been undertaken in large groups through leisure package sold in bulk, or in large organized business groups, future travelers will be in smaller groups or alone, and for a much wider range of reasons.

Significant new traveler segments, such as female business traveler. The small business traveler and the senior traveler, all of which have different aspirations and requirements from the travel experience.

Moreover, Asia tourism market will start to exist behaviors in the adoption of newer technologies, a giving the traveler new ways to manage the travel experience, creating new behaviors. This with provide new opportunities for travel providers. The use of mobile devices, smartphones, tablets etc. and social media are the obvious findings to become an integral part of the travel experience. Thus, quality method can attempt to predict Asia Pacific tourism market development in the future. It is such as (AI) big data gathering tool can give traveler quality opinions to any travelling businesses to make the more accurate where will be the popular travel destination choice next month or next half year or next year.

However, improving the predictive power of travel behavior models and to increase understanding travel behavior which lies in the use of panel data(repeated measures from the same individuals). Whereas, cross-sectional data only reveal inter-individual differences at one moment in time, panel data can reveal intra-individual changes over time. In effect, panel data are generally better suited to understand and predict (changes in) travel behavior. However, a substantial proportion was also observed to transition between very different activity/travel patterns over time, indicating that from one year to the next, many people renegotiated their activity/travel patterns.

How to apply advanced traveler information systems (ATIS) to predict future travelling behavior?

Nowadays, information can impact on traveler behavior and network performance. For example, when steadily growing levels of vehicle ownership and vehicle miles traveled information has been identified as a potential strategy towards man aging travel demand, optimizing transportation networks and better utilizing available capacity. Toward, this goal to predict further tourist behavioral consumption. Many countries, government tourism development institutes has applied advanced traveler information systems (ATIS) which travel behavior models and high-fidelity network performance models made increasingly feasible through the rapid advances in computer power. Crucial components of this problem domain are the modeling of individual tourist drivers' response to travel information and the development accurate guidance of relevance to real would trip makers. So, this advanced traveler information systems (ATIS) can assist the tourist who like to rent travelling car tools to travel in any countries own free traveler information systems service conveniently. Also, this travel information system can be intended to assist travelers to make better travel choices. e.g. this system can improve the decision making of individual traveler rather than improvements of network performance overall. So, we need to understand how tourists make their travel plans. Also, understanding decision process that lead to booking of the trip is equally important, as it allows of a potential behavior.

How can online tourism sale channel influence traveling consumption of behavior?

Nowadays, internet is popular, it seems that booking air ticket behavior of using internet is predicted to influence overall tourism air tickets payment method. Tourism industry has grown in the previous several decades. Despite its global impact, questions related to better understanding of tourists and whose habits. Using online travel air ticket booking benefits include booking electronic air tickets can be made from entering any electronic travel agents websites in the short time and electronic travel ticket payers do not need leave home, who can pay visa card to pre booking any electronic travel ticket from online channel conveniently.

How can analyze activity based travel demand ?

Nowadays, human are concerning the traffic congestion and air quality deterioration, the supply oriented focus of transportation planning has expanded to include how to manage travel demand within the available transportation supply. Consequently, there has been an increasing interest in travel demand management strategies, such as congestion pricing that attempts to change aggregate travel demand. The prediction aggregate level, long term travel demand to understanding disaggregate level (i.e. individual levels) behavioral responses to short term demand policies, such as ride sharing incentives, congestion pricing and employer based demand management schemes, alternate work schedules, telecommuting limitation of travel agent traditionally work nature shall influence oriented trip based travel modelling passenger travel demand indirectly.

Finally, online travel purchase will be popular to influence the number of travel behavioral consumption nowadays. Any travel package products can be sold from websites to attract travelers to choose to pre-book air ticket for any trips conveniently. In the past ten years, the internet has become the predominant carrier of all types of information and transactions. Regarding travel decisions, internet has also become an important sales channels for the travel industry, because it is associated with comparably lower distribution and sales costs, but also because it adapts to high supply and demand dynamics in this industry. Consequently, the travel and tourism industry tries to increase the internet sale specific share of sales volumes. So, internet sale channel has changed travel consumption behavioral pattern and characteristics and travel experience. For example, Switzerland has one of the highest population-to-computer ratio in Europe. It is also one of the most highly internet penetrated countries in terms of use of the WWW on a day-to-day basis, with more than 75 percent of the population older than 14 years using the WWW daily (ICT, 2005).

The reason of booking online tourism may include: convenience, fast transaction, finding traveling package choice easily, more airline seats available. So, online booking tourism will influence the traditional tourism agents visiting of sales and air tickets and travelling package numbers to be decreased. Finally, the online booking tourism market shares will be expanded to more than traditional tourism agents visits sale market in the future one day. So, the travel agents who still use the traditional tourism visiting sale channel which ought raise whose features to compare to differ to online tourism sale channel if these traditional tourism agents want to keep competitive ability in tourism industry for long term.

What is actively based patterns of urban population of travel behavioral prediction method?

Actively based patterns of urban population. It is a method of motivational framework means in which societal constraints and inherent individual motivations interact to shape activity participation patterns. It can be used to predict one city or urban the numbers of travel demand in the year. It has two elements: First, capability constraints refer to constraints are imposed by biological needs, such as eating and sleeping and/or resources, such as income, availability of cars etc. to undertake the urban or city's family activities in the year. Second, coupling constraints define where, when and the duration of planning activities that are to be pursued with other individuals. So, this method needs to gather information (data) to get the relationship between activities, travel and spending work time and space time to evaluate whether there are how many families who have real needs to spend time to go to travel in the year.

What is trip based versus activity based approaches?

What is trip based versus activity based approaches? The fundamental difference between the trip-based and activity based approaches is that the former approach directly focuses on trips without explicit recognition of the motivation or reason for the trips and travel. The activity based approach , on the other hand, views travel as a demand derived from the need to pursue travel activities. So, it is better understand the individual or family behavior basis for individual or family travelling decision regarding participation in travelling activities in certain places or cities or countries at given times and hence the resulting travel needs. This behavioral basis includes all the factors that influence the why, how, when and where of performed activities and resulting individuals and household, the cultural/ social norms of the community and the travel surrounding environment.

Another difference between the two approaches is in the way travel is represented. The trip based approach represents travel as a collection of trips. Each trip is considered as independent of other trips, without considering the inter-relationship in the choice attributes , such as time, destination and mode of different trips. As tours are chains of trips beginning and ending at a same location , say home or work. The tour based representation helps maintain the consistency across and capture the interdependency and consistency of the modeled choice attributed among the trips of the same tour.

In addition to the tour based representation of travel, the activity based approach focuses on sequences or patterns of activity participation and travel behavior, using the whole day or longer periods of time is the unit of analysis. Such as approach can address travel demand management issues through an examination of how people modify their activity participation, for example, will individuals substitute more out-of-home activities for in home activities in the evening of who arrived early form work due-to a work schedule change?

The major difference between trip based and the activity based approaches is in the way, the time dimension of activities and travel is considered. In the trip based approach, time is reduced to being simply a cost making a trip and a day's viewed as a combination, defined peak and off peak time periods. On the other hand, activity based approach views individuals' activity travel patterns are a result of their time use decisions with a continuous time domain. As individuals have 24 hours in a day or multiples of 24 hours for longer periods of time and decide how to use that travel among or allocate that time to activities and travel and with who, subject to their socio-demographic, transportation system and other and scheduling of trips. So, determining the impact of travel demand management policies on time use behavior is an important step to assessing the impact of such policies on individual travel behavior. The final major difference between this two approaches relates to the level of aggregation. In the trip based approach, most aspect of travel, e.g. number of trips etc. are analyzed at an aggregate level.

Consequently, trip based methods accommodate the effect of socio-demographic attributes of households and individuals in a very limited fashion, which limits the activity of the method to evaluate travel impacts of long term socio-demographic characteristics of the individuals who actually make the activity travel choices and the travel service characteristics of the surrounding environment. So, the activity based models are better equipped to forecast the longer term changes in travel demand in response composition and the travel environment of urban areas. Also, using activity based models, the impact of policies can be assessed by predicting individual level behavioral responses instead of employing trip based statistical averages that are aggregated over defined demographic segments.

Can apply (AI) big data gathering method predict senior age will be main travelling target?

In the past, Germany government had established tourism survey analysis to analyze survey data in order to arrive at reliable conclusions on future trends in travel behavior. To aim to find how demographic change will influence the tourism market and how the industry can adapt to those changes. The travel analysis provided data on tourism consumer behavior, including attitudes, motives and intentions. Since, 1970 year, it is based on a random sample, representative for the population in private households aged 14 years or older. Then, a continuous high scientific standard combined with a national and international users makes the travel analysis a useful tool and reliable source for tourism industry and policy decisions. It aimed to gather statistical data. e.g. on the age structure and on demographic trends, quantitative and qualitative analysis with time series data from the travel analysis. It shows e.g. not only the future volume , quite different from today's seniors, or how who will travel of family holidays will change, e.g. single parents of low, but grandparents of growing significance for tourism.

Demographic change is said to be one of the important drivers for new trends in consumer traveling change behavior in most European countries (e.g. Lind 2001). Because the growing number of senior citizens in the European Union and other industrialized countries, such as the USA and Japan, looks to become one of the major marketing challenges for the tourism industry. United Nations statistics predict that the share of people being 60 age or older will grow dramatically in the coming future, and is expected to rise from 10 percent of the world population in 2000 year to more than 20 percent in 2050 year (United Nations Population Division, 2001). From its statistic, some data showed that travel propensity increased throughout life until the age of about 50 years of age and was then kept stable until very late in life 75 age. The most important results is that the travel propensity when getting older is not going down between 65 and 75 age of course, the overall development of this variable is influenced by a lot of other factors which are responsible for quite a variation over time. It is now possible to suggest that the general pattern of travel propensity is one of the key indicators for holiday life cycle travel behavior, includes three stages. The growth stage tends to increase from early adult hood until 45 age old or when reaching some 80%. The next stage is stabilization from the ages of around 50 age, until 75 age old, starting with a lower increase.

Finally, the decrease stage is a slight decrease occurs once people reach the more advanced age of 75 age to 85 age old (Lohmann & Danielsson 2001).

So, it seems Germany government tourism prediction to future travelers' behavior indicated these findings, such as on how future senior generations will travel, who had used survey data to examine the patterns of travel behavior of a generation getting older and applied the findings to draw conclusions on the future. Also, it predicted that on the future of family trips, family segmentation will be the travel behavior patterns in the future. These findings together with the statistical data on demographic change allowed for a better understanding of the coming tends in family holidays. It's aim developed in consumer behavior related to demographic change and predicted what will happen future of tourism one had to consider other influences and drivers as well, for example, trends on the supply side. e.g. low cost airlines or in travelling consumption behavior in general whether how the past may provide a key to predict travel patterns of senior citizens to the future.

Given the projected growth of the senior citizens market, designing specific marketing strategies to meet the prospective needs of elderly tourists will become increasingly important. It has been an implicit assumption that it will be a close relationship between the travel behavior of today's senior citizens and the those of future ones. The growing number of senior citizens in the world. e.g. China, Hong Kong, Japan, USA etc. countries. Global senior citizen tourism market will be based solely on demographic predictions about the future of the population's age structure. However, many of these seniors won't only live longer but will be fitter and more active until later in life. Many of the will also have plenty in life. Many of them will also have plenty of time and money to spend on travel. So, will these new seniors behave like today's senior citizens? Will they adopt the same travel behavior as the previous generation or become a new market of oldies for the leisure and tourism industry? However, to determine the actual number of senior citizens who will be travelling and to sought to evaluate and specify certain difficult to predict the actual numbers of senior citizen to any country. However, they can be based on the implicit assumption that there is a close relationship between the travel behavior of past, present and future seniors. But is this a valid assumption? As the revise- analysis travel analysis survey, which was conducted in Germany every year, offered some interesting data possibilities. It was designed to monitor the holiday travel behavior, opinions and attitudes of Germans and has been carried out since 1970 year, questions in the questionnaire. Data are based on face to face interviews, with a representative sample of more than 7,500 respondents, the interviews being carried out in January each year. All results refer to the average for the defined generated, which ranges generally over ten years. The group of people then at the age of 60 to 69 age is described. This corresponds to the same generation ten years ago, when they had an age of 50 to 59 age. When this methodological approach is not necessarily very sophisticated, it does have the important advantages of being cost effective.

IS (AI) big data gathering method a better psychological method to compare human marketing research method predict travel behavioral consumption?

On the psychological view point, I think individual traveler's character will have those kind of personal characteristics. First, simplicity searchers value above everything ease not transparency in their travel planning and holiday making, and are willing to avoid having to go through extensive research. Second, cultural purists use their travel as an opportunity to immerse themselves in an unfamiliar looking to break themselves entirely from their home lives and engage. Sincerely with a different way of living. Third, social capital seekers understand that to be well travelled is a personal quality, and their choices are shaped by their desire to take maximum of social reward from their travel. They will exploit the potential of digital media to enrich and inform their experiences, and structure their adventures always keeping in mind they are being watched by online audiences. Finally, reward hunters seek a return on the investment who make in their busy , high-achieving lives. Linked in part to the growing trend of wellness, including both physical and mental self-improvement who seek truly extraordinary and often indulgent or luxurious' must have experiences.

Why needs to know the personal character of individual traveler's characteristics? Because if travel agents could feel which kinds of individual traveler's character, then who can predict which kind of travel package to design to them more easily. For example, how to determine future travel behavior from past travel experience and perceptions of risk and safety? We need to concern that the influences of past international travel experience, types of risk associated with international travel and the overall degree of safety feeling during international travel on individual's travelling experiences likelihood of travelling to various geographic regions on their next international vacation trip or avoidance of those regions, due to perceived risk. Because individual traveler's experience of safety risk degree to the countries, it will influence who chooses to go to the countries/country to travel again.

Why travelers avoid certain destinations are as relevant decision making as why who choose to go to the country(countries) to travel. Perceptions of risk and safety and travel experiences are likely to influence travel decisions; efforts to predict future travel behavior can benefit to individual tourist's decision making.

As Weber & Bottom (1989) defined risky decision is as "choices among alternatives that can be described by probability distributions over possible outcomes" (p.114). Some psychologists judge subjective perceptions of physical reality, i.e. image of a particular tourist destination, whereas value judgement refers to the way individual rank destinations according to whose attributes. i.e. attractiveness, safety, risk etc. factors to form on overall image. So, if the individual traveler had unhappy and worried and unsafe experiences to go to where the place(country) to travel during whose vacation time before. Then, this negative travel experience will influence who is afraid to go to the place (country) to travel again. Risk of place, country, destination or region means the danger is relatively high to the place, i.e. increasing in airplane accidents, crime or terrorist activity targeting citizens of potential traveler's nationality or the probability of occurrence is great , i.e. recent occurrences involving travel regions/destinations under consideration or effective actions to control consequences exist. i.e. selecting safe regions and destinations, taking extra precautions when traveling to risky destinations. These risk factors will influence the individual traveler who chooses to cancel travel plan to go to the country again.

Another interesting research, how to predict behavioral intention of choosing a travel destination, which has focus of tourism research for years, but the complex decision making process leading to the choice of a travel destination has not been well researched. The planned behavior model using its core constructs, attitude, subjective norm and perceived behavioral control, with the addition of the past behavioral variable on behavioral intention of choosing a travel destination.

Understanding why people travel and what factors influence their behavioral intention of choosing a travel destination is beneficial to tourism planning and marketing. Understanding travel motivation is the push and pull model. The idea of the push and pull model is the decomposition of an individual's choice of a travel destination into two forces. The first force is the push factor that pushes an individual away home and attempts to develop a general desire to go somewhere else, without specifying where that may be. The second force is the pull factor, that pulls on individual toward a destination, due to a region specific travel location or perceived attractiveness of a destination. The respective push and pull factors illustrate that people travel because who are pushed by their internal motives and pulled by external forces of a destination. Nevertheless, how push and pull factors guide people's attitude and how these attributes lead to behavioral intentions of choosing a travel destination have rarely been investigated. The decision making process leading to the choice of a travel destination is a very complex process. The planned behavior model is as a research framework to predict the behavioral intention of choosing a travel destination. The model based on the three constructs of attitude, subjective norm, and perceived behavioral control (Fishbein & Ajzen, 1975).

In conclusion, the factors can influence travelers who decide to choose to travel the country, which include personal safety was perceived to the highest motivation factors among the important factors which include, scenic beauty, cultural interests, friendliness of local people, price of trip, services in hotels and restaurants, quality and variety of food and shopping facilities and services. The factors include both push and pull. Push factors include knowledge, prestige, and enhancement of human relationship etc., whereas, the most significant pull factors include high technologic image, expenditure and accessibility etc. For example, Japanese travelers visiting Hong Kong. Push factors are such as exploration dream fulfillment and pull factors are such as benefits sought, attractions and good climate city. It will be the factor of future travel patterns and motivations of sub-cultural and ethic groups for Japanese choice to go to Hong Kong travelling.

How can apply (AI) digital channel (big data gathering method) predict travelling consumer behaviors?

(AI) big data digital channel can be applied to help travelling businesses to evaluate whether how much the e-ticket price and travelling package price is the most attractive or reasonable to persuade travelling consumers feel it is the most reasonable price to choose to buy the airline's e-tickets or the travel agent's travelling package product from internet channel . It helps travelling consumers to feel which airlines or travelling agents which ought change their e-ticket and/or travelling package price to let travelling consumers to choose to buy the airline e-ticket or the travelling agent's travelling package products from internet channel. It can be applied to predict whether how many travelling consumer numbers can be increased or decreased when the airline e-ticket price is variable or the travelling agent travelling package price is variable . It aims to give opinions to help any online airlines or travelling agents to judge whether which e-ticket or travelling package price is the most reasonable to let travelling consumers to accept to choose to buy which airline's e-tickets or traveling agent's package products more attractive.

Thus, (AI) e-ticket or e-travelling package price measurement technology can be preference to be applied online communication ecommerce and mobile phone internet platform aspect. As traveling businesses can enter their past e-ticket or travelling package prices data and past travelling customer number data into computer or mobile. Then, (AI) price measurement technology can gather these data to analyze these e-ticket or travelling package product prices and past travelling customer number to compare their e-ticket and/or travelling package prices variable changing range level to find their e-ticket and /or travelling package price variable difference to measure to make conclusion about every travelling package or/and e-ticket product's price variable changing will influence how many travelling customer number increase or decrease changing to choose to sell their different kinds of travelling package or e-ticket products more accurate. Then, (AI) price measurement software will help them to analyze all past e-ticket and/or travelling package price variable changing data to compare whether which e-ticket and/or travelling package price range can let travelling customers to feel it is more reasonable and attractive to influence them to choose to buy their e-ticket or travelling package product among different airlines and travel agent choices. Because any e-ticket or travelling package product's price is one important factor to influence travelling consumers to choose to buy the airline's e-tickets or travelling agent's travelling package products.

For example, Amazon publish has applied (AI) price measurement technology to help authors to decide how much every different topic of e-book or paper book price, it can attract the largest number of readers to buy. Any one author only needs to type whose book name to Amazon publish author himself/herself Amazon website. Amazon publish (AI) price measurement learning machine will help them to auto-calculate and judge how much e-book or paper book price is the most attractive and the most reasonable in order to increase reader number to buy their e-books or paper books to read. So, (AI) online price measurement machine will gather past similar book names and past every similar book readers' reading times and the number of readers to give opinions to let every author to judge whether his/her very new e-book or paper book ought charge how much price to the e-book or paper book which can attract many readers to choose to buy. Although, it is not ensure that the e-book or paper book price must let readers to feel it is the most reasonable price to choose to buy in reader's view point. However, it has other factors to influence readers' choice to buy the e-book or paper book, e.g. whether the book content is attractive to public, the author's familiarity, the book's page is enough or not to satisfy readers to read etc. factors. But, instead of all these extra factors to influence readers to choose to buy the book to read. (AI) price measurement learning machine can real give opinions to every author to let them to judge the e-book or paper book different price range whether is too high to influence readers to choose to buy to read or tool low to influence readers feel it is possible poor content book to compare other similar content books. Thus, (AI) price measurement machine can help authors to predict every reader's reading behaviors or reading experience and reading habit from online channel in short time easily. The author only enter the book name to let Amazon publish price measurement machine to check, it will follow past reader's reading habit and reading experience to judge whether the similar all book topic sale record to judge how much price is the reasonable price to attract many readers to buy the book.

Hence, (AI) can be applied to digital channel to help travelling businesses to predict travelling consumer behavior in the future. In the future, mobile/smartphone, laptop, desktop will be most frequent used ecommerce channels to develop online business. So, (AI) can be also applied to these platforms to gather data to make analysis to help travelling businesses to predict travelling consumer purchase behaviors popularly. Due to , ecommerce is popular to global, so digital online and instore channels can be one good channel to let (AI) learning machine to make platform to gather past every online travelling consumer purchase (buying) experience data to help travelling businesses to build airline or travelling agent brand personality and having a responsible, positive impact on society.

To apply (AI) learning machine technology to understand travelling customer online purchase behavior, it will raise business e-commerce successful chance: For example, (AI) learning machine can help travelling businesses to gather data to analyze to determine whether short-term or long-term signals in the online travelling consumer behavior that indicate higher purchase intents to let every online travelling business to know. (AI) learning machine can find that online users with long-term purchasing intent tend to save and click through on more content.

However, as online travelling users approach the time of purchase their activity becomes more topically focused and actions shift from saves to searches from online travelling consumption channel. Then, (AI) learning machine will further find that the brand airline and/or travelling agent purchase signals in online travelling consumption behavior can exist weakness before an online travelling purchase is made and can also be traced across different online travelling purchase categories. Finally, (AI) learning machine synthesize these insights in predictive models of online travelling user purchasing intent to the brand of airline or/and travelling agent travelling package product. Taken together, it's work identifies a set of general principles and signals that can be used to model online travelling user e-ticket and/or travelling package purchasing intent across many online content discovery applications. Thus, (AI) learning machine can help online travelling businesses to gather any online travelling users' click online travelling behaviors data to judge whether there are how many online travelling users will choose to find their online travelling business websites to make final decisions to buy their travelling package or/and e-ticket products from online channels. Then, it will give opinions to help the online travelling businesses to let it to judge whether what are the important website factors will help its online travelling business to attract many online travelling consumers, e.g. designing unattractive travelling website issue, online unattractive scene photos issue, unclear website travelling photo color issue, unclear website travelling advertisement message, contents and words impressions issue, lacking image movement frequent attractive seeing issue etc. different website factors. Thus, online digital channel will be one good choice to apply (AI) learning machine to help travelling businesses to predict travelling consumer behaviors.

Thus, (AI) big data technology can also assist travelling consumers to gather different manufacturers' data to compare what their advantages and disadvantages of their travelling package products are. Then, travelling consumers can make comparison to choose which airline or travelling agent is the suitable to whom to buy e-ticket or pre-booking travelling package in online travelling consumption market.

.

Thus, I believe that artificial intelligent "big data" gathering method can be suggested to be applied to attempt to predict travelling consumer behavioral changes in global online travelling business environment, the reasons are as below:

On the travelling consumer's beneficial hand, travelling consumers can apply this (AI) big data gathering method to attempt to gather any global airline e-tickets and/or travelling agent's package product data to be analyzed by this artificial intelligent learning system to compare human general marketing research method, e.g. survey, questionnaire, marketing plan etc. different human judgement methods to predict traveler consumption behavioral change model. Then, it analyzed all the different data to compare what are the range of the most reasonable e-ticket and/or travelling package online purchase history and sale in order to make more accurate prediction to future traveler change traveling consumption behavioral model in next month, or next half year or next year short term period traveling consumption change prediction. Thus, it seems that future AI tool can be attempted to apply to predict any industries price behavior, e.g. deciding what level of price is the attractive level to attract consumer in these industries, e.g. fuel, education, tourism, health, entertainment, etc. different product purchase. It can give more absolute price suggestion to any merchants to set their price change predict in order to increase many customer numbers to buy their products in every year, or every quarter every month, or month week, even every day etc. different sale period.

Reference

Backman and others "motivation is conceptually viewed as " a state of need, a condition that services as a driving force to display different kind of behavior toward certain types of activities, developing preferences, arriving at some expected satisfactory outcome.", 1995, p.15.

Fishbein & Ajzen, "The model based on the three constructs of attitude, subjective norm, and perceived behavioral control". 1975.

Hsu et al. "A tourist behavior model has been developed, called the expectation, motivation and attitude " (EMA) model ,2010.

ICT,WWW . "Switzerland has one of the highest population-to-computer ratio in Europe." Switzerland, 2005.

Jorea Ministry of Environment, " For South Korea environmental attitude is a major factor in decision making vis-a-vis the consumption of " green" food and services", Korea, 2015.

Korea Ministry Of Environment. Public Organizations spend 2.2 Trillon Korean Won To

Purchase green Products in 2014; Ministry Of Environment: Sejoung, Korea, 2015.

Lind , Lohmann & Danielsson , United Nations Population Division, "Demographic change is said to be one of the important drivers for new trends in consumer traveling change behavior in most European countries". 2001.

Mayne, Lonnie. " Evolve of die in the age of the consumer". Entrepreneur, N.P. , 16 Apr. 2014. web of Oct. 2016.

Lee, D.; Kim, M. ; Lee, J. adoption of green electricity policies: Investigating the role of environmental attitudes via big data-driven search-queries. Energy policy 2016. 90, 187-201.

Lee, Terrence, " Tech in Asia-connecting Asia's startup system " Tech. in Asia- connecting Asia's startup ecosystem, N.p.,4 July 2016.

Weber & Bottorn "risky decision is as choices among alternatives that can be described by probability distributions over possible outcomes" , 1989, p.114.

What factors can influence travel behavioural consumption

Prediction travel behavioral consumption from traditional human's mind of tourism market research method

How to predict travel consumption? It is one question to any travel agents concern to use what methods which can predict how many numbers of travelers where who will choose to go to travel more accurately. I think that who can consider how to predict travel behavioral consumption from psychology view and computer science view both.

On the psychology view, It has evidence to support the relationship between self-identify threat and resistance to change travel behavior to any travelers, controlling for whose past travelling behavior, resistance to change if a psychological phenomenon of long standing interest in many applied branches of psychology. Past travelling behavior has been acknowledged as a predictor of future action. Such as travelling behavior that is experienced as successful is likely to be repeated and may lead to habitual patterns. Some psychologists differentiate habit between two concepts, such as goal oriented and automatic oriented both. Although repeated past travelling behavior is addition goal oriented and automatic oriented. Further non-deliberative nature of habit may make appeals to judge and to predict future individual traveler's behaviour accrately. However, repeated travelling behavior without a necessary constraint of goal orientation and automatic oriented both. So, it seems that psychological factor can influence any individual traveler why and how who choose to decide whose travelling behaviour.

On the computer statistic view, structural equation modeling is an extremely flexible linear-in-parameters multivariate statistical modeling technique. It has been used in modeling travel behavior and values since about 1980 year. It is a software method to handle a large number of variables, as well as unobserved variables specified as linear combinations (weighted averages) of the observed variable.

Whether climate change can influence travelling behaviours.

The flexibility of human travelling behavior is at least the result of one such mechanism, our ability to travel mentally in time and entertain potential future. Understanding of the impacts is holidays, particularly those involving travel. Using focus groups research to explores tourists' awareness of the impacts of travel own climate change, examines the extent to which climate change features in holiday travel decisions and identifies some of the barriers to the adoption of less carbon intensive tourism practices. The findings suggest many tourists don't consider climate change when planning their holidays. The failure of tourists to engage with the climate change to impact of holidays, combined with significant barriers to behavioral change, presents a considerable challenge in the tourism industry.

Tourism is a highly energy intensive industry and has only recently attracted attention as an important contributions to climate change through greenhouse gas emissions. It has been estimated that tourism contributes 5% of global carbon dioxide emissions. There have been a number of potential changes proposed for reducing the impact of air travel on climate change. These include technological changes, market based changes and behavioral changes. However, the role that climate change plays in the holiday and travel decisions of global tourists. How the global tourists of the impacts travel has on climate change to establish the extent to which climate change, considerations features in holiday travel decision making processes and to investigate the major barriers to global tourists adopting less carbon intensive travel practices. Whether tourists will aware the impacts that their holidays and travel have on climate changes.

When, it comes to understand indvidual traveler's behavioral change, wide range of conceptual theories have been developed, utilizing various social, psychological, subjective and objective variables in order to model travel consumption behavior. These theories of travel behavioral change operate at a number of different levels, including the individual level, the interpersonal level and community level. Whether pro-environmental behavior can be used to predict travel consumption behavior in a climate change. However, the question of what determines pro-environmental behavior in such a complex one that it can not be visualized through one single framework or diagram.

Despite the potentially high risk scenario for the tourism industry and the global environment, the tourism and climate change ought have close relationship. Whether what are the important factors and variables which can limit tourism? e.g. money, time, family problem, extreme hot or cold weather change, air ticket price, journey attraction etc. variable factors. Mention of holidays and travel were deliberately avoided in the recruitment process, so as not to create a connection factor to influence traveler's individual mind. However, the dismissal of alternative transportation modes can be conceived as either a structural barrier, in the sense that flying is perhaps the only realistic option to reach long-haul holiday destination, or a perceived behavioral control barriers in that an individual perceives flying as the only option open to whom. The transportation tool factor will be depend to extent on the distance to the destination. This can also be interpreted in a social perspective as an intention with the resources available where much international tourism is structured around flying. To increase the availability of different transportation modes, tourists could choose holiday destination closer to home.

Finally, also how to predict future travel behavioural consumption. I feel that travel agents need to predict whether any country's random daily variation of weather factor is also important to influence travel behaviour. e.g. in weather, temperature, rainfall adn snowfall with traffic accidents factors will have relationship to cause travel demand. Some scientists estimate suggest that when warmed temperatures and reduced snowfall are associated with a moderate decline in non-fatal accidents, they are also associated with a significant increase in fatal accidents. Thus increase in fatalities and temperature. Half of the estimated effect of temperature on fatalities is due to changes in the exposure to pedestrians, bicyclists and motorcyclists as temperature increase. So, if any countries have rainfall, snowfall and low temperature to cause traffic accidents, whether this accident occurrence will influence the travelers who liking climb snow hills, riding bicycle, running sports who will avoid to travel to these countries' bad weather after occurs. So, why I feel that this natural climate factor will also be one serious factor to influence travel behavioral consumption.

Market method predicts future travel consumption behavior

Whether individual habitual behaviour can influence travelling behaviour : e.g. renting travel transportation tools

Whether habit can be intended to predict of future travel behavior to people are creatures of habits. Many of human's everyday goal-directed behaviors are performed in a habitual fashion, the transportation made and route one takes to work, one's choice of breakfast. Habits are formed when using the some behavior frequently and a similar consistency in a similar context for the some purpose whether the individual past travel consumption model will be caused a habit to whom. e.g. choosing whom travel agent to buy air ticket or traveling package; choosing the same or similar countries' destinations to go to travel ; choosing the business class or normal (general) class of quality airlines to catch planes. Does habitual rent traveling car tools use not lead to more resistance to change of travel mode? It has been argued that past behavior is the best predictor of future behavior to travel consumption. If individual traveler's past consumption behavior was always reasoned, then frequency of prior travel consumption behavior should only have an indirect link to the individual traveler's behavior. It seems that renting travel car tools to use is a habit example. So, a strong rent traveling car tools useful habit makes traveling mode choice. People with a strong renting of traveling car tools of habit should have low motivation to attend to gather any information about public transportation in their choice of travelling country for individual or family or friends members during their traveling journeys.

Even when persuasive communication changes the traveler whose attitudes and intention, in the case of individual traveler or family travelers with a strong renting travel car tools habit. It is difficult to change whose travel behaviors to choose to catch public transportation in whose any trips in any countries. However, understanding of travel behavior and the reasons for choosing one mode of transportation over another. The arguments for rent traveling car tools to use, including convenience, speed, comfort and individual freedom and well known. Increasingly, psychological factors include such as, perceptions, identity, social norms and habit are being used to understand travel mode choice. Whether how many travel consumers will choose to rent traveling car tools during their trips in any countries. It is difficult to estimate the numbers. As the average level of renting travel car tools of dependence or attitudes to certain travel package policies from travel agents. Instead different people must be treated in different ways because who are motivated in different ways and who are motivated by different travel package policies ways from travel agents.

In conclusion, the factors influence whose traveler's individual behavior either who chooses to rent traveling car tools or who chooses to catch public transportation when who individual goes to travel in alone trip or family trip. It include influence mode choice factors, such as social psychology factor and marketing on segmentation factor both to influence whose transportation choice of behavior in whose trip.

How to determine future travel behavior from past travel experience and perceptions of risk and safety for the benefits to travel consumers?

How to determine future travel behavior from past travel experience and perceptions of risk and safety for the benefits to travel consumers? Why does individual traveler avoid certain destination(s) is(are) as relevant to tourist decision making as why who chooses to travel to others. Perceptions of risk and safety and travel experience are likely to influence travel decisions. If travel agents had efforts to predict future travel behavior to guess whether travelers will feel where is(are) risk and unsafe to cause who does not choose to go to the country to travel. Then, the travel agents will avoid to choose to spend much time to design the different traveling package to attract their potential travel consumers to choose to travel. The reason is because in the case of individual traveler's tourism experience, the traveler whose past disappointment travel experience (psychological risk) will be a serious threat to the traveler's health or life (health, physical or terrorism risk). The past safety or unhealthy risk to the country(countries) will influence the traveler decides to choose not to go to the countries(country) to travel again in the future.

What is push and pull factors to influence any
traveler who chooses where is whose preferable travelling destination

How to predict individual traveler's behavioral intention of choosing a travel destination. Understanding why people travel and what factors influence their behavioral intention of choosing a travel destination is beneficial to tourism planning and marketing. In general, an individual's choice of a travel destination into two forces. The first force is the push factor that pushes an individual away from home and attempt to develop a general desire to go somewhere, without specifying where that may be. The other force is the pull factor that pull an individual toward in destination, due to a region-specific or perceived attractiveness of a destination. The respective push and pull factors illustrate that people travel because who are pushed by whose internal motives and pulled by external forced of a destination. However, the decision making process leading to the choice of a travel destination is a very complex process. For example, a Taiwanese traveler who might either choose new travel destination of Hong Kong or another old travel Asia destinations again or who also might choose any one of Western country, as a new travel destination. The travel agents can predict where who will have intention to choose to travel from whose past behavior and attitude, subjective and perceived behavioral control model.

The factors influence where is the traveler choice, include personal safety, scenic beauty, cultural interest, climate changing, transportation tools, friendliness of local people, price of trip, trip package service in hotels and restaurants, quality and variety of food and shopping facilities and services etc. needs. So, whose factors will influence where is the individual travel's choice. It seems every traveler whose choice of travel process, will include past behavior. e.g. travelling experience, travelling habit, then to choose the best seasoned travelling action to satisfy whose travel needs. This process is the individual traveler's psychological choice process, who must need time to gather information to compare concerning of different travel packages, destination scene, climate change, transportation tools available to the destination, air ticket price etc. these factors, then to judge where is the best right destination to travel in the right time.

Why expectation, motivation and attitude factor can influence travelling behaviour.

Social psychology is concerned with gaining insight into the psychological of socially relevant behaviors and the processes. For instance, on a global level bad influence to global warming, it influences some countries extreme cold or hot bad climate changing occurrence, then it ought influence some travelers' behavioral decision to change their mind to choose some countries to go to travel at the moment which do not occur extreme hot or cold climate (temperature). e.g. above than 40 degree in summer or below than 0 degree in winter. Due to the extreme climate changing environment in the countries, it will cause them to feel uncomfortable to play during their trips. So, the global warming causes to climate changing factor will influence the numbers of travel consumption to be reduced possibly. This is global climate changing environment factor influences to bad or uncomfortable social psychological feeling to global travelers' mind of traveling decision. What is individual traveler expectation, motivation and attitude? Tourism sector includes inbound (domestic) tourism and outbound (overseas) tourism both incomes to any countries. According to recent article, a tourist behavior model has been developed, called the expectation, motivation and attitude (EMA) model (Hsu et al., 2010).

This model focuses on the pre-visit stage of tourists by modeling the behavioral process by incorporating expectation, motivation and attitude. Travel motivation is considered as an essential component of the behavioral process, which has been increasing attention from the travel; industry. The economic approach defines "tourism" is an identifiable nationally important industry. It includes the component activities of transportation, accommodation, recreation, food and related service. So, tourism behavioral consumption is concerned the individual tourist's usual habituate of the industry which responds to whose needs, and of the impacts that both the tourist and the tourism industry have on the socio-cultural, economic and physical environment.

However, travel motivation means how to understand and predict factors that influence travel decision making. According to Backman and others (1995, p.15), motivation is conceptually viewed as " a state of need, a condition that services as a driving force to display different kind of behavior toward certain types of activities, developing preferences, arriving at some expected satisfactory outcome." So, motivation and expectancy which has close relationship to any tourist before who decided to do any tourism of behavior. Some economists confirmed motivation and expectancy which has relations, such as expectation of visiting an outbound destination has a direct effect on motivation to visit the destination;

motivation has a direct effect on attitude toward visiting the destination; expectation of visiting the outbound destination has a direct affect on attitude toward visiting the destination and motivation has a mediating effect on the relationship in between expectation and attitude.

What methods can predict future travel behavioural consumption

How to use qualitative of travel behavioural method to predict future travel consumption?

I also suggest to use qualitative of travel behavioural method to predict future travel consumption. Methods such as focus groups interviews and participant observer techniques can be used with quantitative approaches on their own to fill the gaps left by quantitative techniques. These insights have contributed to the development of increasingly sophisticated models to forecast travel behavior and predict changes in behavior in response to change in the transportation system. First, survey methods restrict not only the question frame but the answer frame as well, anticipating the important issues and questions and the responses. However, these surveys methods are not well suited to exploratory areas of research where issues remain unidentified and the researched seek to answer the question "why?". Second, data collection methods using traditional travel diaries or telephone recruitment can under represent certain segments of the population, particularly the older persons with little education, minorities and the poor. Before the survey, focus group for example can be used to identify what socio-demographic variables to include in the survey, how best to structure the diary, even what incentives will be most effective in increasing the response rate. After the survey, focus, focus groups can be used to build explanations for the survey results to identify the "why" of the results as well as the implications. One Asia Pacific survey research result was made by tourism market investigation before. It indicated the travel in Asia Pacific market in the past, had often been undertaken in large groups through leisure package sold in bulk, or in large organized business groups, future travelers will be in smaller groups or alone, and for a much wider range of reasons. Significant new traveler segments, such as female business traveler. The small business traveler and the senior traveler, all of which have different aspirations and requirements from the travel experience.

Moreover, Asia tourism market will start to exist behaviors in the adoption of newer technologies, a giving the traveler new ways to manage the travel experience, creating new behaviors. This with provide new opportunities for travel providers. The use of mobile devices, smartphones, tablets etc.

and social media are the obvious findings to become an integral part of the travel experience. Thus, quality method can attempt to predict Asia Pacific tourism market development in the future.

However, improving the predictive power of travel behavior models and to increase understanding travel behavior which lies in the use of panel data(repeated measures from the same individuals). Whereas, cross-sectional data only reveal inter-individual differences at one moment in time, panel data can reveal intra-individual changes over time. In effect, panel data are generally better suited to understand and predict (changes in) travel behavior. However, a substantial proportion was also observed to transition between very different activity/travel patterns over time, indicating that from one year to the next, many people renegotiated their activity/travel patterns.

How to apply advanced traveler information systems (ATIS) to predict future travelling behaviour?

Nowadays, information can impact on traveler behavior and network performance. For example, when steadily growing levels of vehicle ownership and vehicle miles traveled information has been identified as a potential strategy towards man aging travel demand, optimizing transportation networks and better utilizing available capacity. Toward, this goal to predict further tourist behavioral consumption. Many countries, government tourism development institutes has applied advanced traveler information systems (ATIS) which travel behavior models and high-fidelity network performance models made increasingly feasible through the rapid advances in computer power. Crucial components of this problem domain are the modeling of individual tourist drivers' response to travel information and the development accurate guidance of relevance to real would trip makers. So, this advanced traveler information systems (ATIS) can assist the tourist who like to rent travelling car tools to travel in any countries own free traveler information systems service conveniently. Also, this travel information system can be intended to assist travelers to make better travel choices. e.g. this system can improve the decision making of individual traveler rather than improvements of network performance overall. So, we need to understand how tourists make their travel plans. Also, understanding decision process that lead to booking of the trip is equally important, as it allows of a potential behavior.

How does online tourism sale channel can influence traveling consumption of behaviour?

Nowadays, internet is popular, it seems that booking air ticket behavior of using internet is predicted to influence overall tourism air tickets payment method. Tourism industry has grown in the previous several decades. Despite its global impact, questions related to better understanding of tourists and whose habits. Using online travel air ticket booking benefits include booking electronic air tickets can be made from entering any electronic travel agents websites in the short time and electronic travel ticket payers do not need leave home, who can pay visa card to pre booking any electronic travel ticket from online channel conveniently.

How to analyze activity based travel demand ? Nowadays, human are concerning the traffic congestion and air quality deterioration, the supply oriented focus of transportation planning has expanded to include how to manage travel demand within the available transportation supply. Consequently, there has been an increasing interest in travel demand management strategies, such as congestion pricing that attempts to change aggregate travel demand. The prediction aggregate level, long term travel demand to understanding disaggregate level (i.e. individual levels) behavioral responses to short term demand policies, such as ride sharing incentives, congestion pricing and employer based demand management schemes, alternate work schedules, telecommuting limitation of travel agent traditionally work nature shall influence oriented trip based travel modelling passenger travel demand indirectly.

Finally, online travel purchase will be popular to influence the number of travel behavioural consumption nowadays. Any travel package products can be sold from websites to attract travellers to choose to prebook air ticket for any trips conveniently. In the past ten years, the internet has become the predominant carrier of all types of information and transactions. Regarding travel decisions, internet has also become an important sales channels for the travel industry, because it is associated with comparably lower distribution and sales costs, but also because ir adapts to hign supply and demand dynamics in this industry. Consequently, the travel and tourism industry tries to increase the internet sale specific share of sales volumes. So, internet sale channel has changed travel consumption behavioural pattern and characteristics and travel experience. For example, Switzerland has one of the highest population-to-computer ratio in Europe. It is also one of the most highly internet penetrated countries in terms of use of the WWW on a day-to-day basis, with more than 75 percent of the population older than 14 years using the WWW daily (ICT, 2005).

The reason of booking online tourism may include: convenience, fast transaction, finding traveling package choice easily, more airline seats available. So, online booking tourism will influence the traditional tourism agents visiting of sales and air tickets and travelling package numbers to be decreased. Finally, the online booking tourism market shares will be expanded to more than traditional tourism agents visits sale market in the future one day. So, the travel agents who still use the traditional tourism visiting sale channel which ought raise whose features to compare to differ to online tourism sale channel if these traditional touriam agents want to keep competitive ability in tourism industry for long term.

Actively based patterns of urban population of travel behavioural prediction method.

Actively based patterns of urban population. It is a method of motivational framework means in which societal constraints and inherent individual motivations interact to shape activity participation patterns. It can be used to predict one city or urban the numbers of travel demand in the year. It has two elements: First, capability constraints refer to constraints are imposed by biological needs, such as eating and sleeping and/or resources, such as income, availability of cars etc. to undertake the urban or city's family activities in the year. Second, coupling constraints define where, when and the duration of planning activities that are to be pursued with other individuals. So, this method needs to gather information (data) to get the relationship between activities, travel and spending work time and space time to evaluate whether there are how many families who have real needs to spend time to go to travel in the year.

What is trip based versus activity based approaches?

What is trip based versus activity based approaches? The fundamental difference between the trip-based and activity based approaches is that the former approach directly focuses on trips without explicit recognition of the motivation or reason for the trips and travel. The activity based approach , on the other hand, views travel as a demand derived from the need to pursue travel activities. So, it is better understand the individual or family behavior basis for individual or family travelling decision regarding participation in travelling activities in certain places or cities or countries at given times and hence the resulting travel needs. This behavioral basis includes all the factors that influence the why, how, when and where of performed activities and resulting individuals and household, the cultural/ social norms of the community and the travel surrounding environment.

Another difference between the two approaches is in the way travel is represented. The trip based approach represents travel as a collection of trips. Each trip is considered as independent of other trips, without considering the inter-relationship in the choice attributes , such as time, destination and mode of different trips. As tours are chains of trips beginning and ending at a same location , say home or work. The tour based representation helps maintain the consistency across and capture the interdependency and consistency of the modeled choice attributed among the trips of the same tour.

In addition to the tour based representation of travel, the activity based approach focuses on sequences or patterns of activity participation and travel behavior, using the whole day or longer periods of time is the unit of analysis. Such as approach can address travel demand management issues through an examination of how people modify their activity participation, for example, will individuals substitute more out-of-home activities for in home activities in the evening of who arrived early form work due-to a work schedule change?

The major difference between trip based and the activity based approaches is in the way, the time dimension of activities and travel is considered. In the trip based approach, time is reduced to being simply a cost making a trip and a day's viewed as a combination, defined peak and off peak time periods. On the other hand, activity based approach views individuals' activity travel patterns are a result of their time use decisions with a continuous time domain. As individuals have 24 hours in a day or multiples of 24 hours for longer periods of time and decide how to use that travel among or allocate that time to activities and travel and with who, subject to their socio-demographic, transportation system and other and scheduling of trips. So, determining the impact of travel demand management policies on time use behavior is an important step to assessing the impact of such policies on individual travel behavior. The final major difference between this two approaches relates to the level of aggregation. In the trip based approach, most aspect of travel, e.g. number of trips etc. are analyzed at an aggregate level.

Consequently, trip based methods accommodate the effect of socio-demographic attributes of households and individuals in a very limited fashion, which limits the activity of the method to evaluate travel impacts of long term socio-demographic characteristics of the individuals who actually make the activity travel choices and the travel service characteristics of the surrounding environment. So, the activity based models are better equipped to forecast the longer term changes in travel demand in response composition and the travel environment of urban areas. Also, using activity based models, the impact of policies can be assessed by predicting individual level behavioral responses instead of employing trip based statistical averages that are aggregated over defined demographic segments.

Why senior age will be main travelling target?

In the past, Germany government had established tourism survey analysis to analyze survey data in order to arrive at reliable conclusions on future trends in travel behavior. To aim to find how demographic change will influence the tourism market and how the industry can adapt to those changes. The travel analysis provided data on tourism consumer behavior, including attitudes, motives and intentions. Since, 1970 year, it is based on a random sample, representative for the population in private households aged 14 years or older. Then, a continuous high scientific standard combined with a national and international users makes the travel analysis a useful tool and reliable source for tourism industry and policy decisions. It aimed to gather statistical data. e.g. on the age structure and on demographic trends, quantitative and qualitative analysis with time series data from the travel analysis. It shows e.g. not only the future volume , quite different from today's seniors, or how who will travel of family holidays will change, e.g. single parents of low, but grandparents of growing significance for tourism.

Demographic change is said to be one of the important drivers for new trends in consumer traveling change behavior in most European countries (e.g. Lind 2001). Because the growing number of senior citizens in the European Union and other industralised countries, such as the USA and Japan, looks to become one of the major marketing challenges for the tourism industry. United Nations statistics predict that the share of people being 60 age or older will grow dramatically in the coming future, and is expected to rise from 10 percent of the world population in 2000 year to more than 20 percent in 2050 year (United Nations Population Division, 2001). From its statistic, some data showed that travel propensity increased throughout life until the age of about 50 years of age and was then kept stable until very late in life 75 age. The most important results is that the travel propensity when getting older is not going down between 65 and 75 age of course, the overall development of this variable is influenced by a lot of other factors which are rsponsible for quite a variation over time. It is now possible to suggest that the general pattern of travel propensity is one of the key indicators for holiday life cycle travel behaviour, includes three stages. The growth stage tends to increase from early aduithood until 45 age old or when reaching some 80%. The next stage is stabilisation from the ages of around 50 age,until 75 age old, starting with a lower increase. Finally, the decrease stage is a slight decrease occurs once people reach the more advanced age of 75 age to 85 age old (Lohmann & Danielsson 2001).

So, it seems Germany government tourism prediction to future travellers' behaviour indicated these findings, such as on how future senior generations will travel, who had used survey data to examine the patterns of travel behaviour of a generation getting older and applied the findings to draw conclusions on the future. Also, it predicted that on the future of family trips, family semgmentation will be the travel behaviour patterns in the future. These findings together with the statistical data on demographic change allowed for a better understanding of the coming tends in family holidays. It's aim developed in consumer behaviour related to demographic change and predicted what will happen future of tourism one had to consider other influences and drivers as well, for example, trends on the supply side. e.g. low cost airlines or in travelling consumption behaviour in general whether how the past may provide a key to predict travel patterns of senior sitizens to the future.

Given the projected growth of the senior citizens market, designing specific marketing strategies to meet the prospective needs of elderly tourists will become increasingly important. It has been an implict assumption that it will be a close relationship between the travel behaviour of today's senior citizens and the those of future ones. The growing number of senior citizens in the world. e.g. China, Hong Kong, Japan, USA etc. countries. Global senior citizen tourism market will be based solely on demographic predictions about the future of the population's age structure. However, many of these seniors won't only live longer but will be fitter and more active until later in life. Many of the will also have plenty in life. Many of them will also have plenty of time and money to spend on travel. So, will these new seniors behave like today's senior citizens? Will they adopt the same travel behaviour as the previous generation or become a new market of oldies for the leisure and tourism indudtry? However, to determine the actual number of senior citizens who will be travelling and to sought to evaluate and specify certain difficult to predict the actual numbers of senior citizen to any country. However, they can be based on the implicit assumption that there is a close relationship between the travel behaviour of past, present and future seniors. But is this a valid assumption? As the reiseanalyse travel analysis survey, which was conducted in Germany every year, offered some interesting data possibiltieis. It was designed to monitor the holiday travel behaviour, opinions and attitudes of Germans and has been carried out since 1970 year, questions in the questionnaire. Data are based on face to face interviews, with a representative sample of more than 7,500 repondents, the interviews being carried out in January each year. All results refer to the average for the defined generated, which ranges generally over ten years. The group of people then at the age of 60 to 69 age is described. This corresponds to the same generation ten years ago, when they had an age of 50 to 59 age. When this methodological approach is not necessarily very sophisticated, it does have the important advantages of being cost effective.

Psychological method to predict travel behavioural consumption.

On the psychological view point, I think individual traveler's character will have those kind of personal characteristics. First, simplicity searchers value above everything ease not transparency in their travel planning and holiday making, and are willing to avoid having to go through extensive research. Second, cultural purists use their travel as an opportunity to immerse themselves in an unfamiliar looking to break themselves entirely from their home lives and engage. Sincerely with a different way of living. Third, social capital seekers understand that to be well travelled is a personal quality, and their choices are shaped by their desire to take maximum of social reward from their travel. They will exploit the potential of digital media to enrich and inform their experiences, and structure their adventures always keeping in mind they are being watched by online audiences. Finally, reward hunters seek a return on the investment who make in their busy , high-achieving lives. Linked in part to the growing trend of wellness, including both physical and mental self improvement who seek truly extraordinary and often indulgent or luxurious' must have experiences.

Why needs to know the personal character of individual traveler's characteristics? Because if travel agents could feel which kinds of individual traveler's character, then who can predict which kind of travel package to design to them more easily. For example, how to determine future travel behaviour from past travel experience and perceptions of risk and safety? We need to concern that the influences of past international travel experience, types of risk associated with international travel and the overall degree of safety feeling during international travel on individual's travelling experiences likelihood of travelling to various geographic regions on their next international vacation trip or avoidance of those regions, due to perceived risk. Because individual traveler's experience of safety risk degree to the countries, it will influence who chooses to go to the countries/ country to travel again.

Why do travellers avoid certain destinations are as relevant decision making? Why do they choose to go to the country(countries) to travel? Perceptions of risk and safety and travel experiences are likely to influence travel decisions; efforts to predict future travel behaviour can benefit to individual tourist's decision making. As Weber & Bottom (1989) defined risky decision is as "choices among alternatives that can be described by prodability distributions over possible outcomes" (p.114). Some psychologists judge subjective perceptions of physical reality, i.e. image of a particular tourist destination, whereas value judgement refers to the way individual rank destinations according to whose attributes. i.e. attractiveness, safety, risk etc. factors to form on overall image. So, if the individual traveler had unhappy and worried and unsafe experiences to go to where the place(country) to travel during whose vacation time before. Then, this negative travel experience will influence who is afraid to go to the place (country) to travel again. Risk of place, country, destination or region means the danger is relatively high to the place, ie. increasing in airplane accidents, crime or terrorist activity targeting citizens of potential traveler's nationality or the probability of occurrence is great , ie. recent occurrences involving travel regions/destinations under consideration or effective actions to control consequences exist. i.e. selecting safe regions and destinations, taking extra precautions when traveling to risky destinations. These risk factors will influence the individual traveler who chooses to cancel travel plan to go to the country again.

Another interesting research, how to predict behavioural intention of choosing a travel destination, which has focus of toursm research for years, but the complex decision making process leading to the choice of a travel destination has not been well researched. The planned behaviour model using its core constructs, attitude, subjective norm and perceived behavioural control, with the addition of the past behavioural variable on behavioural intention of choosing a travel destination.

Understanding why people travel and what factors influence their behavioural intention of choosing a travel destination is beneficial to tourism planning and marketing. Understanding travel motivation is the push and pull model. The idea of the push and pull model is the decomposition of an individual's choice of a travel destination into two forces. The first force is the push factor that pushes an indvidual away home and attempts to develop a general desire to go somewhere else, without specifying where that may be. The second force is the pull factor, that pulls on individual toward a destination, due to a region specific travel location or perceived attractiveness of a destination. The respective push and pull factors illustrate that people travel because who are pushed by their internal motives and pulled by external forces of a destination. Nevertheless, how push and pull factors guide people's attitude and how these attributes lead to behavioural intentions of choosing a travel destination have rarely been investigated. The decision making process leading to the choice of a travel destination is a very complex process. The planned behaviour model is as a research framework to predict the behavioural intention of choosing a travel destination. The model based on the three constructs of attitude, subjective norm, and perceived behavioural control (Fishbein & Ajzen, 1975).

In conclusion, the factors can influence travelers who decide to choose to travel the country, which include personal safety was perceived to the highest motivation factors among the important factors which include, scenic beauty, cultural interests, friendliness of local people, price of trip, services in hotels and restaurants, quality and variety of food and shopping facilities and services. The factors include both push and pull. Push factors include knowledge, prestige, and enhancement of human relationship etc., whereas, the most significant pull factors include high technologic image, expenditure and accessibility etc. For example, Japanese travelers visiting Hong Kong. Push factors are such as exploration dream fulfillment and pull factors are such as benefits sought, attractions and good climate city. It will be the factor of future travel patterns and motivations of sub-cultural and ethic groups for Japanese choice to go to Hong Kong travelling.

Bibliography

Backman, K., Backman, S., Uysal, M. And Sunshine, K. (1995). Event Tourism : An Examination Of Motivations And Activities. Festival Management And Event Tourism, 3(1), 15-24.

Fishbein, M., & Ajzen, Z. (1975). Belief, Attitude, Intention And Behaviour: An Introduction To Theory And Research, Boston: Addison Wesley.

Hsu, C.H.C., Cai , L.A., Li, M(2010). Expectation, Motivation And Attitude: A Tourist Behavioral Model. Journal Of Travel Research, 49(3), 282-296. http://dx.doi, org/10.1177/004728750 9349266.

ICT Information And Communication Technology Switzerland, 2005. ICT Fakten (ICT facts). Available from http://www.ictswitzerland.ch/de/ict%2fakten/factsfigures.asp(retrieved Dec.12, 2005) in German.

Lind, (2001): Befolkningen, Familjen, Livscykeln- Och Ekonomisk Tillvaxt. Institutet For Tillvaxtpo-litiska studier/Vinnova/Nutek.

Lohmann, Martin (2001): The 31 st. Reiseanalyse-RA 2001. Tourism: vol. 49, no.1/2001;pp.65-67, Zagreb.

United Nations Population Division (2001). World Population Prospects: The 2000 year Revision, New York.

Weber E.U., & W, P.Bottom (1989). "Axiomatic Measures Of Perceived Risk: Some Tests And extensions." journal of behavioral decision making, 2 (2): 113-31.

However, green or nature tourism strategy may include these elements : Quality, tourism should have an impact on the quality of life for all members of the tourist process, exploitation of nature resources should be optimal and ensure their generation, balance, distribution of benefits among participants in the tourist process must be fair. So, future any kinds of green or nature tourism will need have these features in order to attract many travelers to visit any countries' green lands, e.g. they may rent cars to travel to green lands. So, developing attractive green lands will be one kind new travelling trend for green tourism in global future travel market.

There are two types of models that contribute to the better understanding of future tourism industry development, explanatory model refer to factors that cause development growth. For example, whether the travelers feel necessary to travel to different destinations, very often nice landscapes and sightseeing, pescriptive modes (e.g. life clcle explanations, physical models) examines tourism from what appears on ground e.g. large hotels facilities etc. Hence, any kinds of tourism leisure must need build these both models in order to attract travelers to choose to buy the tourism package from the travel agent more easily. It is important tourism leisure element to any one travel agent's tourism service package if it hopes to develop its tourism service success. So, the expansion of the tourist region over the natural boundaries of the city centre that occured in the first place as a result of the growth of tourism demand, is the end causing this very expansion to continue.

Butler (1980) involves a six stage evoluation of tourism, namely explanation, involvement, development, consolidation, stagnation, and post-stagnation. The last stage is further characterized by a period of decline, rejuvenation or stabilization. The applicability of the model to a given area has been assessed and judged of a tourist destination's development matched the six phases conceptually described by Butler reference

Butler, R.W. (1980). the concept of a tourist area cycle of evolution: Implications for management of resources. Canadian Geographer, 24, 5-12.

Hence, our tourism industry is facing decline life cycle stage because COVD 19 human mouth disease has influenced many travelers feel fear to catch airplanes to travel, even they also feel to contact the potential COVD 19 human mouth disease people when they arrive the country , they feel that they may contact these sick people, instead of airplanes. So, this kind disease had influenced many travel agents reduce tourism service package number , due to many travelers' tourism leisure activities will reduce, due to travelers number reduces, they only carry cargos to transport to replace travelers COVD 19 disease influence our tourism industry is experiencing decline life cycle stage nowadays. Unless, COVD 19 human mouth attacking to lung disease can be treated by new medicine invention . Otherwise, tourism industry can not re-grow to mature life cycle stage easily.

The most used framework for examing stagnation and possible decline in tourism destinations has been tourist area life cycle model (Butler, 1980). The model has been operationalized frequently in the tourism lierature. It includes series of stages in tourism development, leadning eventually to the stagnation and post-stagnation stages. When a nature destination can either decline, however, it does not offer a systematic explanation of hoe tourism destination might avoid decline . Such as COVD 19 human mouth disease may influence travelers feel fear to catch air planes. So, even the country has beautiful nature scene to attract people to travel, althoug it is a nature attractive destination, but due to COVD19 disease occurs, it may influence this country's this nature attractive destination to enter decline life cycle stage at this moment.

Hence, tourism industry's life cycle stage , sometime it can be influenced by non predicted factor, such as COVD19 disease factor, it can influence travelers' travelling desire to be reduced suddenly from 2019 , due to they feel afraid to catch air planes to avoid to get this kind COVD 19 human mouth disease to bring lung disease when they are sitting in closed window inside air plane environment. So, COVD 19 human counth disease causes global tourism industry is facing serious decline life cycle stage. The question is that any one does not know when this kind COVD 19 disease will be treated by new medicine invention, so if this kind COVD 19 disease still can not be killed by new medicine invention, then it will continue to influence global tourism development to be improved , even any nature attractive scenes, they can not persuade any travelers to catch air planes to visit any countries to travel easily. But, however, we still need to keep our natural environment to prepare future COVD 19 diease disappears , e.g. parks are important places for the protection of ecological systems and natural resources as well as for the provision ot recreational and tourism opportunities for the public. Then, nature or green tourism can be continue to develop to attract many travelers to travel after COVD 19 disease disappears in the future.

● What are the characteristics of birth life cycle stage to tourism industry ? Butler , R.W. (1980)'s model begins with a discovery and exploration or birth stage in which a location is discovered by a small, select group of people as a place with desirable assets often, this discovery is nature population who may see the perceived assets. As just ordinary aspects of their environment or local culture. The early tourists have very little support in the form of amenities, and typically, this is preferred and is part of a location's of being undiscovered. The early tourists, therefore rely heavily on and interact frequently with the residents of the region. This small group of early tourists is largely in dependent and shares information about a destination by word of mouth or by select affinity groups. Over time, as more people are introduced to the destination, the number of visitors begins to increase. So " word of mouth" will be traveler information to persuade them to make travelling destination choices in the tourism industry beginning. It is tourism industry's birth life cycle stage characteristics . However, internet invention can let any one see any countries' scene photos, so it is one kind of good advertisement method to introduce any countries' scene, instead of travelling magazine in tourism growth and maturity life cucle both stages.

Moreover, space tourism is at the birth life cycle stage. It needs travelers feel interest to travel space, if this kind space tourism service providers hope to implement their any space journeys in success. These factors may influence its development succeeds. Nowadays, its target market is wealthy travelers group, wealthy individual are needed, as they serve as the main consumers for space tourism . For space tourism to succeed there must be enough demand from those who are able to afford to expensive ticket. To date there have only been seven commercial space travelers, or space tourists, although they prefer to be called space flight participant, as they see themselves as pioneers and adventers as opposed to ordinary tourists. So, any future space tourism that price must need to reduce to general public, e.g. ordinary income level people, they can spend, if space tourism hopes to reach from stage stage rapidly. So, space tourism is still far to mature stage.It depends on whether how long time its any space journey ticket price can be reduced to any one can pay. So, when its customer target is not only wealthy travelers, many ordinary or common income level people, they can pay to any one space jounrney. It may mean to reach growth life cycle stage.

● What characteristics to space tourism growth stage?

When human space tourism of commericalization of activities in outer space can bring these feeling to let any one space traveler feels then, it may mean that it can reach growth stage, such as they may feel their any space journeys may bring positive impacts that outer. Space recreation can produce, in order to come up with space tourism, exploring and untravelling the hidden anystories of the space are needed. Also they can feel need drastically broadens and enrichs human's technical awareness and constructive knowledge need from any one space tourism journey package. When space tourism reachs mature life cycle stage? What its characteristics are? When any one space travelers can feel that not only earth based attractions that simulate the space experience , they must need to catch airships to experience this different tourism experience, such as space theme parks, space training camps, virtual reality facilities , space hotels (skotel), multimedia interactive games and tele robotic moon rovers controlled from earth, but also parabolic flights, lasting up to three days or week long stay at floating space hotel, including participatory educational ,as well as sports competitions (i.e. space olympics). Hence, above these will be nay space tourism development. It can reach mature life cycle stage characteristics when any one can feel the real travelling mouth to compare to travel our earth anywhere, they can not find that they feel space tourism may be same to our earth's holiday (need to rela) or cultural (know different places or specialized tourism, e.g. expectations of adventures , even space scientists discover new experiences to expectations of adventure or get more information, scientific interest feeling. Then, at this moment, we can call space tourism has reached the mature stage. However, I believe that to develop space tourism in success. We must need to control space tourism ticket price to be reduced to general low income people. They may spend budget level. So, ticket price may be one major factor to influence future space tourism growth when it can reach mature stage. Also, it mean that whether space tourism may become another kind of popular tourism lesiure activities to use. It depends on ticket price factor, instead of its any space tourism trip arrangement factor. So, any one space tourism service provider must need long time to spend in order to implement its different strategies, e.g. ticket price, space trip arrangemet to achieve its their space tourism to achieve its their space tourism different destination package in success if they hope their future space tourism business can grow up in short time.

Airport service life cycle stage improvement strategy
Any organizations will have life cycle stage from birth, growth , mature to decline. In airport service organizations have theis life cycle stages in service aspect. Airports organizatins aim to provide safe, comfortable , even shopping environment to let passengers to stay and to wait to transfer another air planes to visit another destination or arrive the country's airport to check out or check in to enter the airport to leave. If airports have life cycle stages, what the characteristics to every stage? How to improve airport service in order to reach mature life cycle stage rapidly? How to implement airport service strategy in order to reach mature life cycle stage to the aorport organization rapidly?I shall explain as below:
Any airports need to be planned in order to raise excellent service to let passengers to let any travelers choose to travel the country whether the country can provide excellent service and facilities. It will bring indirect

emotion impact to influence the travelers chooce to revisit the country to travel again. However, soft or hard element or) staff service performance or airport facility), they will influence whether the different countries travelers to choose to travel to re-visit the country again. So, learning how to keep the mature or airport service life cycle stage to stay long time, it will be one important factor to influence any airport business in success.

In the birth life style stage to airport, airport organizations must maintain the capability to provide expert advice to airport owners an matters including operational safety, during construction, environmental compatibility, and airport development standards. No other private or public organization can be expected maintain this level of proficiency. These value-added services enhance public trust when assuring consistant application of standards for the nation's airport system. So, it seems that when the new airport is built if it hopes its passenger customers can consider themselves emotion need. So, it ought concentrate on nowadays airplane landing cunways or airport transfer free service transport etc. facilities can let them to feel safe when they were walking in any airport places. If they feel anywhere are dangerous when they are walking or staying in the ne sirport, then new airport non safe or dangerous factor may influence travelers to choose the country to travel again.

Any new airports will need have good new national airport plan in order to it might operate in the near future with respect to safety areas. The plan elements may include as below:

Achieving zero accidents aim, establish standard safety areas at all commercial service airports , achieving the most minimum 85% of all passenger flights operate on runways with safe feeling, increase measure to 100% of all passenger flight operating on runways with standard safety areas after three months. Within 5 years, 95% of all passenger flights begin and end on runways with standard safety areas.

On benefits aspect, aims to mobilize work force to improve safety area performance describes realistic investment benefits. So, in any new airports birth life cycle stage, they must need to consider safety and expenditure for repair aspect in order to keep its service performance to avoid passengers have dissatisfactory feeling when they are staying in their new airports.

When the country has many travelers travel to the country , then the country's new airport passengers number must increase. It is its the new airport growth life cycle stage. These are critical success factors influence the airport, whether it can improve service performance in order to excite different countries travelers visiting the country's airport desire or grow up the visitors number successfully. The critical success factors may include: Having necessary support from internal and externa stakeholders to implement and willing to share information and identify anywhere the total airport facilities of repair needs that are both reliable and feasible projections to let passengers to feel more safe feeling when they are staying in the airport, understand its future service vision and mission, set strategic direction and goals to process/product specific objectives and decision-making across and doen the organization, define, model and prioritize planning prcesses critical for mission performance, practice hand-on sernior management ownership of planning process and allow field, personnel flexiblity in performing jobs, adjust organizational structures , an essessment program to evaluate planning process and product management , e.g. national airport system performance, create organizational understanding of the value management to customer and stakeholder current and future expectations developing human resources management strategies to support new process that solves needs planners and engineers, building information resources strategies change, especially for entering data at the source and maintains data integrity and timeliness.,establish central support group to support reengineering efforts, outreach and training efforts across the organization, phase in short-and long-term results that achieve set goals and objectives over the next two years.

Thus, when one new airport begins to feel passengers number is increasing. It ought experience the growth life cycle stage to the new airport , if it hopes that it can reach mature life cycle stage rapidly as well as keeps its mature life cycle stage to stay in this stage long time or reachs the airport service performance to the most satisfactory level in this mature life cycle stage. It must need to attempt to plan these strategies to implement in order to avoid decline life cycle stage occurs in short time. So, it explains why some new airport can experience the development to mature life cycle stage from grow life cycle stage in short time,even when it reachs mature life cycle stage. It can keep to stay in this stage long time. The reason is that it had prepared effective strategies to achieve how to improve its airport service performance aim in order to satisfy passenger needs. When they are staying in the country's airport any time. Hence, every year revising service performance is needed to any airports.

Any airports must have development processes. The question is that whether the airport needs how long time to reach growth or mature life cycle stage from birth stage or decline life cycle stage will be delayed how long to occur. The development processes may mean that the airport development life cycle stages changes that had toard a particular result or even as a series of continuous actions or operations coducting to an end (Merriam-Webster, 2013).

reference

Merriam-webster (2013). On line dictionary. Available at: https://www.merriam-webster. com/(last accessed July , 8 2013).

Hence, any airport organizations with experience development pricess. When the new airport is built, it must be in the birth life cycle stage. Its passengers number can not increase rapidly. It needs time to grow their number. But, when the new airport operates a period, many different countries begin feel this new airport is existence in the country. They will attempt to catch airplance to visit this country airport to catch airplane to visit tis country airport to travel. If they feel this country airport service performance can satisfy their short time staying feeling or its passengers or airports visitors number may increase rapidly. It meand that this airport is experiencing growth life cycle stage. So, if the airport can attract many visitors in short time. It will reduce time to growth life cycle stage from birth life cycke stage.

So , service performance may be one important factor to inflow the airport grows. When the airport develops to the period, passengers number can not increase rapidly, it may be the airport's mature life cycle stage. Due to it's passengers number can not grow rapidly, its passengers number also may reduce. When its passengers number has significant decrease, if its reduction number is increasing more. It implies that the airport is experiencing decline life cycle stage. All any country's airport may experience whole life cycle stages. If the country's airport can not implement successful strategies, it may experience birht life cycle stage in long time because it can not grow its passengers number significantly. So, any airports need to learn how to help them to change growth life cycle stage, even mature life cycle stage can stay in long time easily. If they hope to attract many different countries passengers to visit their airports or travel themselves countries or enjoy to stay short time in themselves airports in order to grow themselves airline industry development.

● How can processes improvement management strategy influence airport service performance?

Overall processes in an airport may involve passengers, luggage, cargo, aircraft movements, ground handling, and crews . All of these operations can be systematised into processes at airport terminal. Three main types of processes can be established departing , arrival and transfer . Departure consists in catching a flight to a final or intermediate destination, arrival consists in landing and leaving the airport, and transfer consists in landing at the airport only to catch another flight to a final or an intermediate destination. Airports also deal with cargo. It involves in the movement of cargo by air, cargo fies from the shopper to the consignee through one or more airlines. However, when the airport can let them freight forwarder, being familiar with the necessary procedures how permits the airline to concentrate on the provision of air transport and to avoid time consuming details of the facilitation and landside distribution system. It will raise efficiency and improve service performance. The services product by the ground handling are crucial to the success and efficiency of the airport operations.

These services are usually provided by specialised companies. Briefly, it includes the luggage treatment, passengers carrying from plan to terminal when needed and aircraft assistance. Also, focusing on crew, there are two majoe processes, one for departures and the other for arrivals. The crew members also have to pass the security and passport controls. However, they have special channels for this. Once they reach the aircraft, the similarities with the passengers' procedure stop. Hence, they have to perform a set of activities , such as check the aircraft load sheets and help passengers to name a few. Also airport terminal operations processes for passengers and luggage, typically for departures , passengers do the check on the airline area, pass security controls, proceed to the general lounge and lastly to the gate holding area. arriving passengers are able to immediately go from the luggage claim area, but the non-passengers have to pass the passport control at first. After this passengers have to decide if they need to declare goods or not as the paths are different . Hence, if the airport can reduce all of this service processes are less complex as immigration check in-out service, liggage claim can be efficient to carry when passengers need to find themselves luggage. Then, it will reduce waste time and let they satisfy airport service absolutely. So, reducing service process time amy also help the airport to increase customers number significantly. When airport role is the middleman between airlines , cargo transport service providers and passengers, e.g. short time transport cargo service and reducing passengers check in or check out service time. then, it will let them to feel more satisfactory service to the airport.

Hence, airport capacity is as a multifactor function leaves open the exact relationship between the factors but stresses that all factors are relevant to assess airport capacity . So , understanding airport capacity and what drives the capacity usage at airports may provide an insight in the set of instructments available to optimise the use of capacity. All of these factors may influence any capacity of an airport, they may include as below:

For example, technical constraints, e.g. ATM per hour service in a runway in a combined arrival and departure fashion, when many passengers are staying at the airport, they can withdraw money from ATM easily. So, ATM number facilities service supply number and location choice to the airport factors will infuence passengers ' satisfactory level, another factor is environmental constraints, it can directly offer the wellbeing of the communities surrounding the negative emotion to passengers and communities surrounding the airprt. For this factor, the change in technology and/or operational procedures can provide more capacity in the system.

Airline business models factor, it can affect the capacity spoke model when other under a point-point one ,these models directly affect the peak hour operational capacity, particularly in big international hubs. Airlines often compete with high frequencies between destinations, thus increasing the number of movements. In addition, conncectivity also has downsides for this model: the delays in one airport might be exported and sometimes in another, due to the connectivity influencing the real capacity. This factor has been setting economic incentives or pricing models. Furthermore, expanding information systems, from one airport to multiple airports gate-to-gate concept, and the use of larger airport to redcuce frequencies.

Hence, above these factors may influence whether the airport needs how long time to reach maturiry life cycle stage when it is staying the growth life cycle stage. It depends on how its strategies implementation and how environment influence its implementation , if it hopes to achieve to reach the maturity life cycle stage in success in short time.

Finally, I shall explain life cycle cst analysis to any country pavement strategy will bring what significant influential benefits to any airports continue to develop in order to avoid to reach decline life cycle stage time in short time easily , when they are staying in the mature life cycle stage. In the construction or rehabilitation investments of highway's pavements, it is already common to perform a life-cycle analysis or life cycle cost analysis for different alternatives to airport pavements. Becauae when any airport pavements are using for a long time, every day has many airplanes need to fly to land on the pavement. It can bring significant repace influence when the airport has many airplanes are needed to land on the pavements every day in the maturity life cycle stages.

Hence, how to evaluate the repair cost expenditure budget in order to satisfy every day air planes land on the airport pavement need. In the calculations are different cost factors (including direct and indirect cost)to any airport itself pavement. Direct costs are related to the critical construction cost landing on pavement activities and are calculated with information from the airport agency and constructors that work for them. The indirect costs are related with the loss of daily revenue of the airport during work activities, such as landing on the airport pavement.

Runways are the most critical pavements area of airport , so it is critical to ensure the quality of these pavement to let airplanes to land on the airport safety, e.g. they need to be constructed with sufficient strength to carry the moving airport and have a high resistance to skidding and aquaplaining. It is most of the time accomplished with reconstructions or deep rehabilitation. Hence, predicting how much will spend on airport pavement facilities expenditure must need in every day.

However, the life cycle assessment (LCA) is a mult step procedure for calculating the life time environmental impact of a product or service is needed to any airport organizations, when they reachs maturity life cycelt stage . The complex process includes goal and cope definition in inventory analysis impact assessment. The process is vaturally iteractive as quality and completeness of information is constantly being testes. When the definition of the aim and scope of the study is done the next step is the development of an inventory, in which all significant environmental burdens during the lifetime of the product,, such as airport pavements or process , such as airplanes landing on the pavement or airplanes leaving from the pavement in the airport.

(Araujo, Oliveria & Silve) 2014 explained that life cycle snslysis of pavements are focused on the activities of extraction, production, transportation application of materials, concisely the construction of the road. Because its difficult to obtain other relevant data knowing that the use phase of the pavement is predominant with repect to energy consumption and also to gas emissions related to the atmosphere. One of the main factors for the use phase is the rolling resistance, this depends on the surface and structural characteristics of the different pavements.

reference

Araujo, J.P.C. Oliveria, J.R.M. & Silva H.M.R.D. (2011) . the importance of the use phase on the LCA of environmentally friendly solutions for asphalt road pavements. transportation research part D: trasport and environment, 32(0), 97-110. Retrieved in March 2015 from://

dx. doi.org/10.1016/j.trd.2014.07.006.

Hence, , if the airport can have good repairment or renew skills to help its pavement to improve. Then, it may bring long time benefit, such as reducing airplanes energy consumption and also to avoid gas emissions or reduce gas emissions accident occurrene, even air plane landing on pavement accident occurrence chance can reduce to the zero. so, defining the expected pavement performance time improvement strategy can influence whether the airport pavement can satisfy all airplane users how long time landing on or leaving on the airport pavement. Also it is the major factor to influence airport main function success for any airplanes arriving to the country's airport pavement or leaving from the country's airport pavement. Hence, calculating any airport pavement life cycle costs factor. It is necessary to analysis and interpret carefully the results to identfy the most economic pavement strategy in any airport's whole life cycle development stages.

CHAPTER FOUR

Factors influence oil industry development recession

Nowadays, global oil industry is experiencing decline cycle stage. From 1950 oil energy product is at the birth cycle stage. When cars , human walking replace tool is invented, human began to drive cars to go to anywhere in habit daily. Because human is often to drive cars to go to offices, or leisure places, so cars can cause gas need increases. Before, 1970, oil energy product is at the growth cycle stage, becuse cars are accepted to Western people more than Asia people only. But, after 1970, in Asia many countries, e.g. China, Japan, Singapore etc. people began to accept cars to replace catching public transport tools, so gas need had been increasing . Till to 1990. oil industy had been experiencing mature life cycle stage, because global car manufacture number had increased, global every family may have at least one car when the parent has children. So, global cars need number increases, it may be one factor to bring gas need increases. Also global travelers number increases, it will cause many airplanes need to fly to different countries frequently. So, it also bring gas need increases. Because global drivers and travelers number increases, this factor may cause gas need increases significantly because driving activities and flying activities are frequently occurence. However, nowadays oil industry is experiencing decline cycle life stage. Because COVID-19 human mouth disease influences many travelers feel fear to catch air planes when they need to sit in closed window airplanes , if one passenger has COVID 19 disease, he/she will bring other passengers to get this kind of lung disease by air contact. So, global travelers number decreases, it can influence airplanes need to fly frequently, so gas need is also influenced to reduce. Also, since electronic vehicle invention, because electronic vehicle is charged battery for its energy, so gas does not absolute need. If global many drivers have environmental protection awareness, they choose to buy electronic vehicles to replace traditional gas vehicles, then gas need must be influenced to decrease. So, these two main factors may influence global oil industry need decrease. The question is that: How gas manufacturers raise gas users need from decline life cycle stage to re-grow life cycle stage? I shall indicate the methods as below:

● How to raise global gas users need desire ?

Future of sustainable resources

scarcity economic and social loss to oil industry

In economic theory, it indicates two major factors are responsible for the emergence of economic problems. They are (i) the existence of unlimited human wants and (ii) the scarcity of available resources, such as limited numbers of food and natural resource shortage. I feel that human need to solve these two problems before 2050 years. How to balance an optimization approach for human and ecological flow needs ? How to solve climate change environment problem and welfare is for the centrality of human need? Because natural environment factor and natural resource and food shortage and our social economic growth which will have close connection relationship. If natural environment is bad, it will influence a lot of crops numbers can't be grown in farms. The reason of crops shortage will be caused, due to numbers of crops supply to be reduced because bad weather can not grow much crops and overpopulation numbers will increase largely at the same time before 2050 year. It will cause the numbers of demand is more than supply seriously. The result of the prices of foods will be increased by overpopulation and food shortage, so that it will cause every country inflation will be risen, it will occur in developing countries urban areas due to which have , such as India , China, Africa etc. countries have no many farms to provide to farmers to grow foods because air and water pollution and factories are built on farm land , so which need to pay higher price to import crops and foods to provide whose overpopulation to eat from overseas developed countries. Experience of developing countries that have succeeded in the reducing hunger and malnutrition shows that economic growth doesn't automatically ensure success, the source of growth matters too. This isn't surprising since 75% of the poor in developing countries live in rural areas and their incomes are directly or indirectly linked to agriculture. Many countries will continue depending on international trade to ensure their food security. It is estimated that by

2050 year developing countries net import of rice will were than double from 135 million tones in 2008/2009 to 300 million in 2050 year. It seems overpopulation will cause developing countries foods shortages in 2050 years.

Climate change and increased biofuel production represent major risks for long term food security. Studies estimate that the aggregate negative impact of climate change on African agricultural output up to 2080 year to 2100 year could be between 15% and 30%. Agriculture will have to adapt to climate change, but it can also help mitigate the effects of climate change. A recent study estimates that continued rapid expansion of biofuel production up to 2050 year would lead to the number of pre-school children in Africa and South Asia being 3 and 1.7 million higher. Thus, policies promoting the use of food based biofuels need to be reconsidered with the aim of reducing the competition between food and fuel for scare resources. The sharp increases in food price that occurred in global and national markets in recent years, and the resulting increases in the number of hungry have sharpened the awareness of policy makers and of the general public. Hence, different countries governments need to concern safe agricultural system to avoid any foods shortage to supply after 2050 year.

The perspective for 2050 year raises a number of important questions. Are current public and private investments sufficient to ensure adequate agricultural production potential, sustainable use of natural resources, information and communication research for technological breakthroughs to avoid foods shortage for the future? What needs to be undertaken to help agricultural meet the challenges of climate change and growing energy scarcity? What can be done to ensure food security in Africa, India , China etc. developing countries. The facing highest population growth rates,. The severest impacts from climate change and the heaviest burden of HIV/AIDS etc. diseases threats.

Finally, on the changing socio-economic environment hand, the main socio-economic factors that drive increasing food demand are population growth, increasing urbanization and rising incomes. In 2007 year, the USA dept. of Economic and Social affairs indicated that in fact, the developed countries population growth is slower than developing countries. However, all of the growth in the world's population will take place in urban areas. By 2050 year, more than 70% of the world's population is expected to be urban. Thus, scientists need to concern to predict developing countries urban area people foods demand and supply both numbers whether global foods can provide enough supply to urban area people in developing countries after 2050 year. On the other side, human will concern whether there be enough natural resource base of land, water and genetic diversity to meet developing countries needs after 2050 year.

What factors cause the resources scarcity and why human need to solve the resources scarcity before 2050 year

In comparison to the past 50 years, the rate at which pressure are building up on natural resources-land, water, bio-diversity will be increasing during the coming 50 years. An expanded use of agricultural feedstock for biofuels and ongoing environment degradation would work in the opposite direction. Much of the natural resource base already in use worldwide shows degradation . These include capture fisheries and water supply . In addition, actions to other ecosystem services, such as the ecosystem service, food production often cause the degradation of others, soil nutrient depletion, erosion, desertification, deflection of freshwater reserves, loss of tropical forest and biodiversity are clear indicators.

Whether natural resource base should be adequate to meet the future demand at global level. Whether any developing countries should still limit commercial natural resource import capacity to let rural area population to use to protect whose domestic natural industry development when rural area population will be increasing seriously in 2050 year. Biodiversity, another essential resource for agricultural and food production is threatened by urbanization , deforestation, pollution and the conversion of wetlands. As a result of agricultural modernization, changes in diets and population density, humankind increasingly depends on a reduced amount to agricultural biological diversity for its food supplies.Thus major reforms and investments are needed in all regions to cope with rising scarcity and degradation of land, water and biodiversity and with the added pressures resulting form rising incomes, climate change and energy demands.

There is a need to establish the right incentives to protect agriculture's environmental services to protect biodiversity and to ensure food production using new agricultural technologies before 2050 year. For the developing countries, in order to ensure that resources are available in the required quantity and quality and in the urban locations where they are needed, large additional investments need to be made in order to avoid rural people of hunger coincides with resource scarcity before 2050 year. Increased investment incentives and provided stable production growth incentives : land, water and biodiversity of three natural resources. The aim should be to stop over-exploitation, degradation and pollution, promote efficiency gains and expand overall capacities as appropriate . To provide the rural population engaging in ecosystem services with win-win solution to improve the sustainability of ecosystems, mitigate climate change and improve rural incomes. Whether and under what conditions the estimated future food demand can be met and how food security can be achieved. Hence, every country needs to have an effective economy system to attempt to solve the basic economic problems. The function of the economy is to allocate scarce resources among unlimited wants. Moreover, every country needs to have effective economic system to study of its citizen behavior in relation to how scarce resources to allocated and how choices are made between alternative uses of the country government's limited expenditure. Due to our earth has scarce resources, it implies human will scarce natural resources to provide us to use. Our governments need to predict whether what our earth's limited natural resources will be all used in order to solve our natural resources to be used in the short time quickly as well as our governments need to apply effective economic system to design soluble methods to avoid our earth will be not to provide any natural resources to satisfy our daily essential needs in one day.

The average U.S. resident , in a year, consumes 275 pounds of meats, uses 635 pounds of paper and uses energy equivalent to 7.8 metric tons of oil. Before, long years ago, the average American ate 197 pounds of meat, used 366 pounds of paper and used energy equivalent to 5.5 metric tons of oil. In the U.S. there is about one passenger car for every two people. Otherwise, Europeans have about one passenger car for every 3.1 people. On the other side, Developing countries have on average, about one passenger car for every 49 people. What does economics have to tell us about these differences in consumption?

Consume sovereignty means the idea that consumer's needs and wants determine the shape of all economic activities. Is this belief valid? That is are the final goals of economic activity all to be found in the act of consumption. Hence, if one day, our earth scarce any kinds of natural resources to be caused shortage, e.g. water, air, oil, land , gas, solar, gas , unclear , wind energy resources as well as foods e.g. vegetables and meats etc. eating resources. Due to human numbers are increasing, such as China, India and Africa etc. developing countries' people numbers are increasing much than the USA, UK etc. developed countries 's people numbers every year. But, our earth's vegetables and pigs, cows, sheet etc. meats foods numbers are decreasing every year. I believe that our foods and vegetables and natural energy resources prices will be influenced to be rose too much due to human demands (wants) are excessive to compare to our earth natural energy resources and meats and vegetables foods supply numbers. On the other side ,if every country's inflation will be increasing , but our salaries will be decreasing, or our salaries will be kept to stable and no changing, even employers will decide to dismiss employees to cause unemployment ratio rising. In result, global consumers' shopping ability will be falling down and crime numbers will be rising by poor, such as developing countries, e.g. Africa, China, India etc. will have many people feel hungry, or who feel diseases , even who will be sick to die from diseases or will be kill to die by crimes. Also , these other factors include foods scarcity, foods and natural energy prices rising, working and home environment pollution etc. factors , these factors can then cause global economic poor , serious inflation ,unbalance incomes reallocation between rich and poor people, discrimination and unfair threat will be caused between countries, even , the war between countries will be caused. Hence, our governments need to concern how to solve our earth natural energy resources and foods and vegetables scarcity challenge , due to which will be caused shortage to supply to human to consume to use or eat in the future on day occurrence. Thus, above reasons can be concluded that as below:

Nowadays, the numbers of human (every country people) are increasing more than just the increasing numbers of consumers' consumption activities , such as our daily essential consumption include meats and vegetables etc. foods and natural energy resources, such as lands, water, gas, oil, wind, water, nuclear, electricity etc. energy . Moreover, natural resources and foods numbers are decreasing due to overpopulation are increasing in developing countries and the numbers of emigration are rising to developing countries, such as UK, USA, France, Germany poor people numbers are increasing due to war or poor issues occur in the developing countries. Moreover, due to the provision consumption activities are most directly address living standard (or lifestyle) goals, which have to do with satisfying basic needs and getting pleasure through the use of natural resources energy provision service demand and vegetables and foods tasty demand by the developed countries' people needs . Also, these poor issues will occur in the developing countries possibly in the future. Due to these factors, I predict our essential consumption , such as foods, vegetables and natural energy resources service provision price will be increasing in global competitive market due to foods and vegetables and energy shortage will be caused by the overpopulation demands rising up and foods and natural energy resources supply numbers falling down factors. Hence, our governments must need to find methods to solve the problem of our essential natural resources shortage and foods scarcity issues occurrence in the future.

Suggestions to solve resources scarcity methods

● Estimation of growth of rural population and income and expected changes of natural resources supply numbers

I recommend developing countries need to estimate growth of rural population and incomes numbers and expected changes numbers in consumption patterns . Taking into account developing countries' known resource capacities and projected development of yields, input use and technologies and making assumptions about their future trading capacity, estimates are also make of future food production level, land use and natural resource numbers import trade demand of developing countries estimation before 2050 year.

Estimation of water natural resources, such as water scarcity agreement on key definitions, the conceptualization of water scarcity in ways that are meaningful for policy development and decision making, the quantification of water scarcity, policy and technical response options available to ensure food security in conditions of water scarcity, criteria and principles that should be used to establish priorities for action to response to water scarcity in agriculture and ensure effective and efficient water scarcity copying strategies. Thus, developing countries will concern to reduce water resources shortage risk. Why is predict water supply important?

During the twentieth century, large multi-purpose dams have served the needs of agriculture, energy and growing cities, and helped protect population from flood hazards. On farm water conservation, particularly the adoption of agricultural practices that reduce runoff to increase the infiltration and storage of water in the soil in rained agriculture is the most relevant local supply enhancement option that farmers have to increase foods production by increasing water availability and decentralized water harvesting conveniently in rural areas for farmers needs. For example, ground water exploitation has grown or in scale. Ground water's capability to provide flexible, on demand water in support of irrigation has been as a major advantage by farmers in rural areas. Thus, farmers need to learn how to reduce water losses increase water productivity and water re-allocation to avoid natural resource of water shortage after 2050 year.

● Renewable natural resources and foods planting sustainability development

The concept of sustainability has become the current answer to absolving our earth of its environment and economic crises in the 21 ST. century. On the one side, the pessimists, usually ecologists and other scientists, who are convinced the earth can't forever support the different countries' demand of renewable and non renewable resources. On the other side, are the optimists, the economists, who are equally convinced that the earth, with market incentives, appropriate public policies, material substitution, recycling and new technology can satisfy the needs and improve the quality of human welfare. Both views are supporting arguments are explored used and sustainable development. Thus, renewable old energy natural resource can keep old energy natural resource to renew to use or research other new energy resource to substitute old natural resource, it will reduce the risk of energy resource shortage if the other new natural resource can be substituted to the old natural energy resource to use in our daily life , such as inventing one kind of new energy resource can be used to substitute gas to drive cars or drive boats or plans or the old gas can be renewed or cycled to use to drive cars or boats or the oil can be renewed or cycled to use to cook. Also, our earth foods, e.g. fruits, vegetables or meats etc. foods if which can be recopied to grow many numbers planting foods from any one kind food or many kinds of foods, such as one meat can be copied to manufacture two to three same kind tasty meats or unlimited same kind tasty meats. I believe the renewable natural resource energy or recopied foods can reduce our foods or energy shortage after 2050 year.

The application of sustainable strategy
between local and national and regional
of international countries

A redefined concept is of the society as whole system, made up of three concentric circles: the economy is found within the society, and both the economy and society exist within the environment. Sustainability indicators are therefore said to attempt to measure the extent to which these boundaries are respected.

I think sustainability measure as a whole concept environment, society and economy. At the bottom of the triangle is the environment or the ultimate means which represents natural resources as a precondition for decent human life. The economy (which includes technology, politics and ethics) is on the next, is not independent but serves as a vehicle for achieving ultimate ends. At the top is equity or society or ultimate end which refers to the wellbeing of the human being.

According to Daly(1990) who indicated "that the economy therefore succeeds to the extent that it conserves and restores ultimate means the environment, and enables the achievement of ultimate ends society equity. This is the application of sustainable strategies to local, national and regional issues, as well as the role of international agencies in local /national strategies." Our earth occurs issues of overpopulation, diseases and political conflict, developed countries also have to deal with problems, such as pollution and unlimited urban expansion with limited resources. Sustainability is the process suggested to improve the quality of human life within the limitations of global environment. It involves solutions for improving human welfare that doesn't result in regarding the environment. We(human) need to concern living within certain limits of the earth's capacity to maintain life, understanding the interconnections among economy, society and environment and maintaining a fair distribution of foods and vegetables and natural energy resources and opportunity for this generation and the next. Thus, on the one side, our governments need to concern three categories: Social/ political, environmental and economic issues are interconnection. Social issues include poverty, consultation, empowerment and culture. Environmental issues include pollution, natural resources and biodiversity/ resilience and economic issues include efficiency, growth and stability. It seems our governments need to considerate social and environment and economic issues to reduce our natural energy resources and foods and vegetables to allocate to let every country people to use fairly.

Reducing global warming and biodiversity
issue occurrence

It seems that we need to know our society will influence our natural environment good or bad. If our society damaged our natural environment, then it will be possible to influence our foods supply of decreasing numbers. e.g. fishes, pigs, cows, sheep and vegetables and fruits etc. foods . Due to bad climate and air and lands and ocean pollution can influence foods can not be grown easily and successfully in farms or fishes can not be lived healthy in ocean. Then, it will cause our meats, fruits and vegetables etc. foods supply shortage. Even, our gas , oil, water etc., natural resources will cause our oceans and lands pollution if human pollute our oceans and lands. In result, our natural resources used numbers will be reduced due to clean lands and oceans are polluted for long time. Finally, natural resources and meats and vegetables and fruits , rice etc. foods prices will be risen due to which are shortage to supply and developing countries' population numbers are increasing which will cause more demand.

Finally, it shall cause many developing countries' poor people who can't eat enough meats, fruits, rice vegetables etc. foods as well as who can't use enough natural resources to attempt to adapt whose past normal daily life, such as lacking enough oil to help them to cook foods to be heat to eat at home or lacked enough water to be boiled to drink. Even, whose health will be poor , then who get diseases to cause die easily when there is no enough oil to buy or enough water to drink. Hence, these developing countries governments need to concern foods and natural resource scarcity problems which will be occurred if who do not find methods to reduce this issue to be occurred after 2050 year.

As Erekson et. al.(1999) concerns about" loss of resources, such as biodiversity or global weather (climate) warming are pacified with the potential of new technology which will lead to greater investments to the future generations for alternative resources and welfare."

Hence, I recommend our governments need to concern global warming or biodiversity issue because of our foods and vegetables and natural resources, such as water, air will be possible polluted to be caused shortage quickly if our earth's global warming or biodiversity issue occurrence to cause our earth's large oceans or lands areas to be polluted. Our governments can attempt to control natural resources , such as oil, gas, water supply into the market and not though the political special conditions to keep them, without considering the political and social standings, which rule the control power and the use of those resources. Such as developed countries can be able to minimize the impact of foods or/and natural resources production and consumption over the natural resources, they are only mechanisms built within an economic rationality, which should be possible to control its people's demand of natural resources, e.g. oil, gas, water and supply of natural resources get more balance. Then these natural resources sale price won't be raised more every year. When there developed countries' people , such as American and Britain who can control to reduce to spend to use the excessive natural resources too much in any time and any place habitually. Then , I believe the developing countries' governments e.g. Africa, China, India, which can buy those developed countries governments' excessive natural resources to raise those developed countries' natural resources supply numbers to provide to whose people to use as well as the most important benefit is that developed countries can gain foreign income from excessive natural resources expectation. Then, these governments will raise GDP economic growth. Hence, if developed countries could control whose people consume natural resource numbers and they could also control to produce natural resource supply numbers . Then, they can gain more excessive natural resources export chance to achieve to raise GDP economic growth aim for long term. As Kirkby et al., (1995)explained "the complexity of sustainable development our natural environment. If our governments can let our earth natural environment gets creation to maintenance, then our natural environment will be reduced the time to degradation. In the long time result, our society rural and urban economy will be growth , then our different countries' global growth will be caused diversity." Hence, it seems different countries' governments need to concern sustainable development to our natural environment .

How to apply agricultural green bio-economy
concept to solve control sustainable food
consumption and production in a resource-
constrained world

Nowadays, challenges for the global food supply have never been so complex. Between now and 2050 year, it has been predicted that growth in the global population and changing diets in developing countries, special in India and China and Africa etc. developing countries which may lead to an increase of around 70% in food demand. At the same time, depletion of fossil hydrocarbons will increase the demand for biomass for biofuels and industrial materials. Hence, developed and developing countries' governments ought need to coordinated to reduce air and water pollution and approached to lands use planning and oceans use planning to supply enough farms to grow potatoes, vegetables, tomatoes, fruits and let cows, pigs, sheep etc. animals can have comfortable and clean farm to live to produce good tasty meats to provide human to eat as well as to reduce pollution to supply fresh and clean water to let fishes to be lived and provides to human to drink clean water. Due to overpopulation will be predicted by scientists after 2050 year, so it will be caused foods and energy shortage possibly. Hence, different countries' governments need have long term perspectives to prepare to have enough foods and energy supply to provide us to eat and use for our earth with resource constraints and environmental limits, and which includes guideline on agricultural research to achieve foods supply aim.

On the one hand, I believe the knowledge-based bio-economy can play in realizing there challenges in particular the balance demand between foods, feed and fuel and the strategic role new technologies can have upon developing a sustainable an green bio-economy. On the other hand, I also think production of the presently high resource dependence and to build more environmentally begin sustainable agriculture system able to feed 9 billion people by 2050 year. I recommend global governments need to concern all aspects of food security including the total food chain and impacts of other land-use and management as well as non food areas, research areas which can be closed to free resources for new priorities, research to manufacture more new unique natural resources, due to gas, oil etc. resources will be used all in one day. On the energy shortage aspect, Substitution of these oil, gas etc. natural resources are needed . For example, nuclear energy is a kind of new natural resource, it can be used to push machines of rockets to be moved in space. In the future, I hope that nuclear energy can be used to drive cars or ships or trains etc. transportation tools in land. Hence, new natural resource research is essential and valid investment to be improved by scientists in the future.

On the global food supply interconnected challenges hand, including climate changes, energy and water supply are further encountered by the financial and economic changes in an increasingly globalized world. As a result, it is unclear how the growing demand for food and bioenergy (both biomass and biofuels) within a wider bio-economy can be met without further compromising ecosystem services on which all economic activities and social depend. I shall emphasizes the interaction of the economic, social and ecological components of our food systems at various levels, with feed backs increasingly the uncertainty and risks relating to future developments.

We need to face the food requirements of a growing world population have to be satisfied and we also need to the face of increasing resource scarcities, such as water, energy and land and foods etc. with the situation further exacerbated by climate change. Thus, we need to focus on our reducing demand through food consumption behavioral changes and structural changes in food systems and food chains change. Due to some developed countries people often to choose to buy these foods to eat excessively e.g. cow meat and pig meat and drink excessive soft drinks, e.g. man-made color juice. So, these developed countries consumers will feel these excessive foods and soft drinks can be rubbish if these developed countries consumers often drink these man-made color juice and eat pig and cow meats often excessively. It seems who ought to change their diet behavior and food consumption to avoid to spend too much money to buy excessive foods and drinks and who often shall not decide to eat and drink them when who feel not hungry habitually . Hence, changing human diet habit is one important psychology factor to reduce water and foods shortage, due to the meats and juices can be reduced to be rubbish if human can learn how to control their diet habit to reduce to consume excessive meats and vegetables and rice and soft drinks etc. kind of foods and drinks. Then, I believe that food and water drinking numbers will be reduced too much in the future. Hence, different countries' governments need to educate whose people to know that why who will face foods and water scarcity possibly and to let who to know how the issue can be avoided to cause by the changing of their diet habit and consumption behavior. Teaching includes, such as let who to learn why resources scarcities are expected to reduce and defining food security concept, the need is for a better understanding of complexity of vegetable systems, the need to improve the diversity and response capacity of food systems to enhance resilience, the need to address both food consumption and production, knowledge generation and innovation through cross-sector approaches is essential and the need for agricultural knowledge and innovation systems that are fit for farming purpose. After developed countries' people are educated to let who to know why who need to reduce to consume excessive foods and soft drinks habitually to aim to avoid the chance of foods and water supply shortage will be occurred after 2050 year.

On the other side, in the case of biodiversity, the loss of functional biodiversity destabilizes ecosystems and weakens their ability to deal with natural disasters or human induced stresses, such as pollution and climate change. Hence, scientists need to research how to reduce new diseases to cause foods and water pollution, even new diseases cause to influence human health. Due to unpredictable new diseases will be caused foods, fruits, vegetables etc. can't be grow easily , even cows, pigs, sheep etc. animals are not health to cause diseases to be died easily. Then, those new diseases will be decreases our foods supply numbers seriously.

Resources scarcities are expected to define future food security. The predominant form of agriculture, food processing and retailing relies heavily on cheap inputs and the potential impact on this of long term resource scarcity trends has been largely overlooked. Scarcities are either biophysical limits, such as resource supply and availability or environment limits relating to pollution and its impacts on ecosystems and the global climate system. Hence, every country's government ought to educate to let whose citizen to discuss how to protect future food security topic to avoid resource scarcities occurrence after 2050 year. We need to know we are facing pollution (e.g. land, water, energy) and related to environmental limits e.g. climate change, ocean acidification and biodiversity loss. They represent a real threat, not only to future food supplies, but also to global stability and prosperity, through increasing poverty to developing countries and impacts on international trade, finance and investments.

Hence, pollution and environmental limits will have direct relationship to influence every countries' foods supply numbers , then it will influence every country's gross domestic product income if the consumption is reduced by foods inflation. For example, the combined effect of climate change and bio-diversity which makes the food production systems poorly due to a reduced resilience to shocks and changes over the long term , such as the limited availability of ore resources, soil degradation to loss of biodiversity. Both of these require a long term strategic approach to research and an openness to new research directions. These will need to help provide solutions towards more sustainable food consumption and production, some of which will need to break with current farmers or food manufacturers way of producing food methods. For example, research into ecological approaches: foods nutrient and water clean management and replacement of energy intensive inputs are priorities. Research to support energy efficient technologies for use in the food chain is also needed. Industry should assist in tackling the forthcoming challenges with new business models that can support the decoupling of resource use and changing consumption excessive foods behaviors and improving health foods production methods. For instance, changing the foods supply chains) e.g. more local purchasing) may have huge impacts on costs and also on creating closer links and confidence between producers and consumers.

In conclusion, different countries need find methods to solve foods and energy scarcity problem before 2050 year. I recommend that who can attempt to solve earth warm climate, innovate agricultural production and supply system, change human diet habit and food consumption of behavior, co-operate the trade of foods and energy demand and supply between countries fairly and reasonably, reduce food and natural resource waste, renew and recopy new kind of foods, research new natural resource substitution etc. different methods. However, if every country government can attempt to find any one or more of these methods to solve food scarcity to avoid to occur before 2050 year. I believe that the food scarcity challenge won't be occur after 2050 year in the future.

Reference

Erekson, O.H., Loucks, O.L. Strafford, N.C. 1999.
The context of sustainability . In: Sustainability
perspectives for resources and business
USA, p. 3-21.

Daly, H.E. 1990, Towards some operational
principles of sustainable development,
ecological economics, 2(1), 1-6.

Kirkby, J; O' Keefe P., Timberlake, L. (eds.) 1995.
The earthscan reader in sustainable development.
Earthscan Publications Ltd., London, 1-14p.

4.1 Suggestions to solve resources scarcity methods to oil supply

I. Estimation of growth of rural population and income and expected changes of natural resources supply numbers

I recommend developing countries need to estimate growth of rural population and incomes numbers and expected changes numbers in consumption patterns . Taking into account developing countries' known resource capacities and projected development of yields, input use and technologies and making assumptions about their future trading capacity, estimates are also make of future food production level, land use and natural resource numbers import trade demand of developing countries estimation before 2050 year.

Estimation of water natural resources, such as water scarcity agreement on key definitions, the conceptualization of water scarcity in ways that are meaningful for policy development and decision making, the quantification of water scarcity, policy and technical response options available to ensure food security in conditions of water scarcity, criteria and principles that should be used to establish priorities for action to response to water scarcity in agriculture and ensure effective and efficient water scarcity copying strategies. Thus, developing countries will concern to reduce water resources shortage risk. Why is predict water supply important? During the twentieth century, large multi-purpose dams have served the needs of agriculture, energy and growing cities, and helped protect population from flood hazards. On farm water conservation, particularly the adoption of agricultural practices that reduce runoff to increase the infiltration and storage of water in the soil in rained agriculture is the most relevant local supply enhancement option that farmers have to increase foods production by increasing water availability and decentralized water harvesting conveniently in rural areas for farmers needs. For example, ground water exploitation has grown or in scale. Ground water's capability to provide flexible, on demand water in support of irrigation has been as a major advantage by farmers in rural areas. Thus, farmers need to learn how to reduce water losses increase water productivity and water re-allocation to avoid natural resource of water shortage after 2050 year.

II. Renewable natural resources and foods planting sustainability development

The concept of sustainability has become the current answer to absolving our earth of its environment and economic crises in the 21 ST. century. On the one side,
the pessimists, usually ecologists and other scientists, who are convinced the earth can't forever support the different countries' demand of renewable and non renewable resources. On the other side, are the optimists, the economists, who are equally convinced that the earth, with market incentives, appropriate public policies, material substitution, recycling and new technology can satisfy the needs and improve the quality of human welfare. Both views are supporting arguments are explored used and sustainable development. Thus, renewable old energy natural resource can keep old energy natural resource to renew to use or research other new energy resource to substitute old natural resource, it will reduce the

risk of energy resource shortage if the other new natural resource can be substituted to the old natural energy resource to use in our daily life , such as inventing one kind of new energy resource can be used to substitute gas to drive cars or drive boats or plans or the old gas can be renewed or cycled to use to drive cars or boats or the oil can be renewed or cycled to use to cook. Also, our earth foods, e.g. fruits, vegetables or meats etc. foods if which can be recopied to grow many numbers planting foods from any one kind food or many kinds of foods, such as one meat can be copied to manufacture two to three same kind tasty meats or unlimited same kind tasty meats. I believe the renewable natural resource energy or recopied foods can reduce our foods or energy shortage after 2050 year.

III. The application of sustainable strategy
between local and national and regional
of international countries

A redefined concept is of the society as whole system, made up of three concentric circles: the economy is found within the society, and both the economy and society exist within the environment. Sustainability indicators are therefore said to attempt to measure the extent to which these boundaries are respected.

I think sustainability measure as a whole concept environment, society and economy. At the bottom of the triangle is the environment or the ultimate means which represents natural resources as a precondition for decent human life. The economy (which includes technology, politics and ethics) is on the next, is not independent but serves as a vehicle for achieving ultimate ends. At the top is equity or society or ultimate end which refers to the wellbeing of the human being. According to Daly(1990) who indicated "that the economy therefore succeeds to the extent that it conserves and restores ultimate means the environment, and enables the achievement of ultimate ends society equity. This is the application of sustainable strategies to local, national and regional issues, as well as the role of international agencies in local /national strategies." Our earth occurs issues of overpopulation, diseases and political conflict, developed countries also have to deal with problems, such as pollution and unlimited urban expansion with limited resources. Sustainability is the process suggested to improve the quality of human life within the limitations of global environment. It involves solutions for improving human welfare that doesn't result in regarding the environment. We(human) need to concern living within certain limits of the earth's capacity to maintain life, understanding the interconnections among economy, society and environment and maintaining a fair distribution of foods and vegetables and natural energy resources and opportunity for this generation and the next. Thus, on the one side, our governments need to concern three categories: Social/ political, environmental and economic issues are interconnection. Social issues include poverty, consultation, empowerment and culture. Environmental issues include pollution, natural resources and biodiversity/ resilience and economic issues include efficiency, growth and stability. It seems our governments need to considerate social and environment and economic issues to reduce our natural energy resources and foods and vegetables to allocate to let every country people to use fairly.

IV. Reducing global warming and biodiversity
issue occurrence

It seems that we need to know our society will influence our natural environment good or bad. If our society damaged our natural environment, then it will be possible to influence our foods supply of decreasing numbers. e.g. fishes, pigs, cows, sheep and vegetables and fruits etc. foods . Due to bad climate and air and lands and ocean pollution can influence foods can not be grown easily and successfully in farms or fishes can not be lived healthy in ocean. Then, it will cause our meats, fruits and vegetables etc. foods supply shortage. Even, our gas , oil, water etc., natural resources will cause our oceans and lands pollution if human pollute our oceans and lands. In result, our natural resources used numbers will be reduced due to clean lands and oceans are polluted for long time. Finally, natural resources and meats and vegetables and fruits , rice etc. foods prices will be risen due to which are shortage to supply and developing countries' population numbers are increasing which will cause more demand. Finally, it shall cause many developing countries' poor people who can't eat enough meats, fruits, rice vegetables etc. foods as well as who can't use enough natural resources to attempt to adapt whose past normal daily life, such as lacking enough oil to help them to cook foods to be heat to eat at home or lacked enough water to be boiled to drink. Even, whose health will be poor , then who get diseases to cause die easily when there is no enough oil to buy or enough water to drink. Hence, these developing countries governments need to concern foods and natural resource scarcity problems which will be occurred if who do not find methods to reduce this issue to be occurred after 2050 year.

As Erekson et. al.(1999) concerns about" loss of resources, such as biodiversity or global weather (climate) warming are pacified with the potential of new technology which will lead to greater investments to the future generations for alternative resources and welfare." Hence, I recommend our governments need to concern global warming or biodiversity issue because of our foods and vegetables and natural resources, such as water, air will be possible polluted to be caused shortage quickly if our earth's global warming or biodiversity issue occurrence to cause our earth's large oceans or lands areas to be polluted. Our governments can attempt to control natural resources , such as oil, gas, water supply into the market and not though the political special conditions to keep them, without considering the political and social standings, which rule the control power and the use of those resources. Such as developed countries can be able to minimize the impact of foods or/and natural resources production and consumption over the natural resources, they are only mechanisms built within an economic rationality, which should be possible to control its people's demand of natural resources, e.g. oil, gas, water and supply of natural resources get more balance. Then these natural resources sale price won't be raised more every year. When there developed countries' people , such as American and Britain who can control to reduce to spend to use the excessive natural resources too much in any time and any place habitually. Then , I believe the developing countries' governments e.g. Africa, China, India, which can buy those developed countries governments' excessive natural resources to raise those developed countries' natural resources supply numbers to provide to whose people to use as well as the most important benefit is that developed countries can gain foreign income from excessive natural resources expectation. Then, these governments will raise GDP economic growth. Hence, if developed countries could control whose people consume natural resource numbers and they could also control to produce natural resource supply numbers . Then, they can gain more excessive natural resources export chance to achieve to raise GDP economic growth aim for long term. As Kirkby et al., (1995)explained "the complexity of sustainable development our natural environment. If our governments can let our earth natural environment gets creation to maintenance, then our natural environment will be reduced the time to degradation. In the long time result, our society rural and urban economy will be growth , then our different countries' global growth will be caused diversity." Hence, it seems different countries' governments need to concern sustainable development to our natural environment .

V. How to apply agricultural green bio-economy
concept to solve control sustainable food
consumption and production in a resource-
constrained world

Nowadays, challenges for the global food supply have never been so complex. Between now and 2050 year, it has been predicted that growth in the global population and changing diets in developing countries, special in India and China and Africa etc. developing countries which may lead to an increase of around 70% in food demand. At the same time, depletion of fossil hydrocarbons will increase the demand for biomass for biofuels and industrial materials. Hence, developed and developing countries' governments ought need to coordinated to reduce air and water pollution and approached to lands use planning and oceans use planning to supply enough farms to grow potatoes, vegetables, tomatoes, fruits and let cows, pigs, sheep etc. animals can have comfortable and clean farm to live to produce good tasty meats to provide human to eat as well as to reduce pollution to supply fresh and clean water to let fishes to be lived and provides to human to drink clean water. Due to overpopulation will be predicted by scientists after 2050 year, so it will be caused foods and energy shortage possibly. Hence, different countries' governments need have long term perspectives to prepare to have enough foods and energy supply to provide us to eat and use for our earth with resource constraints and environmental limits, and which includes guideline on agricultural research to achieve foods supply aim.

On the one hand, I believe the knowledge-based bio-economy can play in realizing there challenges in particular the balance demand between foods, feed and fuel and the strategic role new technologies can have upon developing a sustainable an green bio-economy. On the other hand, I also think production of the presently high resource dependence and to build more environmentally begin sustainable agriculture system able to feed 9 billion people by 2050 year. I recommend global governments need to concern all aspects of food security including the total food chain and impacts of other land-use and management as well as non food areas, research areas which can be closed to free resources for new priorities, research to manufacture more new unique natural resources, due to gas, oil etc. resources will be used all in one day. On the energy shortage aspect, Substitution of these oil, gas etc. natural resources are needed . For example, nuclear energy is a kind of new natural resource, it can be used to push machines of rockets to be moved in space. In the future, I hope that nuclear energy can be used to drive cars or ships or trains etc. transportation tools in land. Hence, new natural resource research is essential and valid investment to be improved by scientists in the future.

On the global food supply interconnected challenges hand, including climate changes, energy and water supply are further encountered by the financial and economic changes in an increasingly globalized world. As a result, it is unclear how the growing demand for food and bioenergy (both biomass and biofuels) within a wider bio-economy can be met without further compromising ecosystem services on which all economic activities and social depend. I shall emphasizes the interaction of the economic, social and ecological components of our food systems at various levels, with feed backs increasingly the uncertainty and risks relating to future developments.

We need to face the food requirements of a growing world population have to be satisfied and we also need to the face of increasing resource scarcities, such as water, energy and land and foods etc. with the situation further exacerbated by climate change. Thus, we need to focus on our reducing demand through food consumption behavioral changes and structural changes in food systems and food chains change. Due to some developed countries people often to choose to buy these foods to eat excessively e.g. cow meat and pig meat and drink excessive soft drinks, e.g. man-made color juice. So, these developed countries consumers will feel these excessive foods and soft drinks can be rubbish if these developed countries consumers often drink these man-made color juice and eat pig and cow meats often excessively. It seems who ought to change their diet behavior and food consumption to avoid to spend too much money to buy excessive foods and drinks and who often shall not decide to eat and drink them when who feel not hungry habitually . Hence, changing human diet habit is one important psychology factor to reduce water and foods shortage, due to the meats and juices can be reduced to be rubbish if human can learn how to control their diet habit to reduce to consume excessive meats and vegetables and rice and soft drinks etc. kind of foods and drinks. Then, I believe that food and water drinking numbers will be reduced too much in the future. Hence, different countries' governments need to educate whose people to know that why who will face foods and water scarcity possibly and to let who to know how the issue can be avoided to cause by the changing of their diet habit and consumption behavior. Teaching includes, such as let who to learn why resources scarcities are expected to reduce and defining food security concept, the need is for a better understanding of complexity of vegetable systems, the need to improve the diversity and response capacity of food systems to enhance resilience, the need to address both food consumption and production, knowledge generation and innovation through cross-sector approaches is essential and the need for agricultural knowledge and innovation systems that are fit for farming purpose. After developed countries' people are educated to let who to know why who need to reduce to consume excessive foods and soft drinks habitually to aim to avoid the chance of foods and water supply shortage will be occurred after 2050 year. On the other side, in the case of biodiversity, the loss of functional biodiversity destabilizes ecosystems and weakens their ability to deal with natural disasters or human induced stresses, such as pollution and climate change. Hence, scientists need to research how to reduce new diseases to cause foods and water pollution, even new diseases cause to influence human health. Due to unpredictable new diseases will be caused foods, fruits, vegetables etc. can't be grow easily , even cows, pigs, sheep etc. animals are not health to cause diseases to be died easily. Then, those new diseases will be decreases our foods supply numbers seriously.

Resources scarcities are expected to define future food security. The predominant form of agriculture, food processing and retailing relies heavily on cheap inputs and the potential impact on this of long term resource scarcity trends has been largely overlooked. Scarcities are either biophysical limits, such as resource supply and availability or environment limits relating to pollution and its impacts on ecosystems and the global climate system. Hence, every country's government ought to educate to let whose citizen to discuss how to protect future food security topic to avoid resource scarcities occurrence after 2050 year. We need to know we are facing pollution (e.g. land, water, energy) and related to environmental limits e.g. climate change, ocean acidification and biodiversity loss. They represent a real threat, not only to future food supplies, but also to global stability and prosperity, through increasing poverty to developing countries and impacts on international trade, finance and investments. Hence, pollution and environmental limits will have direct relationship to influence every countries' foods supply numbers , then it will influence every country's gross domestic product income if the consumption is reduced by foods inflation.

For example, the combined effect of climate change and bio-diversity which makes the food production systems poorly due to a reduced resilience to shocks and changes over the long term , such as the limited availability of ore resources, soil degradation to loss of biodiversity. Both of these require a long term strategic approach to research and an openness to new research directions. These will need to help provide solutions towards more sustainable food consumption and production, some of which will need to break with current farmers or food manufacturers way of producing food methods. For example, research into ecological approaches: foods nutrient and water clean management and replacement of energy intensive inputs are priorities. Research to support energy efficient technologies for use in the food chain is also needed. Industry should assist in tackling the forthcoming challenges with new business models that can support the decoupling of resource use and changing consumption excessive foods behaviors and improving health foods production methods. For instance, changing the foods supply chains) e.g. more local purchasing) may have huge impacts on costs and also on creating closer links and confidence between producers and consumers.

In conclusion, different countries need find methods to solve foods and energy scarcity problem before 2050 year. I recommend that who can attempt to solve earth warm climate, innovate agricultural production and supply system, change human diet habit and food consumption of behavior, co-operate the trade of foods and energy demand and supply between countries fairly and reasonably, reduce food and natural resource waste, renew and recopy new kind of foods, research new natural resource substitution etc. different methods. However, if every country government can attempt to find any one or more of these methods to solve food scarcity to avoid to occur before 2050 year. I believe that the food scarcity challenge won't be occur after 2050 year in the future.

Environment Economy-Pollution and illness influences oil consumer behavior

How the economic consequences of outdoor air pollution influences consumer behaviors ? Air pollution can increase number of respiratory and cardiovas cular diseases. How they can impact economic growth, e.g. on human health, mortality and morbidity and agriculture aspects ? Whether when this diseases are caused from outdoor air pollution, why it can influence consumer behavior or brings negative consumpton emotion?

The macroeconomic costs of these impacts of outdoor air pollution that are linked to economic activity, and it raises welfare costs related to activity morality and pain and suffering from illness to consumers. For example, market costs are those that are associated with biophysical impacts that directly affect economic activity, e.g. lower crop yields affect agricultural production . Non market costs may also include the monetised welfare costs of morality (premature deaths) , and of the disutility of illness (pain and suffering).

Raising emissions reflect the assumptions on economic growth with increasing GDP and energy demand, especially in fast growing economies, such as the high population countries, India and China. These large changes are due to the increase in the demand for agricultural products and energy (include transport and power generation). For continuousing increase in energy demand to China and India car drivers, when they need to drive their cars to go to anywhere often. The higher emission will bring serious pollution. The environment protecting householders will decrease to use emissions from energy demand for, with reflects technology improvement in energy efficiency, the use of cleaner fuels, and biomass in open fire to cleaner energy sources including LPG, ethanol or enhanced cooking stoves. Hence, when many people get the diseases from air pollution. It will increase the medical (healthcare) cost to governments or when government needs to give welfare assistance to patients.

The three different market impacts of air pollution may include: reduced labor productivity, increased health expenditures and crop yield losses. They may reduce the GDP pollution feedback on the economy. At the global level, the consequences of labor productivity and health expenditure may impact to market cost increases,because increases expenditure to labor productivity, health expenditure and value added generated in agriculture from low productivity changes in crop yields.

What is the welfare costs of mortality and illness ? It is possible to attribute a cost to non-market impacts, such as the premature deaths and the costs of pain and suffering from illness . The welfares cost of the premature deaths caused by air pollution are calculated using the value of a statistical life to any one. Large costs can also associated with the pain and suffering from illness. So, pollution causes diseases to bring welfare cost increases, they include hospital living day to every patient when he is caused illnesses from air pollution. Moreover, it will impact government pollution expenditure to raise welfare cost to assist the low income level pollution illness patients' hospital living welfacre cost when they need to live long days in hospitals.

How does air pollutin impact on consumer automobile choices ? Air pollution levels can bring negatively affect the sales of fuel inefficient cars to China or India car drivers. They will choose to buy electronic cars to drive to replace fuel cars, because electronic cars only need to charge battery and it can reduce air pollution. When China or India their big city people's income level is rising, they will have more money to buy electronic cars to drive to reduce air pollution. Moreover, they believe that electronic cars can have better car quality and reduced air pollution need to charge battery fuel efficiency to compare fuel cars, when they need to often drive cars on roads. Som electronic cars demand will be the preference choice battery fuel efficiency or green driving tools to compare general fuel cars to satisfy China and India car purchasers when they are living in serious air pollution environment cities.

When the high environment protection awareness car buyers number is increasing in the countries, environment protection awareness will influence their car choice decison on which car to buy , when they are living in more heavily polluted cities tend to buy less fuel-inefficient cars. So, the electronic cars number need will increase in China and India both car market, because these two countries have similar characteristics, they have high population and gardens and farms number is less and there are many people are living in cities and many people are high income level , they usually have one car at least. So, they must feel cities are serious polluted by their diving behaviors. So, their environment protection awareness are ususally higher to compare other countries , they have less cities. So high air pollution to cities can excite the environment protection awareness to China and India car purchasers as well as they will prefer to choose to buy electronic cars to replace fuel cars to drive in possible, because they do not hope to live a high car dirty cities to cause their poor health when they have high income level. Also, it implies that it has direct relationship between China and India cities have high income level people number increases and air pollution level increases and electronic car demand number increases and fuel car demand number decreases in China and India car market in micro economic China and India electronic car and fuel car demand and supply market.

I assume that each China and India car consumer makes a relatively fuel or electronic car choice among possible car transmissions, between the option of buying no car and buy car or between the option of buying electronic car and fuel car. However, air pollution will be one major factor to influence China and India car purchase demand number on electronic and fuel car supply number. If china and India's air pollution can reduce, then car purchase number will increase, as well as the fuel car demand number will also increase ,because China and India have many cities are polluted serious. It can influence car purchase buyers how to decide car choice to make car or no car purchase decision, even purchase either fuel car or electronic car decison.

● How consumer decisions are impacted on environment?

Environmental impacts may occur on households, when they need to buy food, mobility, house, household goods and appliances for home use in household consumer behavior view. It can bring direct impacts, that occue because of the use of householder products and services during householders are staying at home. When householders feel need to raise living quality, they will considerate how they use services and related household products. When minimizing the use of natural resources and toxic materials as well as the emissions of waste and pollutants over the life cycle of the service or household product, e.g. using electricity or fuel time at home, cooling time and bathing time at home activities. So, for on householder who has high environment protection awareness and energy protection awareness, he will reduce long time to use electricity or fuel use time for cooking, bathing, watching television, listening radio time activities at homes, because he does not hope energy waste and protect air fresh at homes.

So, consumption is concerned by environment factors, such as demographics, technology, income and prices, psychological, social , cultural environments, e.g. consumers economic behavior is influenced by habt, routines, conventions etc. different environment factors influence. So, economic assumptions of rational and regular behavior is based on long-established principles, such as utility maximization. For example, when one country is encountering serious air or water pollution, then consumers will spend long time to search any data (marketing research activities) when they need to make purchase decision on pollution environment as well as pollution environment is dependent on (e.g. attitude, intention to the consumers).

Because when pollution environment will influence consumption behavior, such as behavioral and experimental economic to consumers. It implies on pollution environment's psychological assumptions on individual consumption motives, such as on the role of mental habits, loss confidence. So, consumers usually feel to spend long time to make purchase choice or decison on pollution environment, exaggerated optimism, expectatons, avoiding miscalculation,short-sightedness more enjoyment etc. psychological factors. When they need to make purchase decision on pollution environment, e.g. when one car consumer will need to make choice to buy one car, when he is living in China city, city is polluted serious. So, he will need to spend long time to gather any car model and brand and quality and fuel quality air polluted level to achieve to choose to buy the most clean fuel and the most least air polluton car to avoid to cause air polluton when he is driving the car in the China's city. So, air pollution way causes the China environment protection awareness car consumers to spend long time to gather any less use fuel car information to avoid to cause air pollution when he needs often to drive the car on the city roads in the China cities.

Hence , air pollution may cause the China car purchasers feel need to spend more time to gather car information in order to decide whether he ought to buy one car or no car purchase choice on the air pollution environment. So, the car must use less fuel to avoid air pollution easily when he drives the car on the China's cities' roads.

Reference

Erekson, O.H., Loucks, O.L. Strafford, N.C. 1999.
The context of sustainability . In: Sustainability
perspectives for resources and business
USA, p. 3-21.

Daly, H.E. 1990, Towards some operational
principles of sustainable development,
ecological economics, 2(1), 1-6.

Kirkby, J; O' Keefe P., Timberlake, L. (eds.) 1995.
The earthscan reader in sustainable development.
Earthscan Publications Ltd., London, 1-14p.

How can positive or negativesocial environment influence airlines oil need

Nowaday, airline industry is entering global competition. So, any some less positive or negative social environment changing which will influence any airlines' passenger behavioral consumption change. For example, air ticket price rises or fuel price rises or the country's season is bad or the global economy is bad or the country has terrible death threat etc. different negative social environment change fastors which will influence any country passenger individual travel consumption desires.

In Special, business class airline transportation demands are also increasing, due to many business travelers need to catch planes to go to any different countries to do business as well as many cargoes need to be carried from planes to transport to different countries to sell. So, business class traveler target group behavioral consumption is difficult to influence travelling consumotion desires from external environmental factors because business class traveler target group concerns to need to catch planes to go to another country to discuss business co-operation with the country's businessmen. So, their business travel desires won't easy to be influenced more than individual entertainment travel consumer's desire.

It seems cargo and business aim of aviation transportation industry has less chance to be influenced to reduce businessmen traveler or cargo transportation numbers to compare to entertainment traveler numbers by external environment change influences, due to the business travelers and cargo transportation travelling desires is difficult to reduce travelling or transportation needs to reduce the " doing businesses to earn profit chance with another country's businessmen". However, ignorance of internal or external market dynamics, catching entertainment travelers business can be detrimental to airline profitability more than carrying cargoes or business travelers business. Because the demands of travelling different countries' travelers' consumption are still more than the demands of businessmen carrying cargoes in any countries every year. So, the global GDP of travelling income sector is still have the important position to any country nowadays.

How can positive or negative social environment change influence any airlines' air ticket prices to be risen or fallen as well as how can these social environment change influence passenger consumption desires ? For example: What is the petroleum price change influence ?In fact, the increase in petroleum price can have chance to affect every airlines passenger has a negative manner to reduce travel consumption because increased oil prices have resulted in the reduction of airline services operations, the number of airline schedules flights, even airline bankruptcies. Whether global economic inflation or deflation, terrorism threats to the country, oil shortage or oil price rising or fallening, bank interest rate increasing or decreasing etc. external factors which have the most influential causes to bring the bad or good effects to cause airline industry share price reducing or increasing or increasing or reducing air ticket price. In result, these external environmental changes will influence the global traveler numbers to be increased or decreased at the time.

To support this hypotheses, this are my research first question, such as : Does a combination of terrorism and price of petroleum significantly influence airline profit changing mostly? The alternative hypothesis was my research second question, such as: Whether a significant relationship exists between terrorism, price of petroleum and airline profitability more than other factors, such as inflation, bank interest rate or air ticket price changing of these factors to influence passenger consumption desires change. I shall indicate that the first assumption was that terrorism has a negative effect on airline profitability and another assumption was that only external factors as oil prices or terrorism affect airline profitability. Finally, the terrorism and oil shortage and oil rising price factors can influence every passenger travel consumption desire to be reduced mainly.

Terrorism attack influences traveller need

However the effects of oil price and terrorism on airline profitability was limited to a regional perspective, so oil price and terrorism external environmental change will only influence some countries' airline traveler numbers to be decreased, e.g. the terrorism attack of plane crash event to USA on 11 Sept. After the terrorism attack happened on USA 11 Sept. incident of terrorism attack was restricted to events of skyjacking, attacks on oil production, refinery and distribution. Then, due oil shortage will be caused due to reducing oil production, refinery and distribution as well as it will influence oil price is risen and airline ticket price is also risen. It will reduce travel consumption desire to some countries if their airlines' ticket prices are also increasing. Other types of terrorist activities, such as attacks on financial targets or senior government officials could have an adverse effect on the petroleum and airline industry. I think the disruption of the production or distribution of petroleum because of incidents of terrorism was costly in terms of loss of business and the inflationary effect on fuel dependent products or services.

In fact, some airlines have adopted more fuel saving technology, so whose fuel consumption would not use more than other non fuel saving technology airlines. It seems fuel price increasing will not be the only factor to influence the airline industry's traveler numbers decreasing due, the owning more fuel saving technologic airlines which air tickets prices won't influence to be risen , due to reducing oil production and shortage influences . However, due to some airlines which have fuel saving technology, so which can avoid to use more fuel to provide planes to use and which fuel costs will be reduced, then which can provide cheaper air ticket fare prices to compare the non fuel saving technology airlines. The result will cause some not owning fuel saving technological airlines which will lose travelling customers in this global airline travelling market, also the not fuel saving technological airlines need to renew their fuel technology if which want to keep their competitive abilities to avoid to close down their businesses. So, what factors will influence the not owning fuel saving technological airlines profitability to be reduce if the oil shortage factor can not influence their planes energy supply to be reduced to cause air ticket prices to be increased? To answer this question, I shall indicate another financial risk factor how it influences airline industry behavioral change.

Also, I shall indicate the financial risk of airline industry evidence from Cathay Pacific airways and China airlines against key determinants of which include interest rate, exchange rate and fuel price risk for the period of January 1996 year to December 2011 year. During this period, these key external factors which were the most serious influence to cause these two airlines choose to change their strategic behaviors. Due to any these financial risks is difficult to predict and it was also changing often, these factors will also affect any airlines stock returns which arise from changing economic conditions, e.g. fuel price movements and fluctuations in exchange rates. These external unpredicted changing factors will attribute to the air tickets cyclical demand, capital investment, fixed costs of labor and landing rights to this global airline industry. Finally, it will cause some airlines need to rise air ticket prices to reduce expenditures increasing.

However, the relationship between fuel price and stock prices varies across economies which will influence travel passenger consumption of desires. For example, the effects of oil price changes in sub-sector indices, such as wood, paper and printing, insurance and electricity. In the past, on global stock exchange market was positively significant in 2011 year. Otherwise, with respect to the U.S.A. aviation industry, some economists suggested that global airlines stock returns were negatively to percentage change in fuel prices related to any airline firm value, e.g. Qantas and Air

New Zealand were negatively share price growth to fuel price risk in the short term in the 2011 year. Thus, due to these two airlines share price went down, it will influence investors who loss confidence to buy their shares as well as it will influence travelling passengers who choose to buy other airlines' air tickets to go to travel because they will feel these two airlines have business challenges, e.g. bad service quality and food quality and uncomfortable airline seat environment and poor management style. etc different bad feeling. So, these two airlines' share prices went down, it will influence every travel passenger's confidence to choose to buy their air tickets to sit their planes to go to travel.

Airlines fuel manufacturing supply strategy

However, there are some airlines which are the characteristic of self organization . It means that they are present in that both of oil fuel production and providing flights service in airline industry. So, these self organization airlines can control the oil fuel price by themselves. However, any self supply airline organization is also evident in efforts by businesses acts of terrorism against economic targets by adopting proactive steps, such as airline and airport security. So, it seems any self suply airline organization can reduce the risk to avoid oil price raising and terrorism attacks in airline industry risk management sector because oil shortage won't influence their air ticket prices need to be raised. Beside, these self supply airline organizations which have high technology of fuel efficient aircrafts, the use of one aircraft model, the adoption of direct routes versus customer loyalty programs and other operational cost reductions are strategies for increased profitability.

To solve oil price, terrorism etc. external risk to airline industry. Instead of high technology of fuel efficient aircrafts and self supply airline organization methods can solve terrorism attacks and oil price rising risks. However, I believe that there are other risks will threaten to airline industry. This risks concern traveller individual psychological factors influence, so it means that any airlines can apply psychological methods to predict which airline passengers' travel consumption desires. The risks include such as (1) user factor, such as : the travel country culture and tradition difference will influence the traveler chooses to prefer to go to the country to travel , the traveler's education level is high , who will choose to go to developed countries to travel, e.g. USA, UK. Otherwise, if the traveler's education level is low, who will choose to go to developing countries to travel, e.g. China, India etc. (2) economic factor, such as air tickets and airline fuel costs,

(3) human resources and macro economic factor, such as political stability, economic development, educational policy, health policy, environmental policy. However, these risks occurrences are resulting in the relationship of cause and effect events. These events are not directly observable.

Such as, the complexity of relationship between terrorism and airline profitability. Hence, if global airline industry can predict when those risks occur to do protective strategic behavior. It is possible that which can understand why these risk events will occur and their protective strategic behaviors also influence their outcomes to be positive to avoid any external risk threats on the long term. However, I think hierarchy, self supply airline organization efficiency methods which are as possible predictors of user preferences to avoid risk threat events to cause whose airline businesses failure occurrences in airline industry because it can reduce oil shortage factor which causes their air ticket prices need to be rised to keep their planes can have enough fuel supply.

● Why tourism and airline industries have close relationship to influence their profitability between of them.

In my study, I suppose terrorism, profitability and the price of petroleum which had properties of distinct and interrelated close relationship. Moreover, these variables (terrorism, profitability and the price of petroleum) displayed differentiation, self replication, efficiency and hierarchy which can cause risk events to airline industry. However, I also think the other internal and external threat factors of airline industry, such as inflation, bank interest rate, business model, service quality, airline fuel or plane engine technology, air ticket pricing, brand loyalty, airline strategic management, government policy and fuel hedging of these factors which can also raise the risks to threaten any airlines existence in airline industry.

There are two basic business models in airline industry. They are network (full service) and low cost (discount) carriers. The network carrier model employs diversification strategy by increased domestic destinations, serving international routes, providing diverse seating arrangements (business, economy and first class), maintaining a complex system of offering high quality service. Otherwise, low cost (discount) airlines focus on lower air fares. To keep operating costs down, discount airlines offer shorter routes and provide point-to-point destinations rather than through sophisticated flights are primarily in domestic destinations.

So, discount airlines operate a common model aircraft fleet, offer a single seating arrangement and cheaper flight services offered to compare network airlines. However, these two basic business models have their unique competitive abilities to provide any airlines existence in airline industry nowadays.

In fact, natural resource of oil is decreasing in our earth. But as the same time, human demand is increasing and oil supply is decreasing, so it also causes the oil fuel price is increasing to supply to airline industry. It influences not only to airline industry, it also impacts of higher oil fuel price to tourism, such as expansion of airports are made based on expected demand increase.

Tourism has been proven to many adverse events, including terrorism, flight disruptions. Beside, the bad natural climate change influences, such as the volcanic ash cloud event occurred in April 2010 year. So, airline industry need to concern climate change because it will cause high fuel prices indirectly. For example, the event occurred the extreme increase in operating costs for airlines in 2008 year, due to unprecedented prices for aviation fuel also meant, that despite the introduction of fuel charges, so this event causes the global airline industry recorded losses seriously. Even if alternative fuels become commercially available for airlines which are still likely to be more expensive than present aviation fuel. Thus, it seems that poor tourism will influence poor travel consumption and low airline tickets sale.

Higher airfares in the future are likely to lead to reduction in travel and cause tourists to shift from more distant to closer destination. When some of the economic responses to higher oil prices are obvious assessing the overall economic impacts on tourism is difficult. However, long term changes in global oil price rises will be similar to global changes in other commodity prices, exchange rates and income. It is therefore important to consider the impact of high oil prices on tourism from a general equilibrium perspective rather than relying only on bottom partial equilibrium. However, I believe tourism and airline industries have close relationship, such as tourism and airline industries are likely to suffer in an environment of high oil prices. Given that tourism destinations receive tourists from a range of origins, it would be useful to understand of some countries are increasing oil prices than others. Such as the net oil importing countries are selling higher oil prices than oil exporting countries generally. For example, New Zealand is an oil import country to provide planes for international visitor arrivals, so its oil fuel price is usually higher to charge to NZ airlines because any NZ airlines need to pay to foreign countries to buy any oil more expensive price. So, NZ airlines usually charge higher airfares to its visitors to compare the other exporting oil countries' airlines.

In economic theory, on income effects indicate negative impacts on tourism demand, the exact effects of higher oil fuel prices for specific destinations are far from clear. However, airline industry's different market segments show different sensitivities to air ticket fares changes. On the first hand, if the visitors are long destinations generally wealthier than average and therefore potentially less affected, as energy costs would be a smaller proportion of their income compared will be those from less wealthy groups. On the second hand, oil prices don't translate into higher transport costs especially not on air routes that are highly competitive and that are maintained for strategic reasons. On the third hand, many other factors shape tourists' decision making, including emotion drivers or those related to images, fashions and perceptions.

Increasing environmental protection awareness of tourists could also be an important factor to influence tourism consumption, instead of oil fuel price raising causes air ticket fares raising factor to reduce traveler numbers. However, oil price raising reason causes also due to high use of cars, vans and domestic air transport in some countries, e.g. Hong Kong, China countries, there are many people like to buy cars to drive. So, the private driver numbers are increasing demand to cause these countries' oil fuel prices raise in the short time suddenly. It will influence HK and China air tickets prices need to be risen , due to there are many cars, vans and domestic air transport tools need to use oil to supply energy to cause oil import numbers will increase to HK and China and HK and China airlines need to pay higher price to buy oil to use. In the result, HK and China airlines air ticket prices will also need to rise and it will influence HK and China travel consumption desire.

Fuel raising price solve methods

● Why oil fuel raising price factor can cause risk to airline.

In long run, implications of changes to supply and demand side conditions of oil fuel energy may differ qualitatively. For example, due to investment responses of producers, consumers and governments in alternative energy sources and more energy efficient plants, vehicles are supplied in order to achieve oil fuel price can't be risen seriously.

However, I believe oil fuel rising charge will be an important factor to influence global airline ticket fares to be also increased. Firstly, on the bank interest changing factor, e.g. bank interest rate rising which only attract more bank saving. But it can not influence the bank savers who choose to reduce relax time to go to other countries travelling. Otherwise, when the bank savers can save more money to earn higher interest in banks, who will prefer to choose to use their saving to consume travelling. Due to who can earn higher interest rate after a period of saving time. So, I believe whose behavioral travelling consumption will be raised when the banks will raise interest rate, then the bank savers won't choose to save more money in banks. So it is possible that who will withdraw more money to consume to go to travelling from their bank saving. It seems bank interest rate changing won't influence bank savers' behavioral travelling consumption to be reduced. Secondly, on the exchange rate changing factor, although any country's exchange changing will cause other countries' money value to be fallen down or risen up. However, it won't influence any travelers' behavioral consumption to be reduced seriously. Although, it is possible that the traveler won't spend too much to go to shopping when who travel to the another country and arrive the country. But, it is not possible to influence the traveler decides to reduce consumption to buy any air ticket to go to travelling. Thirdly, any country inflation also can not reduce travelers' travelling consumption easily because inflation can influence consumers who choose to buy cheaper foods and clothing and reduce entertainments in their every day life. But, one country's inflation can not influence it's citizen do not spend much travelling expenditure because travelers only spend one time or two times of travelling every year usually. So, the travelling expenditure rate of any households is not too much to compare daily essential expenditure. So, it seems that bank interest rate and exchange rate changing and inflation factors won't influence any travelers' travelling consumption of decisions to be reduced easily. Otherwise, if the oil fuel price raises too much, then global airlines' cost will be raised. So, the airlines only choose to increase their air fare prices to aim to avoid loss possibly. It seems that oil fuel price has direct influence airline income.

● Methods to solve rising air fare prices demand.

I. Why will biofuels energy be demanded ?

I suggest these methods how to avoid the oil raising price factor to cause airline air fare prices to be risen to lead the risk of traveler numbers to be reduced.

The first method: Whether aviation fuel markets will have what benefits from biofuels supply to planes. I shall refer the scope includes trends in jet fuel price, airline response to fuel price, increases and volatility and environmental goals for aviation. The aviation fuel supply industry includes production, distribution and consumption of aviation fuel and it outlines players in the aviation fuel supply chain. For example, at each airport, fuel supply chain organization and fuel sourcing could differ with regard to the role of oil companies, airlines, airport owners and operators and airport service companies. However, major jet fuel purchasers are airlines, general aviation operators, corporate aviation and the military, with most of the jet fuel in global different countries demanders being used for domestic commercial and civilian flights carrying passengers, cargos or both. Commercial aviation fuel efficiency has improved dramatically over time, largely due to aircraft and engine upgrades and operational and air traffic control improvements. So, it seems that fuel supply factor can influence airline fare prices majorly.

However, jet fuel prices generally correlate with prices of crude oil and other refined petroleum products, such as diesel. So, increasing prices and the persistent price volatility of jet fuel markets import airline industry finances in any countries. However, airlines use various strategies to manage aviation fuel price certainty, including financial hedges, increased vertical integration and adjustments in aircraft utilization and size to avoid the jet fuel raising price risk. Investments in alternative aviation fuel could be a mechanism to diversity expose to the price of petroleum. It seems the use of alternative aviation fuel would serve to diversify the fuel mix to reduce the risk of jet fuel monopoly raising price threat. If a diversified fuel mix were to avoid either fuel raising price in short term or to avoid fuel raising price in long term. Potential benefits include reduced actual fuel costs from only choice of jet fuel supply increased price certainty and lessened fuel costs. This diversify could allow airlines to become more consistently profitable and to make other investments in their businesses.

So, biofuels have potential to meet aviation industry needs, possibly including managing risks of upward fuel price trends and fuel price volatility and avoid risks with greenhouse gas emissions. So, the aviation fuels market could use biofuels to reduce greenhouse gas emission and mitigate long-term upward price trends, fuel price volatility or both.

What are the challenges of high priced oil for aviation? In fact, nowadays not the resources of oil as such, but much more the insecurity of supply, due to geopolitical instability in combination with a tight oil market makes a scenario with much higher oil prices than the world is currently experiencing not unlikely. Aviation is completely dependent upon oil as its fuel source. Since no practical energy substitute is readily available for commercial aviation, a scarcity of petroleum relative to demand will present a major aviation policy. In addition, efficiency gains, due to operational measures and new aircraft medium term. In particular, it has been demonstrated that the annual reduction rate in fuel consumption traffic unit is not a constant, but is itself also falling, in contrast to past estimates.

So, a high-priced oil scenario will have severe consequences for demand, airline revenues, the competitive position of airports and eventually airline networks, strategies and fleet development. In particular, transfer demand, short-haul and leisure traffic can be expected to be heavily affected by high oil prices, due to their relative high price sensitivity. So, different countries' governments or/and airlines are valuable to research another new and potential biofuel energy to substitute oil energy to supply our planes to reduce the threat of oil monopoly supply to influence the cause of air fare raising prices. Because the elasticity is very high to travelers, when the travelers feel air fares are rising high or even low level to influence travelers who will choose not to buy the air tickets to go to travel easily.

Will the fuel (oil based inputs) risk be higher to compare other costs to cause air ticket prices to be increased?, e.g. engineering maintenance, employees salaries, general cleaning, security office expenses etc. expenditures to airlines? If the probability-weighted upside effect on firm value when a risk is resolved favorably is greater the risk than the probability-weighted downside effect if the risk is resolved badly, then expected value work not be enhanced by hedging. So, the risk will be resolved badly to any commercial airlines. Airlines are an interesting case because the direct effect of source of risk resides squarely within the no offset in revenue functions (unlike for oil producers, for example), so value effects from costs feed directly into equity value. Most directly, the risk source is fuel costs to commercial airlines. Jet fuel is of course, a mix product of crude oil, so airlines indirectly face oil price risk. There are reasons to expect that airlines' fuel costs might to convex in oil price (i.e. absent any hedging). For example, oil prices, being generally pro-cyclical in recent times, tend to be highest when airline demand is strong. Airlines are therefore apt to use more high priced fuel than low-priced fuel over time. Airlines can raise air fare benefit is limited by the elasticity of demand. Also, cost functions could be influenced from fuel cost corresponds to upturns in economic activity overall (due to demand pressures on oil related prices), so it causes that airline's capacity delivers their services given their level of fixed capital. The essence of airlines basis risk in the case of jet fuel is essentially the time profile of the refining margin between crude and jet fuel, or the time profile of the price differential between other refined distillates and jet fuel. Thus, it is far from clear that risk management with oil is sure to add value to any airlines. It seems the impact of airline energy and any countries' domestic or foreign airline passenger travel numbers which have direct close relationship.

II. Whether the relationship between terrorism and oil prices has close relationship.

Whether the relationship between terrorism and oil prices has close relationship. It needs to judge to determine if a combination of terrorism and the price of petroleum significantly predicted airline profitability and which variable whether the further period was the most significant between the terrorism occurrence and the price of petroleum influence. So, different countries' governments or airlines need to collect samples of financial records from which country's any airline commercial passengers and cargo airlines on costs of fuel and any airline profitability. Also, gathering the terrorism data were comparison of terrorist attacks on petroleum in oil-producing nations, and incidents of high jacking aboard any country's aircraft. When any countries' airlines or governments can judge whether the impact of airline energy and terrorism risk level is high or middle or low level. Then, which can use this sample data to measure how to do positive social change to whether to increase or reduce employment in commercial aviation industry, or ought need to invest other higher commercial activity in tourist and other travel related service businesses and when is the most right time to adopt of green technologies by the civil aviation manufacturing industry after the terrorism attacks occurrence to any country. It seems that any countries' governments or airlines which ought concern that the event of when the terrorism attacks will occur and gather past sample data to predict when the next time terrorism attacks event will be occurred and the risk will be high or middle or low level to influence global airline industry development.

III. What factors will influence airline industry's price elasticity of supply and demand?

In fact, the airline industry is largely dependent on the supply of the oil industry. Otherwise, the oil industry is inelastic. However, the increase or decrease of the price of airfare is directly related to the increase or decrease of the oil's price to fuel the aircrafts because there has no any new energy which can be substituted to oil fuel to airline industry. So, it seems oil fuel producers are monopolies to control its sale price to be raised easily.

Another factor that can affect airline industry to be directly targeted by a tragedy brought about by terrorism. The past four years, from 2001 year to 2005 year, there had been at least $40 billion worth of losses in the airline industry because of the September 11 date terrorism attacks in 2000 year. There had been an expected and significant decrease in the demand for the airline industry services because of the attacks that involved planes hijacking and crashing into key locations like the World Trade Center and the Pentagon in USA. Although, terrorism attacks can bring risk to influence fuel price rising in airline industry. However, this risk occurrence to airline industry is only that after the terrorism attacks occurred. It is possible that terrorism attacks won't occur again in the future.

Otherwise, our concerning ought be the greenhouse emissions and how it affects global warming. The air quality would be better once this new regulations are adopted. However, it would affect large airlines. So, it would increase the price of airfares because of economic fees that airline companies have to cover. Air pollution can give a negative impact on the domestic or oversea owned airline companies for long term. If airlines' planes can use clean fuel to fly, e.g. biofuel, then it will bring benefits to global airlines for long term. On the positive side, the environment would be healthier as the earth's temperature would rise, and greenhouse effect would be dramatically reduced. This positive effect can come at a cost that is greater than most people perceive. So, the environment protection travellers who will reduce travelling times to avoid air pollution is caused to influence human health. It seems that airlines need to concern to apply psychological method to predict whose travelling consumption of behavior which is more suitable than behavioral economy method.

On the psychology view point on travelers, who will be more preferable to catch planes to go to different countries to travel, due to the chance of air pollution and global environmental warm issues will be reduced to low risk to influence our health if planes can use biofuel to be energy to fly in the future one day. It seems that spending expenditure to research other non polluted biofuel new energy is one solvable method to global airline industry in the future. To solve, any airlines or countries' governments or oil producers ought choose to spend more time to research new biofuel. Otherwise, the predicting when terrorism attacks event will be occurred, it is more difficult to predict the time more than researching to produce new biofuel energy method in the future.

So, I recommend that researching the new biofuel energy or other kinds of energy to substitute the oil energy and air pollution risk these two factors are the urgent behavioral economy method is used to solve this challenge which the airlines or oil producers or different countries' governments which need to concern nowadays. Because these two negative environment factors are the most influential to cause traveller individual travelling consumption desire to be fallen among of other negative environment factors.

The difference between online and offline travel agents

The main cost related factors to offline or online travel agents

Nowadays,many online or offline travel agents have interest to find what the main factors that can affect their strategies to reduce airline costs. The main factors include route structure, type and characteristics of the aircracft, cost of labor and management quality, which will influence whether which airline routes are the most suitable to let online travel agents or offline travel agents to help them to sell paper air tickets or electronic air tickets to attract travel consumption more easily.

Thus, a cost-related strategy is the main important factors to influence travel consumption choice between online or offline travel agents. For example, considering that advantages in costs is an important strategy for carriers to remain in travel transportation market.

The deregulation process of travel markets and increasing opportunities for competition have created excess capacity in many markets that causes lower rates, even with its rising costs. Thus, the travel strategic costs management as well as travel consumers that their behavior under different influences can bring competitive advantages over travel players.

Cost reduction in the travel market -based industry is a very important way of being competitive between offline and online travel agents, when facing travel air ticket prices decreasing for every trip. So reduce to total travel cost, e.g. fuel, maintenance, labor etc. is relevant, but the influence of each component on every total trip cost depends on factors that are related or not to airline operation. For example, some airline can adopt the lowest cost model to sell air tickets from offline or online travel agents which compete for travel passengers with traditional modes as self driving road transport trip in large areas of countries domestic travel market, such as US, UK domestic travel market.

However, the decision about the relevance of one cost is not a simple matter. The effectiveness of reduction of each item that comprises the total cost of airline can change over time, depending on both the business model and the scope of the airline company or online /offline travel agent company as well as external factors.

However, there are three types of competition advantage between online and offline travel market: They are such as agility, differentiation cost and the differentiation may be related to a product of superior quality, higher value f the brand or the company's positive reputation. Such as the online travel agent's providing the different airline cheap air ticket price and kind of trips to provide to travel consumer consumer comparison or the offline travel agent's famous brand or positive reputation to let travel consumers feel travel agents can provide many actual trip package to let them to compare by oral clearly. Thus, the online travel agent's weakness is lack of travel agent individual exploration to let every travel consumer to understand every trip package more clearly.

But online travel agent's strength is it can provdide one website to let travel consumer attempt to compare different trip air ticket and/or hotel price to make personal travel pre-booking decision at home. The another advantage is related to techniques that reduce production cost, making it is possible to offer cheaper air ticket, or hotel room rents, or cheap trip package, than the competition. Such as online travel agent can sell more cheape electronic air ticket price to compare traditional offline travel agent's paper air ticket price.

Finally, agility refers to the speed which the company responds to market demands. For example, if the online travel agent can make statistics to analyze how many online travel consumers to choose to buy which airlines' electronic or paper air tickets, e.g. which airline trip destinations and trips and hotels choices are the most popular attraction to them. Then, the online airline has possible to respond to provide to the most popular airline trips choices, electronic air ticket price comparison choices and hotel rooms prices choices to attract many online travel consumers to enter their online travel websites to choose different airline electronic tickets to buy or prebook hotel rooms from travel agent websites. Also, if the traditional offline travel agents can attempt to gather every travel consumer's destination trips, hotels , airline paper or electronic ticket prices enquires to make statistics to make which travel trip journeys or destinations and airline paper travel ticket prices are the most popular. Then, it is possible that they can respond to every travel consumer individual demand more to attract whose travel agent choice more easily.

Airline travel agency AirAsia in the domestic airline low cost strategy

There are three major characteristics of the airline industry namely is product nature, its expenditure structure and its market entry conditions. Airline agent's product is homogeneous or undifferentiated , causing significant competition in airline domestic travel or foreign travel both markets, which are free from regulations and economic barriers. However, high capital and operating expenditure is another important characteristic of the airline industry. Aircrafts, airlines' major capital expenditure are very costly to acquire . For operating expenditures, aviation fuel and labor make up the two major costs in the industry.

Another important characteristic of the airline industry is the conditions for market entry, which differs between international and domestic airline markets . In the international travel market, airline travel agency entry is very difficult as international flights and routes are the results of regotiations between governments . On the other hand, in the domestic and regional travel market, travel agency entry depends on the level of deregulation or liberalisation.

More and more countries, however are opening up their domestic travel markets for more competition. In addition, government plays an important role to regulate the travel markets and existing players may significant influence over now travel agent entrants.

In fact, the mjor factors influence to international or domestic travel consumption increasing numbers are the global economy and safety issues, instead of other different economic factors, such as travel destination choice, electronic air ticket or paper air ticket price, hotel price , the country's political change, e.g. war occurrence, bad weather , e.g. very cold or very hot etc. different factors infuence. Because generally , the world or any region of it is in an economic crisis or depression , the demand for airline services will fall. The late 1990 year Asian financial crisis for example, resulted in minimal increase in the number of worldwide airline passengers incrased only minimally from 1997 to 1998 year. Another factor of influencing the travel passenger number to be decreased, it concerns safety issues are also an important driver of the travel industry, which is subject to very safety standards to influence travel passengers' travel choice to the country. In addition, they are also unexpected safety related events, such as the 11 Sept. 2001 year tragedy in the US, which caused reduction in passengers . The increasing popularity of low cost airlines is the newest trend in the airline industry if which hope many passengers choose to buy whose electronic air ticket or paper air ticket to catch which planes to fly from online travel agent or offline travel agent channels.

The rise of low cost airlines, such as AmericaWest, JetBlue and Airtran in US, Ryanair and EasyJet in Europe and Vigin Blue in Australia. The share of low cost airline strategy is popular in the US and European airline market. For example, the Southwest airline low cost strategy is the basis of most low cost airlines operations. The key of the strategy is to reduce costs when at the same time offering low prices to passengers. History showed that the low cost airline strategy is easy to replicate , but difficult to implement successfully.

However, I suggest airlines need to know what functions which can attract passengers to chose to catch their planes to fly if they expect to rise passenger numbers. For example, the critical function of the Malaysia airline travel is to connect the major towns and remote interior areas within East Malaysia, which has poor road systems and limited availability of other significant means of transportation . In contrast, West Malaysia has more developed and extensive rod and railway systems.

Therefore, airline travel is not the main mode of long distance transportation. It implies Malaysis airline ought concentrate on focusing short distance transportation strategy for passenger beneficial choice function. For example, a new small Malaysia airline serving one or two routes may enter easily. Otherwise, a larger airline servicing multiple routes may be harder to enter Malaysis airline market. It also means access to capital and labor are the major obstacles for new airline entrants to Malaysia airline market. Thus, small airlines into a larger airline is probably more likely to be successful as in Air Asia's case to Malaysia airline market.

Thus, the airline low cost strategy competition positions include very low or minimal pressive from other airline similar service substitute products, low or medium power of airline similar input suppliers. In conclusion, low cost airline strategy is a god method to be attempted to win competitors in airline market.

How consumers select travel service between online and offline mode in travel industry

Nowadays, the travel industry is operating through two different modes, online and offline respectively. It involves the identification of the competitive strategies adopted by the tour operators. For example, it was found that e-retil travel is platform that is bringing two market forced the demand and supply tour operators and the customers together, and both parties and more inclined towards online mode in near future. Tour operators are gaining by operating at low cost and increasing their business reach when customers get what they desire as per their convenience. For example, many tour operators had promoted tourism destination through website that allow user to use interface for booking transporttion, foreign exchange etc. However, the role of travel operators (agents) should be assisted any airlines to promote their travel package service by internet more easily , such as tourism destination , arrangement of hospitality, restaurants, transportation tools during their trips.

The reasons why consumers choose online travel service include:

Firstly, it is online researching hospitality service. Online travel websites can provide many different accommodation furniture, such as seeking hotel locations, rooms prices comparison, prepaid hotel rooms by visa card payment transaction method, range from luxury five stars deluxe category hotels to small guest houses. The primary need of tourist is to find a place for residing in foreign country or domestic country to ensure whose safety and relaxing needs. Online travel website channel can help whom to find a place , according to his/her needs and paying capacity in the most shorten times.

Secondly, it is online restaurant (food and beverages researching) service. Full service restaurants are divided into two categories, fine dining and casual dining restaurants . Fine dining restaurants are usually located in the premises of luxury hotels, provide high quality food at premium price with good ambience and highly trained professionals. Thus, travel consumers can also compare the different restaurant food price and seek where is the restaurant and find.

What food taste of food supply from the travel agency or travel operator website easily 250 + tour operators are registered with the ministry of tourism (website of tourism ministry) , and the major players in the industry are dealing online and are dominating the travel industry. The major online travel players are Thomas cook, Cox and Kings, make any trips, clear trip, gatra.com and Expedia.

The tour operators whether online or offline offers a large number of services to the tourists including customized package where the customer selects each element of the tour package, specialized tourism package and complete tour guide package.

Nowadays, the tour operational travel (agents) are working through two different modes: offline online . Big brands with luge investment are dealing online and enjoying low cost benefits and huge profit margins. When the small tour operators have their market niche and managing have their market niche and managing their profits by dealing offline.

It is generally prefer offline mode that is the opportunity for small capital investment or employee number for tour operators. But the large scenario is changing as with the usage of internet by the tour operations have given convenience to the customers and now the customers of modern age have started developing preference for online modern. Thus, internet technology change any countries' travel agents or tour operators' air ticket sale method. So, it brings electronic ticket sale method is more popular to compare to traditional travel paper air ticket sale method.

However, online electronic ticket sale method has its disadvantages such as online transaction is unsafe, if the consumer 's name and address and visa card number is stolen to let any internet users to know to be used to buy any products from internet channel easily. Otherwise, traditional walk in offline travel paper ticket sale method is more safe, because the travel consumers can pay cash to the travel agents directly.

However, offline travel agent disadvantages include that the research identified that information communication and technology has very crucial role for tourism industry. Tourist can access any kind of information about tourism destination and tourism products from any part of the world. Tourism comprehends with social media. For example, it was found that (ICT) is bosting up tourism industry. (ICT) helps in searching the location, search for information on tourism products, and e-booking of airline tickets and hotel reservation.

The online travel sale service attraction is that the recent development in the field of information communication and technology and its practical application in tourism and hospitality industry. Generally , online travel sale service must have consumer side and the supplier side.

The decision making prcess of consumer was analyzed and it was found that travel information search and traveller individual electronic ticker pre paid to prebook any plane seat, hotel rooms and restaurants prices comparison to prebook service of traveler individual purchase behavior are corresponding with the usae of (ICT).

What is the online travel sale service strategy?

The two most important things for travel operators (agents) are online travel marketing and strategic management. Former can enhance business operations. Use of (ICT) develops financial capabilities , however, it depends on management choice, financial condition and position. Some researchers recommended that the usage of IT should not be restricted at operational level, however it should be extended up to senior level and should be used for decision making. Social media is regarded as a platform where the tourists and travel operators/agents (suppliers) of tourism industry cross each other. Thus, the role of social media has been directed for future research in tourism industry. Hence, it seems online travel sale service has these features to attract travel consumers to choose to use this online mode to buy electronic air ticket. Such as, airline electronic air ticket price comparison, pre-booking plan seats to avoid full seats flights to delay consumer individual trip plan, pre-booking hotel rooms and prices comparison as well as prebooking restaurant seats and food price and taste comparison, travel destination easy search. Otherwise, these features to attract travel consumers to choose to walk in to travel agents to buy paper air ticket directly. They include: safe cash or visa card payment to avoid personal information is stolen by website payment channel, e.g. via card number, address, name , birth date personal information. Also the travel consumer can enquire any questions from the travel agent and gets individual feedback from the travel agent by oral before who ensure to choose to buy which kind of travel package for whose travel destination. In special, when the travel consumer has much time to spend to enquire any travel trip question, walk in travel agent is the best enquire methods to let the travel consumer to know the trip information clearly.

● Online/offline travel operators
(agents) maketing strategies

Offline walk in travel unique segment service strategy

Nowadays, online and offlce travel operators competitions are serious. In fact, tourism marketing , there will be more need for online travel operators in the future, due to online travel sale service is popular to be accepted by online travel consumers. Thus, I recommend walk in offline travel agents need to concentrate on focusing some unique travel service to attract new or old travel consumers if who hope to survive.

I recommend that they can focus on specific specialized services, such as travel consultation (specialization) hypothesizing that systematic differences exist between the usage of travel agents for different travel contexts and travel agents can survive if they focus on specific segments of the market, such as older travelers (segmentation; hypothesizing that systematic differences exist between the usage of travel agents depending on the personal characteristics of travellers). The unique travel needs include: specific services related to package holidays, transport services, beach on city holidays, as well as destinations travellers are not familiar with.

I shall give my opinions to provide insight into alternative strategies for travel agencies in a matured travel market with a high internet penetration as below:

The internet online travel sale service is a reality of popular to let travel consumers to feel convenient to pre-book air seat, hotel rooms , air electronic ticket prices comparison. In order to make final purchase decision very easily in the shortest time. Consequently , it has penetrated the decision making process of travel to attract them to choose to buy electronic air ticket, prebooking hotel rooms or restaurant seats from online travel agent channel more than walk in offline travel agent channel. This is especially true in the tourism business where consumption to consume (booking) and the purchase-related information search (Bieger & Lasesser 2004; Crotts 1998).

In fact , apply website to provide travel sale method has these good consequence. From travel operator (agent) supplier's perspective, the success potential derived from operating a website consist of lower distribution costs, higher revenues and a larger potential market share (due to the ubiquitous access). From traverler's perspective, the internet allows direct communication with tourism suppliers facilitatinf requests for information and allowing services and travel related products, e.g. prebooking hotel rooms, restaurant seats , electronic or paper air tickets, travel trip arrangement package products to be purchased at any time and any place from online travel agents /operators conveniently.

Offline / online travel agency (operator) business depends on earn commissions on behalf of airlines. Thus, offline walk in travel agency (

operator) business model that would extend existence as a booking agency (thus focusing on consultation and interpersonal contact) strategy.

As a matter of fact, commission -cutting , which began in the US well ahed of Europe, has had a profound effect specially on business travel agents . Consequently , many of them have re-invented themselves as " travel managers", instead of selling tickets and making arrangements, they charge consultancy fees for reducing the amounts client companies spend on travel (Daneshku, 1999).

● Systematic differences strategy applies to offline walk in travel agent

Thus, I recommend systematic differences strategy can be applied offline walk in travel agent (operator). It means that walk in travel agents could reorient their offline walk in travel agent business to focus on contexts that are less substitutable by other channels and media . Factors hypothetically attributing to the delineation of travel contexts include: helping travellers to choose best travel destinations, helping travellers to attempt to find the number of previous trips (indicating the familiarity with a destination) for their travel reference, helping them to find the cheapest, the most convenient and the most close transportation to ctch during their trips, helping them to find the different types of accommodation and rooms price comparison , nature/type of the trip comparison , arrangement of time of booking (as indicator of spontneous / planned travel) nd helping them to budget overall travel expenditure .

Systematic differences in travel agent use exist in dependence of personal (characteristics with with tourists. Walk in offline travel agents could benefit from a travelling client segmentation strategy and customize and target their services to those travellers that are most likely to be and remain their customers.

Factors hypotheticlly attributing to the traveller segment include: travel expenditure per day, useful travel information as indicator for perceived risk and socio-demographic (age, gender, highest completed and education, professional positions) . Generally, the role of walk in offline travel agent with regard to the travel infrormation search and booking behavior have take an incoming perspective. Such as looking at visitors from different travel markets at a similar destinations. The comparison of central importance in determining whether specialization of travel contexts or market segments is the more promising strategy for walk in offline travel agents.

However, travel package tours strategy must b offline walk in travel attraction . Due to some walk in travellers target segmentation market has still needs. Generally, this travel package tours of travel segmentation consumer who like to enquire the travel agents to concern what the hotel rooms price are the cheapest to provide to them to live, what transportation tools the travel agent can arrange to them to catch anywhere the country destination, the travel agent can provide them to visit during their tour journey. Thus, the travel trip package service is still popular need to offline walk in travel agent (operator). This market is only belonged to offline walk in travel agents (operators) nowadays.

Service fees and commission cuts strategy

The reduction or removal of airline commission continues to challenge travel agencies' profitability It is crucial to understand what trends travel agencies need to be aware of to ensure how to profitability and increase travel agencies' revenues with service-fee models.

Service fees are not only a way to compensate for the loss of airline commission but also a way to generate new revenue sources for travel agencies that guarantee their long term profitability. Many travel agencies are expanding their service fee models, both in terms of the mounts changed and the number of service to airline.

However, if travel agent charge too much service fee to exceed the general airline travel market service fee reasonable or standard level. It will influence many airlines do not choose to find the travel agent to help them to sell air tickets. Travel agents apply fees most often for airline related services. They charge differentiated fees depending on the destination, type of reservation (e.g. frequent flyer), number of tickets sold or type of airline (e.g. full service versus).

However, service fee increases can raise customer loyalty and satisfaction. It won't reduce client numbers or result in a lose in clients.. The reason is that service fees can be tailored to suit individual customer. This helps travel agencies target their clients, with tailored services based on their past purchasing patterns and identity services for which clients' willingness to pay is greater , such as trip planning identity service for which pay , such as hotel only or special promotion.

To revenue mix for travel agencies is increasingly shifting to service fes as airlines have lowered or cut commissions. Successful travel agencies in many European countries are fast adopting, and constantly upgrading , their service fee schemes. Thus, it seems reasonable service fee level is one important factor to influence travel agents and airlines good relationship. In fact, even travel agents raise service fee, it won't influence travel consumer number to be reduced , even they raise air ticket price. It they can provide the informations concerning the reasonable hotel rooms prices and food quality comparison to satisfy travel consumers' living arrangement or helping them to find the reasonable restaurants' food prices and where are their location arrangement or providing the reasonable airlines' electronic air tickets or paper air tickets sale service, even arrangement any high entertainment quality of travel destination trips to let travel consumers to feel satisfactory.

However, I believe the raise air ticket price factor won't influence the travel consumer number to be decreased. Any offline or online travel agents will encounter this crisis. By cutting travel agents' commission. Airlines decreased their dependence on travel agencies as a distribution channel. In fact, three key variable factors will influence travel agents' commission income to be decreased. They include below:

● The unsustainable or no change financial losses by airlines , due to the growth of low cost carriers, leading to an increase in the number of bankruptcies.

● No negative consequences from previous commission cuts: airline had progressively lowed the commission payments.

● No effective resource for travel agencies to satisfy airlines needs.

● The appearance of now airlines and air routes to provide to travel agencies to fall down air ticket price to attract consumers' choices, due to who don't feel to spend much money to go to this new air routes or catch new airline plans , whether these new air routes are excite to entertainment or whether they are safe planes to catch.

● An increase in the number of bankruptcies to cause travel comsumption desire to be reduced.

● New competition forced down air fares.

● The necessity to cut production costs, especially with low cost meaning low production costs and low fares, even if the two are closely linked.

Internet negative influences to travel agents

Although, on the one hand, internet creates offline travel agents to use websites to help them to sell electronic air ticket or travel related products, such as prebooking hotel rooms , restaurants, transportation tools etc. travel service. However, on the other hand, internet also brings travel agencies competitive disadvantage with regad to suppliers' direct websites , when airlines are able to control seat availability and prices. Indeed internet cause the decision is made by the airlines to reduce and/or eliminate travel agency commission has led them to use technology that many of their distrust or are not inclined to use, and to compare prices and travel schedules constantly.

As a result of this travel sale service environment, traditional offline travel agencies are at a competitive disadvantage with regard to online travel agencie and to airline carriers, which have developed their own direct websites where they are able to control seat availability and prices.

Nevertheless, travel agents' pay programmes remain. From some airlines, travel agents receive negotiated incentive commission closely linked to their performance as incentive . However, airlines still need travel agents' assistance to help them to promote air tickets to sell, due to travel agents can provide trip packages, transportation tools, prebooking hotel rooms, restaurants and air tickets arrangement and they can give any enquiries to every individual travel consumer. It is free charge travel professional enquiry service for travel agency's competitive features.

Consequently, how agencies can reduce their reliance on airline commission payments. I recommend these following strategic options to them to apply as below:

● Streamlining operations, controlling staff costs, when ensuring the client feels as little impact as possible.

● Expanding or moving into the leisure business, where commissions on ono-air products remain high (cruise, hotel, railway travel)

● Specializing in geographic areas or becoming niche players for specific leisure products, e.g. destination weddings, student travel group cultural travel, cruises only, cruise and railway travel etc.

● (d) establishing a service fee driven business model.

Concentrating on business travel marketing strategy

The certain characteristics to the business travel market allowed this sector to adapt more easily to the disappearance of commission. Business travel systems have always had different relationship with different customers. They usually have long term buyer relationships, set up long before the commission cap. Some of them quickly renegotiated their contracts to include a transaction or management fee, knowing that the majority of these fee arrangements are specific the need of the client.

The reasons why airlines reduce commission to paid to travel agents. They include petrol costs increasing, e.g. indirect and by pass the established distribution chain by developing airlines' their own websites; reducing or removing commission paid to travel agencies. Consequently, the decision to cut travel agencies' commission clearly shows that airlines wanted to decrease their reliance and dependence on travel agencies as a distribution channel. Thus, the internet appears to be an efficient and cost-effective distribution channel. Also, by creating airlines' own websites and setting directly to their clients, airlines are also to control seat availability to their clients and prices to their websites.

What an e-commerce strategy is used by internet travel websites?

Nowadays, the commercial use of electronic travel ticket travel is common, the most purchased online products include, for example, the name brands in online travel Epedia.travel .com and cheap tickets have been or are being integrated in large online travel firms.

Generally, online travel websites apply these strategies to attract travel consumers as below:

Firstly, shopping mall strategy, means to conduct a comprehensive factors for e-commerce. The online service provider needs to organize catalogs of services, take orders through their websites, accept payments securely, send service or related document, such as airline tickets to consumers and manage client data , such as client profiles.

Secondly, portal strategy, portal websites , such as yahoo give visitors the chance to find almost everything , they are working for in one place. Websites , such as Altavista.com and yahoo.com provide users with a shopping page that links them to many sites carrying a variety of products. Once a client is familiar with a website, who will be more likely to use the online service.

Thirdly, pricing strategy, low price is as a major competitive weapon. It includes a comparison pricing on discount price or price negotiation to let online travel consumers to get the best electronic travel ticket price choice to buy any airline tickets.

Travel agents vs online booking: Tackling the shortcomings and strengths

Consequently, however, one travel consumer who chooses either online booking sale service or traditional walk in offline travel agent to enquire travel service. These both of travel sale methods have shortcomings also. Such as it is possible that online electronic travel ticket purchase has personal data ,e.g. visa card, name, birth data, address, which will be stolen by online crime internet users more easily, who can not enquire any travel questions to get clear travel information concern whose travel destination package service choice or hotel room choice or transportation tool or restaurant choice and airline choice by travel agent. Also, it is possible that walk in travel agent paper travel ticket purchase shortcomings include that the travel consumer can not check any airlines' seat and pre book hotel room or transport tool or restaurant in the shorten time if who needs to fly immediately. Thus, it seems that online travel agent's client group is business travel intention, who does not need to enquire travel agent and has desire to per book airline seat in the short time. Otherwise, the offline walk in agent's client group is entertainment intention , who need to walk in to travel agent to enquire whose travel package and has no desire to pre book airline seat in the short time. Thus, online travel agent ought concentrate on design good travel package for the business travel consumers. Otherwise, offline travel agent ought concentrate on design good travel package for the entertainment travel consumers. Thus, they can have themselves unique travel target package to adopt to their different travel need. Such as business travel consumers need to live cheap and comfortable hotels, catching cheap and fast transportation tools in their business trips, eating in cheap and good taste food in restaurant and spending the less time to catch the airline plan to arrive the destination and cheap and comfortable business class plan seat. Such as entertainment travel consumers need the travel agent can help them to design cheap and enjoyable travel package, includes living comfortable hotel room, exciting and enjoyable trip, good taste food and railway, travel bus, cruise and plane provision in trip.

In conclusion, In fact, tourism is a quite unique area of business in a sense that is a travel sale service product and it can't be observed or manipulated through direct experience prior to purchase . Instead clients have to purely rely on indirect or virtual experience. Thus, every online or offline travel agent ought attempt to design different travel package to attract every business traveler or entertainment traveller trip need because every traveler will have personal unique trip need in this competitive travel sale service market in the future.

Reference

Bieger. Th., and Ch. Laesser (2004). " Information sources for travel decisions: Toward a source process model," Journal of travel reserch, 42(4): 357-371.

Daneshku, S. (1999). " Unwived travel agents unworried bi internet, " Financial Times , London. June 16, 1999:10.

Foucault, B. Lery, N. Rifkin, A. & Silfies , 2000.
" Comparision of textbook prices by retailer and by college" working paper. Cornell University, Ithaca, Ney.

The difference between new and old economic explain the relationshiop between tourism and oil industries

Why is economic theory, a worthwhile thing to do ? e.g. helping organizations to solve challenges, helping society to solve challanges in macro economic view, part of the attraction and the promise of economics is that it cliams to decribe policies that will improve people's lives. This is unlike most other physical and social sciences. Sociology and political science have a policy component, but for the most part, they are concerned with understanding the function of standards of living, but this is really a by-product of science as an intellectual activity matters, physical science, has the potential to improve people standards of living.
What is the role of theory in a policy science? When my view that economic is a policy science. I mean that however either old or new economic theories one useful in policy. Theory is as a substitute for data. For example, we want to determine how a market price will respond to a tax, we could estimate this effect by running a regression of market price, against tax rates, controlling for as many other variable as possible. This would give us an equation that we could use to product how prices respond to change in taxes of one country has many unemployment people, then if it's government change a little 2 to 3 % import tax to private cars. Then, it may cause the country's car buyers number to import car demand decreases. The elastic to car import tax is high because the country has many people are unemployment. Hence, society is continue changing. So, some economists will research how to apply old economic theories to change other new theories to attempt to solve social and organizational challenges. In new economic theories, they are applied new modelling techniques to old real world problems, they add something to economic knowledge to the extent that we accept formalisation as a source of progress in economic.

Some economists focus new economic theory on the dynamic of regional growth and economic activity aspect. When the former foucs on long-run regional growth and later is linked to the " new growth theory". For example, the traditional trade theory is unable to explain the existence of different production structures , e.g. the country's geographical positions in similar regions. Also, trade should lead to conflice face greater market competition and loose incomes. Finally, countries having complementary factors were the best condidates to the formation of trading, so that they will specialize in different commodities. In addition, the traditional trade theory performs poorly when there is high mobility of production factors.

I shall indicate what the difference between new and old economic theories below:

In old economic theories, they may include: Scarcity means that the condition in which our wants and greates than our limited resources. So, we must make choices on how we will use resources. Hence, economic-social concerned with the efficient use of limited resources to achieve maximum satisfaction of economic wants; micro-economic studies such as individuals, firms and industries (competitive markets, labour markets, personal decision making etc.) Otherwise, macro-economics studies the large economy as a whole or in its national economic growth. Government how spends, inflation, unemployment etc. Marginal analysis involves making decisions based on the additional benefits vs. the additional cost.

- Old economic theory
- production possibilities curve

Everyone acts rationally by comapring the marginal costs and marginal benefits of every choice. For example, if you decide to go to college, the opportunity cost of going to college may include work to earn money, production possibilities have four assumptions: Only two goods can be produced, full employment of resources, fixed technology, resources. For example, when one firm produces two products . One is pizza food, another is robots. It produces many robots, then it will produces less pizzas. If it hopes to involve to produce pizzas, but it won't reduce to produce robots. It must need to improve technology in order to improvements in pizza ovens, but robots producing number won't be reduced . If the country has mad cow disease kills 85% of cows, then it will influence the demand for pizza decrease. Then, it may avoid to improve technology to produce many pizza, it can concentrate on applying technology to produce new robot making technology.

In the production possibiliteies curve and efficiency refers this firm can have productive efficiency when robots are being produced in the least costly way, due to pizzas produced number is reduced, this is any point on the production possibilities curve as well as allocative efficiency, when this firm's robots being produced are the ones most desired by society. This optimal point on the ppc depends on the robotic products desires of society.So, the less demand to pizzas, it will influence it applies less technology to produce pizzas, but more technology to be improved to concentrate on producing robotic products.

● Specialization of trade theory

Specialization of trade explains one country can earn comparative advanage when the producer will be lowest opportunity cost to produce. So, countries should trade if they have a relatively lower. For example, US specializes and makes only wheat. Brazil makes only sugar. So, US can export wheat and Brazil can export sugar to earn comparative advantages . When there two countries only concentrate or producing on kind of food in order to earn specialization trade advantages. Free market means little government involvement in the economy, (laissez faire), individuals own resources and the opportunity to make profit gives people incentive to produce items efficiently, wide variety of goods available to consumers and competition and self-interest work together to regulate the economy keep computers and only one company is making them, other making computers to earn profit.

● Invisible hand

This lead to more competition, which means lower prices, better quality, and more product variety. Consequently, most efficient production of the goods, that consumers want, produced at the lowest prices and the highest quality. What does invisible hand mean? It is the concept that society's goals will be met as individuals seek their own self-interest. For example, when society wants fuel efficient cars. Profit seeking producers will make more, then competition between firms results in low prices,high quality and greater efficiency . Consequently, the government does not need to get involved since the needs of society are automatically met. Thus competition and self-interest act as an invisible hand that regulates the free market.

I shall indicate some new economic theories as below:

● Organizational behavioral economic theory

In new economic theories, it may include behavioral economics, it explains how has changes views of consumer theory and finance, hoe to deal climate change and analyze new ways to deal with international environmental problems, farm economy how to raise crop, vegetable, food productivities, how farmers' agriculture growing behavior can achieve crop, raising productivites aim more easily, e.g. predicting climate when is bad change time.

In new miceo economic theory, economists have recommended new economic theory to help organizations to solve problem effectively and efficiently. The problem solving steps include as below:

Identifying the problems, identifying current successes and strengths, analyzing the causes of the problems, identifying the factors that enable our success, envision our desired future, treating the problems, innovating to build more support for those factors that enable success and move us toward the future we desire. For example, whether or not a team is able to sell the big picture and engage in effective strategic planning depends on members' feeling hoping and looking toward a positive future. By appropriate , they mean information that is realistic and timely information that is true and relevant to the situation. Negative information is approriate when it provides the specific boundaries within which a challenge must be met.

In an economic tightening scenario, for example, appropriate negativity might include a target budget reduction amount and time frame. It might also include recognition that staff and elected officials will have to make hard decisions. Hence, in new micro economic theory, it mains to help organizations to find to avoid target budget exceeds to any projects implementations and avoid prolong time to finish any projects for any organizations, less spending and time reducing or raising efficiency and effective achievement will be applied new nicro economic theory to help any organizations to be applied new micro economic theory to help any organizations to achieve benefits (intangible , i.e. reducing time and raising efficiency, tabgible , i.e. less salaries spending and project team members number to any projects).

Hence, new micro economy theory aims to research new organizational behavior can achieve raising efficiency and improving productivities aims. For graphic organizers theory aims to help organizatins to enhance any organizations members' thinking skills by encouraging brainstorming, generating new ideas, connecting parts to the whole, drawing sequence, analyzing causes and effects etc. There are exactly important traits of economic students to make sense out of economic phenomena and to make effective decisions about economic issues. Thus, in new micro economy view to organizations. It explains that every organizational member ought be independent graphic organizer:

They will ought need to be enhanced skills to help that organizations to achieve any aim easily. They may include : organizations show events in chronological orders multiple timeline (sequential organizers), or hierarachy diagram (hierarchical organizers), such as organizers showing the relation between a concept and its subordinate levels of characteristics, ccyclical organizers (organizers showing the sequence of events in a process , e.g. circle organizer), conceptual organizers . (organizers showing how a mian concept is supported by facts, evidence and characteristics, e.g. concept definition map).

So, new micro economic thoery explains that every organizational memeber may explain that every organizational memeber may have different organizer role when they need to cooperate with other members in themselves organizations any time. When they know whether what their organizer role is in the time. They can make thinking strategy skill more easily in short time , it will bring any organizations much intangible economic benefits, such as reducing meeting time, avoiding over-spending and prolonging time to finish any projects for the organization efficiently.

● Division of labor theory

The another new micro economy theory is divison of labor, organizational coordination and market mechanisms in collect time, problem solving skills. It is a view of economic organizations as problem-solving driven by trial -and error learning and collective selection. It assumes any one economic organization ought produce " well constructed" goods and services, achieves productivity among workers and solving problems by technological search and economic production activities raising skills, the most cheap and the most useful function in order to raising the product productivities and quality improvement.

● Logical process theory

For logical process theory , it implies that most technologies and industries and born with a highly vertically-integrated structure, undergo a distintegration process as the industry grows in the expansion phase, and then re-integrate in the maturity phase, but often along integration proles that differ signicantly from those of the original infant industry. Thus, the degree of vertical integration of an industry undergoes major changes along its life cycle. For IBM computer company example, its needs to find any new product to make new market share, such as IBM electronic book publish will be on new technological product market. Due to ecommerce is popular, many readers began to accept to apply internet technological tool to read any books. So, IBM had attempted to sell electronic books in this new ecommerce e-book publishing market. So, IBM needs to expand its traditional computer sale market to (AI) artificial intelligent mobile and electronic book publish both markets. IBM's computer products has reached maturity phase, it needs to change its another new technological products market. It ought not follow its old logical process to continue research how to invent new computers. It ought change to research how to invent new (AI) mobiles and innovate its electornic book reading platforms to attract many electronic books attractively as well as invent new (AI) mobiles to attract many (AI) mobile users. If it still hopes to continue to win its computer competitions in technological product industry.

● Managerial economics

Another new economic theory is managerial economics, it means tha application of economic methods to the managerial decision making process. It is a fundamental part of any business. It is more attention in business as mergers become more aware of its potential as an aid to decision making, and this potential is increasing all the time. For example, global warming challenge will riase cost to our socity, how governments assess the possible scale of cuture green-house gas emissions, and hence of man-made global warming, involves economic forecasts and economic calculations. Those forecasts and calcualtions will provide the basic for poicy on environment pollution issue how to avoid future social cost raises in possible.

Hence, managerial economics may mean how managers find the most efficient way of allocating scarce resources ans reaching their objectives. It aims to predict and compare the cost and benefit may occur when the manager chooses to do the action. In a neoclassical framework, it treats the individual elements within the economy (consumers, firms , workers) as rational agents with objectives that can be expressed as quantitative functions (utilities and profits) that are to be optimized, subject to certain quantitative constraints.

What is the relevance of the managerial economic theory? For example, protesting against global capitalism that economics is of no use in answering the fundamental questions involving value judgements, like reducing pollution, indeed, economists themselves often admit that their science can only make positive impression of the limitations of economics. Hence, in managerial economic view, government should make use of market forces in order to achieve a more efficient solution.

In the terms of reducing pollution, would governments aim to reduce pollution by 90% in the next ten years? But rich and poor countries would suffer overall from a policy of reducing pollution by 90% and that future generations might not benefit either. So, managerial economic theory aims to let policy maker how to make the more reasonable analysis to conclude and to solve any issue for organization leader or government leader, even individual consumer.

● Social entrepreneurship theory

The final new economic theory is social entrepreneurship for each country, regardless of its socio and economic development, one of the main key indicators of success is the social stability of society. Impossibilty of market and government, are the factors that contribute to the need of social enterprise that provides partical and dynamic solution for local social problems. This social innovation form an environment that promotes scientific, technical , technological and informational innovations increase efficiency of new techniques and technologies reduce innovation costs. So, the new economic theory explains society needs to change. So, social entrepreneurship is needed because society is needed to innovate that serves to adopt social changes and development.

Some economists believe that social enterprise is a new way to solve social and economic problems and focus of social innovation and brings positive change to society. In any one social entrepreneurship, it needs coordinational strategy for the development of social entrepreneurship .So, every one is stakeholder to the social entreprenership. Thus, today a significant theoretical basis for this new economic theory , " social entrepreneurship" concept in the new economic model is formed . Consequently, social entrepreneurship is an innovative form of business, which successfully combines social aims and commercial practice .

Consequently, social entrepreneurship is a innovative form of business, which successfully combines socail aims and commercial practice. Social entrepreneurship ought may solve these social challenges, such as unemployment, poverty, skillful workers number shorten . However, socail entrepreneurship works where the government can not work , due to the lack of funding, and the business does not want to become of low profit ability.

Hence, social entreprensurship is a charity and business approaches to solving social problems. Also unlike traditional business that works for the seeking profit only , social enterprise, performs social functions and works where the government can not work , due to the lack of funding , and the business does not want to become of low profitability. Social enterprise changes the traditional economy model, it does not depend on external sources (donors, grants and donations) , the necessary start up capital , receives income from its own activities. It carries on non-profit activities. It includes socio-oriented structure, the goal of activity is to mitigate or solve the specific social problems. Consequently, profits are reinvested in activity expansion or for social purposes in case of charity organization there is no profit and in traditional business the profits share between shareholders.

How can positive or negativesocial environment influence airlines oil need

Nowaday, airline industry is entering global competition. So, any some less positive or negative social environment changing which will influence any airlines' passenger behavioral consumption change. For example, air ticket price rises or fuel price rises or the country's season is bad or the global economy is bad or the country has terrible death threat etc. different negative social environment change fastors which will influence any country passenger individual travel consumption desires.

In Special, business class airline transportation demands are also increasing, due to many business travelers need to catch planes to go to any different countries to do business as well as many cargoes need to be carried from planes to transport to different countries to sell. So, business class traveler target group behavioral consumption is difficult to influence travelling consumotion desires from external environmental factors because business class traveler target group concerns to need to catch planes to go to another country to discuss business co-operation with the country's businessmen. So, their business travel desires won't easy to be influenced more than individual entertainment travel consumer's desire.

It seems cargo and business aim of aviation transportation industry has less chance to be influenced to reduce businessmen traveler or cargo transportation numbers to compare to entertainment traveler numbers by external environment change influences, due to the business travelers and cargo transportation travelling desires is difficult to reduce travelling or transportation needs to reduce the " doing businesses to earn profit chance with another country's businessmen". However, ignorance of internal or external market dynamics, catching entertainment travelers business can be detrimental to airline profitability more than carrying cargoes or business travelers business. Because the demands of travelling different countries' travelers' consumption are still more than the demands of businessmen carrying cargoes in any countries every year. So, the global GDP of travelling income sector is still have the important position to any country nowadays.

How can positive or negative social environment change influence any airlines' air ticket prices to be risen or fallen as well as how can these social environment change influence passenger consumption desires ? For example: What is the petroleum price change influence ?In fact, the increase in petroleum price can have chance to affect every airlines passenger has a negative manner to reduce travel consumption because increased oil prices have resulted in the reduction of airline services operations, the number of airline schedules flights, even airline bankruptcies. Whether global economic inflation or deflation, terrorism threats to the country, oil shortage or oil price rising or fallening, bank interest rate increasing or decreasing etc. external factors which have the most influential causes to bring the bad or good effects to cause airline industry share price reducing or increasing or increasing or reducing air ticket price. In result, these external environmental changes will influence the global traveler numbers to be increased or decreased at the time.

To support this hypotheses, this are my research first question, such as : Does a combination of terrorism and price of petroleum significantly influence airline profit changing mostly? The alternative hypothesis was my research second question, such as: Whether a significant relationship exists between terrorism, price of petroleum and airline profitability more than other factors, such as inflation, bank interest rate or air ticket price changing of these factors to influence passenger consumption desires change. I shall indicate that the first assumption was that terrorism has a negative effect on airline profitability and another assumption was that only external factors as oil prices or terrorism affect airline profitability. Finally, the terrorism and oil shortage and oil rising price factors can influence every passenger travel consumption desire to be reduced mainly.

Terrorism attack influences traveller need

However the effects of oil price and terrorism on airline profitability was limited to a regional perspective, so oil price and terrorism external environmental change will only influence some countries' airline traveler numbers to be decreased, e.g. the terrorism attack of plane crash event to USA on 11 Sept. After the terrorism attack happened on USA 11 Sept. incident of terrorism attack was restricted to events of skyjacking, attacks on oil production, refinery and distribution. Then, due oil shortage will be caused due to reducing oil production, refinery and distribution as well as it will influence oil price is risen and airline ticket price is also risen. It will reduce travel consumption desire to some countries if their airlines' ticket prices are also increasing. Other types of terrorist activities, such as attacks on financial targets or senior government officials could have an adverse effect on the petroleum and airline industry. I think the disruption of the production or distribution of petroleum because of incidents of terrorism was costly in terms of loss of business and the inflationary effect on fuel dependent products or services.

In fact, some airlines have adopted more fuel saving technology, so whose fuel consumption would not use more than other non fuel saving technology airlines. It seems fuel price increasing will not be the only factor to influence the airline industry's traveler numbers decreasing due, the owning more fuel saving technologic airlines which air tickets prices won't influence to be risen , due to reducing oil production and shortage influences . However, due to some airlines which have fuel saving technology, so which can avoid to use more fuel to provide planes to use and which fuel costs will be reduced, then which can provide cheaper air ticket fare prices to compare the non fuel saving technology airlines. The result will cause some not owning fuel saving technological airlines which will lose travelling customers in this global airline travelling market, also the not fuel saving technological airlines need to renew their fuel technology if which want to keep their competitive abilities to avoid to close down their businesses. So, what factors will influence the not owning fuel saving technological airlines profitability to be reduce if the oil shortage factor can not influence their planes energy supply to be reduced to cause air ticket prices to be increased? To answer this question, I shall indicate another financial risk factor how it influences airline industry behavioral change.

Also, I shall indicate the financial risk of airline industry evidence from Cathay Pacific airways and China airlines against key determinants of which include interest rate, exchange rate and fuel price risk for the period of January 1996 year to December 2011 year. During this period, these key external factors which were the most serious influence to cause these two airlines choose to change their strategic behaviors. Due to any these financial risks is difficult to predict and it was also changing often, these factors will also affect any airlines stock returns which arise from changing economic conditions, e.g. fuel price movements and fluctuations in exchange rates. These external unpredicted changing factors will attribute to the air tickets cyclical demand, capital investment, fixed costs of labor and landing rights to this global airline industry. Finally, it will cause some airlines need to rise air ticket prices to reduce expenditures increasing.

However, the relationship between fuel price and stock prices varies across economies which will influence travel passenger consumption of desires. For example, the effects of oil price changes in sub-sector indices, such as wood, paper and printing, insurance and electricity. In the past, on global stock exchange market was positively significant in 2011 year. Otherwise, with respect to the U.S.A. aviation industry, some economists suggested that global airlines stock returns were negatively to percentage change in fuel prices related to any airline firm value, e.g. Qantas and Air New Zealand were negatively share price growth to fuel price risk in the short term in the 2011 year. Thus, due to these two airlines share price went down, it will influence investors who loss confidence to buy their shares as well as it will influence travelling passengers who choose to buy other airlines' air tickets to go to travel because they will feel these two airlines have business challenges, e.g. bad service quality and food quality and uncomfortable airline seat environment and poor management style. etc different bad feeling. So, these two airlines' share prices went down, it will influence every travel passenger's confidence to choose to buy their air tickets to sit their planes to go to travel.

Airlines fuel manufacturing supply strategy

However, there are some airlines which are the characteristic of self organization . It means that they are present in that both of oil fuel production and providing flights service in airline industry. So, these self organization airlines can control the oil fuel price by themselves. However, any self supply airline organization is also evident in efforts by businesses acts of terrorism against economic targets by adopting proactive steps, such as airline and airport security. So, it seems any self suply airline organization can reduce the risk to avoid oil price raising and terrorism attacks in airline industry risk management sector because oil shortage won't influence their air ticket prices need to be raised. Beside, these self supply airline organizations which have high technology of fuel efficient aircrafts, the use of one aircraft model, the adoption of direct routes versus customer loyalty programs and other operational cost reductions are strategies for increased profitability.

To solve oil price, terrorism etc. external risk to airline industry. Instead of high technology of fuel efficient aircrafts and self supply airline organization methods can solve terrorism attacks and oil price rising risks. However, I believe that there are other risks will threaten to airline industry. This risks concern traveller individual psychological factors influence, so it means that any airlines can apply psychological methods to predict which airline passengers' travel consumption desires. The risks include such as (1) user factor, such as : the travel country culture and tradition difference will influence the traveler chooses to prefer to go to the country to travel , the traveler's education level is high , who will choose to go to developed countries to travel, e.g. USA, UK. Otherwise, if the traveler's education level is low, who will choose to go to developing countries to travel, e.g. China, India etc. (2) economic factor, such as air tickets and airline fuel costs, (3) human resources and macro economic factor, such as political stability, economic development, educational policy, health policy, environmental policy. However, these risks occurrences are resulting in the relationship of cause and effect events. These events are not directly observable.

Such as, the complexity of relationship between terrorism and airline profitability. Hence, if global airline industry can predict when those risks occur to do protective strategic behavior. It is possible that which can understand why these risk events will occur and their protective strategic behaviors also influence their outcomes to be positive to avoid any external risk threats on the long term. However, I think hierarchy, self supply airline organization efficiency methods which are as possible predictors of user preferences to avoid risk threat events to cause whose airline businesses failure occurrences in airline industry because it can reduce oil shortage factor which causes their air ticket prices need to be rised to keep their planes can have enough fuel supply.

● Why tourism and airline industries have close relationship to influence their profitability between of them.

In my study, I suppose terrorism, profitability and the price of petroleum which had properties of distinct and interrelated close relationship. Moreover, these variables (terrorism, profitability and the price of petroleum) displayed differentiation, self replication, efficiency and hierarchy which can cause risk events to airline industry. However, I also think the other internal and external threat factors of airline industry, such as inflation, bank interest rate, business model, service quality, airline fuel or plane engine technology, air ticket pricing, brand loyalty, airline strategic management, government policy and fuel hedging of these factors which can also raise the risks to threaten any airlines existence in airline industry.

There are two basic business models in airline industry. They are network (full service) and low cost (discount) carriers. The network carrier model employs diversification strategy by increased domestic destinations, serving international routes, providing diverse seating arrangements (business, economy and first class), maintaining a complex system of offering high quality service. Otherwise, low cost (discount) airlines focus on lower air fares. To keep operating costs down, discount airlines offer shorter routes and provide point-to-point destinations rather than through sophisticated flights are primarily in domestic destinations. So, discount airlines operate a common model aircraft fleet, offer a single seating arrangement and cheaper flight services offered to compare network airlines. However, these two basic business models have their unique competitive abilities to provide any airlines existence in airline industry nowadays.

In fact, natural resource of oil is decreasing in our earth. But as the same time, human demand is increasing and oil supply is decreasing, so it also causes the oil fuel price is increasing to supply to airline industry. It influences not only to airline industry, it also impacts of higher oil fuel price to tourism, such as expansion of airports are made based on expected demand increase.

Tourism has been proven to many adverse events, including terrorism, flight disruptions. Beside, the bad natural climate change influences, such as the volcanic ash cloud event occurred in April 2010 year. So, airline industry need to concern climate change because it will cause high fuel prices indirectly. For example, the event occurred the extreme increase in operating costs for airlines in 2008 year, due to unprecedented prices for aviation fuel also meant, that despite the introduction of fuel charges, so this event causes the global airline industry recorded losses seriously. Even if alternative fuels become commercially available for airlines which are still likely to be more expensive than present aviation fuel. Thus, it seems that poor tourism will influence poor travel consumption and low airline tickets sale.

Higher airfares in the future are likely to lead to reduction in travel and cause tourists to shift from more distant to closer destination. When some of the economic responses to higher oil prices are obvious assessing the overall economic impacts on tourism is difficult. However, long term changes in global oil price rises will be similar to global changes in other commodity prices, exchange rates and income. It is therefore important to consider the impact of high oil prices on tourism from a general equilibrium perspective rather than relying only on bottom partial equilibrium. However, I believe tourism and airline industries have close relationship, such as tourism and airline industries are likely to suffer in an environment of high oil prices. Given that tourism destinations receive tourists from a range of origins, it would be useful to understand of some countries are increasing oil prices than others. Such as the net oil importing countries are selling higher oil prices than oil exporting countries generally. For example, New Zealand is an oil import country to provide planes for international visitor arrivals, so its oil fuel price is usually higher to charge to NZ airlines because any NZ airlines need to pay to foreign countries to buy any oil more expensive price. So, NZ airlines usually charge higher airfares to its visitors to compare the other exporting oil countries' airlines.

In economic theory, on income effects indicate negative impacts on tourism demand, the exact effects of higher oil fuel prices for specific destinations are far from clear. However, airline industry's different market segments show different sensitivities to air ticket fares changes. On the first hand, if the visitors are long destinations generally wealthier than average and therefore potentially less affected, as energy costs would be a smaller proportion of their income compared will be those from less wealthy groups. On the second hand, oil prices don't translate into higher transport costs especially not on air routes that are highly competitive and that are maintained for strategic reasons. On the third hand, many other factors shape tourists' decision making, including emotion drivers or those related to images, fashions and perceptions.

Increasing environmental protection awareness of tourists could also be an important factor to influence tourism consumption, instead of oil fuel price raising causes air ticket fares raising factor to reduce traveler numbers. However, oil price raising reason causes also due to high use of cars, vans and domestic air transport in some countries, e.g. Hong Kong, China countries, there are many people like to buy cars to drive. So, the private driver numbers are increasing demand to cause these countries' oil fuel prices raise in the short time suddenly. It will influence HK and China air tickets prices need to be risen , due to there are many cars, vans and domestic air transport tools need to use oil to supply energy to cause oil import numbers will increase to HK and China and HK and China airlines need to pay higher price to buy oil to use. In the result, HK and China airlines air ticket prices will also need to rise and it will influence HK and China travel consumption desire.

Fuel raising price solve methods

● Why oil fuel raising price factor can cause risk to airline.

In long run, implications of changes to supply and demand side conditions of oil fuel energy may differ qualitatively. For example, due to investment responses of producers, consumers and governments in alternative energy sources and more energy efficient plants, vehicles are supplied in order to achieve oil fuel price can't be risen seriously.

However, I believe oil fuel rising charge will be an important factor to influence global airline ticket fares to be also increased. Firstly, on the bank interest changing factor, e.g. bank interest rate rising which only attract more bank saving. But it can not influence the bank savers who choose to reduce relax time to go to other countries travelling. Otherwise, when the bank savers can save more money to earn higher interest in banks, who will prefer to choose to use their saving to consume travelling. Due to who can earn higher interest rate after a period of saving time. So, I believe whose behavioral travelling consumption will be raised when the banks will raise interest rate, then the bank savers won't choose to save more money in banks. So it is possible that who will withdraw more money to consume to go to travelling from their bank saving. It seems bank interest rate changing won't influence bank savers' behavioral travelling consumption to be reduced. Secondly, on the exchange rate changing factor, although any country's exchange changing will cause other countries' money value to be fallen down or risen up. However, it won't influence any travelers' behavioral consumption to be reduced seriously. Although, it is possible that the traveler won't spend too much to go to shopping when who travel to the another country and arrive the country. But, it is not possible to influence the traveler decides to reduce consumption to buy any air ticket to go to travelling. Thirdly, any country inflation also can not reduce travelers' travelling consumption easily because inflation can influence consumers who choose to buy cheaper foods and clothing and reduce entertainments in their every day life. But, one country's inflation can not influence it's citizen do not spend much travelling expenditure because travelers only spend one time or two times of travelling every year usually. So, the travelling expenditure rate of any households is not too much to compare daily essential expenditure. So, it seems that bank interest rate and exchange rate changing and inflation factors won't influence any travelers' travelling consumption of decisions to be reduced easily. Otherwise, if the oil fuel price raises too much, then global airlines' cost will be raised. So, the airlines only choose to increase their air fare prices to aim to avoid loss possibly. It seems that oil fuel price has direct influence airline income.

● Methods to solve rising air fare prices demand.
    I. Why will biofuels energy be demanded ?
I suggest these methods how to avoid the oil raising price factor to cause airline air fare prices to be risen to lead the risk of traveler numbers to be reduced.

The first method: Whether aviation fuel markets will have what benefits from biofuels supply to planes. I shall refer the scope includes trends in jet fuel price, airline response to fuel price, increases and volatility and environmental goals for aviation. The aviation fuel supply industry includes production, distribution and consumption of aviation fuel and it outlines players in the aviation fuel supply chain. For example, at each airport, fuel supply chain organization and fuel sourcing could differ with regard to the role of oil companies, airlines, airport owners and operators and airport service companies. However, major jet fuel purchasers are airlines, general aviation operators, corporate aviation and the military, with most of the jet fuel in global different countries demanders being used for domestic commercial and civilian flights carrying passengers, cargos or both. Commercial aviation fuel efficiency has improved dramatically over time, largely due to aircraft and engine upgrades and operational and air traffic control improvements. So, it seems that fuel supply factor can influence airline fare prices majorly.

However, jet fuel prices generally correlate with prices of crude oil and other refined petroleum products, such as diesel. So, increasing prices and the persistent price volatility of jet fuel markets import airline industry finances in any countries. However, airlines use various strategies to manage aviation fuel price certainty, including financial hedges, increased vertical integration and adjustments in aircraft utilization and size to avoid the jet fuel raising price risk. Investments in alternative aviation fuel could be a mechanism to diversity expose to the price of petroleum. It seems the use of alternative aviation fuel would serve to diversify the fuel mix to reduce the risk of jet fuel monopoly raising price threat. If a diversified fuel mix were to avoid either fuel raising price in short term or to avoid fuel raising price in long term. Potential benefits include reduced actual fuel costs from only choice of jet fuel supply increased price certainty and lessened fuel costs. This diversify could allow airlines to become more consistently profitable and to make other investments in their businesses.

So, biofuels have potential to meet aviation industry needs, possibly including managing risks of upward fuel price trends and fuel price volatility and avoid risks with greenhouse gas emissions. So, the aviation fuels market could use biofuels to reduce greenhouse gas emission and mitigate long-term upward price trends, fuel price volatility or both.

What are the challenges of high priced oil for aviation? In fact, nowadays not the resources of oil as such, but much more the insecurity of supply, due to geopolitical instability in combination with a tight oil market makes a scenario with much higher oil prices than the world is currently experiencing not unlikely. Aviation is completely dependent upon oil as its fuel source. Since no practical energy substitute is readily available for commercial aviation, a scarcity of petroleum relative to demand will present a major aviation policy. In addition, efficiency gains, due to operational measures and new aircraft medium term. In particular, it has been demonstrated that the annual reduction rate in fuel consumption traffic unit is not a constant, but is itself also falling, in contrast to past estimates.

So, a high-priced oil scenario will have severe consequences for demand, airline revenues, the competitive position of airports and eventually airline networks, strategies and fleet development. In particular, transfer demand, short-haul and leisure traffic can be expected to be heavily affected by high oil prices, due to their relative high price sensitivity. So, different countries' governments or/and airlines are valuable to research another new and potential biofuel energy to substitute oil energy to supply our planes to reduce the threat of oil monopoly supply to influence the cause of air fare raising prices. Because the elasticity is very high to travelers, when the travelers feel air fares are rising high or even low level to influence travelers who will choose not to buy the air tickets to go to travel easily.

Will the fuel (oil based inputs) risk be higher to compare other costs to cause air ticket prices to be increased?, e.g. engineering maintenance, employees salaries, general cleaning, security office expenses etc. expenditures to airlines? If the probability-weighted upside effect on firm value when a risk is resolved favorably is greater the risk than the probability-weighted downside effect if the risk is resolved badly, then expected value work not be enhanced by hedging. So, the risk will be resolved badly to any commercial airlines. Airlines are an interesting case because the direct effect of source of risk resides squarely within the no offset in revenue functions (unlike for oil producers, for example), so value effects from costs feed directly into equity value. Most directly, the risk source is fuel costs to commercial airlines. Jet fuel is of course, a mix product of crude oil, so airlines indirectly face oil price risk. There are reasons to expect that airlines' fuel costs might to convex in oil price (i.e. absent any hedging). For example, oil prices, being generally pro-cyclical in recent times, tend to be highest when airline demand is strong. Airlines are therefore apt to use more high priced fuel than low-priced fuel over time. Airlines can raise air fare benefit is limited by the elasticity of demand. Also, cost functions could be influenced from fuel cost corresponds to upturns in economic activity overall (due to demand pressures on oil related prices), so it causes that airline's capacity delivers their services given their level of fixed capital. The essence of airlines basis risk in the case of jet fuel is essentially the time profile of the refining margin between crude and jet fuel, or the time profile of the price differential between other refined distillates and jet fuel. Thus, it is far from clear that risk management with oil is sure to add value to any airlines. It seems the impact of airline energy and any countries' domestic or foreign airline passenger travel numbers which have direct close relationship.

II. Whether the relationship between terrorism and oil prices has close relationship.

Whether the relationship between terrorism and oil prices has close relationship. It needs to judge to determine if a combination of terrorism and the price of petroleum significantly predicted airline profitability and which variable whether the further period was the most significant between the terrorism occurrence and the price of petroleum influence. So, different countries' governments or airlines need to collect samples of financial records from which country's any airline commercial passengers and cargo airlines on costs of fuel and any airline profitability. Also, gathering the terrorism data were comparison of terrorist attacks on petroleum in oil-producing nations, and incidents of high jacking aboard any country's aircraft. When any countries' airlines or governments can judge whether the impact of airline energy and terrorism risk level is high or middle or low level. Then, which can use this sample data to measure how to do positive social change to whether to increase or reduce employment in commercial aviation industry, or ought need to invest other higher commercial activity in tourist and other travel related service businesses and when is the most right time to adopt of green technologies by the civil aviation manufacturing industry after the terrorism attacks occurrence to any country. It seems that any countries' governments or airlines which ought concern that the event of when the terrorism attacks will occur and gather past sample data to predict when the next time terrorism attacks event will be occurred and the risk will be high or middle or low level to influence global airline industry development.

III. What factors will influence airline industry's price elasticity of supply and demand?
In fact, the airline industry is largely dependent on the supply of the oil industry. Otherwise, the oil industry is inelastic. However, the increase or decrease of the price of airfare is directly related to the increase or decrease of the oil's price to fuel the aircrafts because there has no any new energy which can be substituted to oil fuel to airline industry. So, it seems oil fuel producers are monopolies to control its sale price to be raised easily.

Another factor that can affect airline industry to be directly targeted by a tragedy brought about by terrorism. The past four years, from 2001 year to 2005 year, there had been at least $40 billion worth of losses in the airline industry because of the September 11 date terrorism attacks in 2000 year. There had been an expected and significant decrease in the demand for the airline industry services because of the attacks that involved planes hijacking and crashing into key locations like the World Trade Center and the Pentagon in USA. Although, terrorism attacks can bring risk to influence fuel price rising in airline industry. However, this risk occurrence to airline industry is only that after the terrorism attacks occurred. It is possible that terrorism attacks won't occur again in the future.

Otherwise, our concerning ought be the greenhouse emissions and how it affects global warming. The air quality would be better once this new regulations are adopted. However, it would affect large airlines. So, it would increase the price of airfares because of economic fees that airline companies have to cover. Air pollution can give a negative impact on the domestic or oversea owned airline companies for long term. If airlines' planes can use clean fuel to fly, e.g. biofuel, then it will bring benefits to global airlines for long term. On the positive side, the environment would be healthier as the earth's temperature would rise, and greenhouse effect would be dramatically reduced. This positive effect can come at a cost that is greater than most people perceive. So, the environment protection travellers who will reduce travelling times to avoid air pollution is caused to influence human health. It seems that airlines need to concern to apply psychological method to predict whose travelling consumption of behavior which is more suitable than behavioral economy method.

On the psychology view point on travelers, who will be more preferable to catch planes to go to different countries to travel, due to the chance of air pollution and global environmental warm issues will be reduced to low risk to influence our health if planes can use biofuel to be energy to fly in the future one day. It seems that spending expenditure to research other non polluted biofuel new energy is one solvable method to global airline industry in the future. To solve, any airlines or countries' governments or oil producers ought choose to spend more time to research new biofuel. Otherwise, the predicting when terrorism attacks event will be occurred, it is more difficult to predict the time more than researching to produce new biofuel energy method in the future.

So, I recommend that researching the new biofuel energy or other kinds of energy to substitute the oil energy and air pollution risk these two factors are the urgent behavioral economy method is used to solve this challenge which the airlines or oil producers or different countries' governments which need to concern nowadays. Because these two negative environment factors are the most influential to cause traveller individual travelling consumption desire to be fallen among of other negative environment factors.

New economic development in Tourism and oil industries
   ● How to develop new economic tourism industry

How to develop tourism industry in new economic environment? Any examination of the new economic development of travel and tourism requires definitions of the subject and its components, which are suitable for economic analysis. However, in new economic development to tourism industry, it is also important to look at tourism conceptually, in order to set the scene for a deeper understanding of the future new tourism industry development.

Tourism is neither a phenomenon nor a simple set if industries, however, in new or old economic development environment. It is a human activity which encompasses human behavior, use of resources, and interaction with other people, economies and leisure enjoyment environment. It is also involved physical movement of tourists to locales other than their normal living places.

In future new economic environment, traditional travel needs to include these element in order to satisfy traveler enjoyment and leisure feeling: They may include: Tourist needs and motivations, tourism selection and behavior and constraints , travel away from home , market interactions between tourists and those supplying products to satisfy tourist needs and impacts on tourists , hosts, economies and environments.

In new economic environment, the tourism products may include: carriers, in any forms of transport for tourist travel accommodation, man-made attractions, which could also include the managed areas of natural attractions, private sector and public sector support services, middlemen, such as tour wholesalers and travel agents.

The tourism resources may also include: Natural resources, lands , minerals, water and biological; labor resources, human work, and enterprise; capital resources, manmade enhancement and other resources. The travel and tourism resources problems may include: As there is frequently a mismatch between producer and consumer perception of what constitutes the tourism product , there may be conflict in ideas of which resources are properly involved as well as many of the resources likely to be in demand for tourism are public goods , or even free resources.

In new economic development to tourism industry view, we need to consider that tourism and travel has the reputation of being a relatively clean and pleasant industry in which to work or invest in order to attract a greater number of resource suppliers than as less well-perceived industry, which therefore keeps rewards prices down by competition, how to attract those retiring from or travel business for example, if their finances are already sound, income from travel is not expected to be optimal , travel and tourism is frequently highly seasonal , offering rewards that are competitive with other industries only some of the time, destination products are often in locations which are of little use to other industries, so that competition for resource use if minimal and hence rewards are low.

In general, tourist purpose may include: recreational purpose : holiday, health and sport and religion as well as business purpose: company business

, e.g. conventions and sales trips. So, in new economic tourism development aim, tourism industry need consider hoe to achieve incentive trips to let these both tourists to feel. For example, the overall type of tourism required, destination arrangement, travel mode, accommodation and attraction visiting and purchasing method or distribution channel. The purchasing method choices may include: whether to buy an inclusive package or separate service, whether to buy direct from suppliers, such as airlines or hotels or use an agent , which tour wholesaler or operate or agent to use.

I predict the tourism development in new economic view, it may have these characteristics: Few enterprises in travel and tourism are large, highly cashed-up and have a large asset base, enterprises within travel and tourism that are not in a financial position to diversify, and those do well success to the above –average growth obtainable in travel and tourism compared with many other industries, they would therefore tend to expand within the sector. The result of individual enterprise growth and integration within travel and tourism is an increase in the concentration of that industry. The degree to which output is produced of fewer and fewer enterprises. This can be only be accounted for realistically with the context of an individual economy, Levels of concentration in any part of travel and tourism in the future are likely to depend on two opposing factors: The constant demand by many tourist market segments for new experiences and products, which encourages the development and survival of more and diverse enterprises, and therefore leads to the reduction of concentration as well as technology, which in travel and tourism frequently calls for large capital outlays and requires mass markets for efficient use, promotes integrations and large scale enterprise, especially in air travel and non-personal services (marketing and information communication, travel insurance , tourism payment methods). IN these areas, concentration will undoubtedly increase in future new economic development environment.

● How new economic development in oil industry

The future global economic growth, it will influence personal incomes and GDP rise. They would carry different weight in different countries at different times. Starting from low levels of incomer and economic development. Household consumption will change from being dominated by basic heat to rapidly rising energy use for higher levels of comfort in space heating and cooling (and large dwellings), and greater use of electrical appliances, finally to a degree of saturation influenced by the income distribution patterns of the country concerned. Income distribution typically changes very slowly, so that the technical market for heart will never be saturated because there will always be a proportion of poor people living in small spaces less comfortably than the average. Industrial energy consumption will be influenced by technical efficiency within each sector, and by changes in the structures of the economy, e.g. changing proportions of agriculture, heavy and light industry, and services. One may eventually see evidence of diminishing marginal returns to additional energy inputs compared to other inputs. Energy consumption in the energy transformation sector may be influenced by income, which drives the demand for electricity to influenced by income, which drives the demand for electricity to grow faster than the demand for heat, but is also subject to the chosen technology of transformation, which is influenced by the cost and availability of primary energy inputs (fuels) in new economic development environment.

IN new economic development environment, it will influences that fuels do not compete in all sectors; for example, the transport sector is dominated by oil. Nuclear and hydroelectric power (and most renewables) reach the user through electricity; electricity itself competes with the direct burning of fossil fuels. Electricity provides the means by which other fuels can compete with oil and gas in sectors, such as space heating and process heat. It also is the only means of powering applications such as motors, computers and lighting: these subsectors are difficult to analyze. However, there is strong evidence that higher incomes do not weaken the demand for electricity so much as the demand for energy in total (in contrast to the effect on the demand for non-electric energy forms).

Econometricians look at the historical record of change in fuel prices and quantities to distinguish several factors between the new economic development and old economic development to oil industry in the future. An income effect. Increasing (reducing) fuel prices reduces (increases) the purchasing power of consumers' income: higher incomes caused by lower prices will increase energy consumption; the consumers' allocation of the increased income to energy purchases may reduce as income rises. Thus income may be heading in a different direction from fuel prices that the effect of fuel price changes when incomes are rising means simply that rising incomes have increased demand. Reducing the cost of using energy through win-win efficiency measures causes a similar problem . On the consequence, in future new economic development environment, it may influence in both cases demand will be less than if the future oil price or efficiency has not changed. The other effect is that an efficiency or substitution effect. An increase in fuel prices may cause consumers to spend more on new equipment, building materials and management operations, which will reduce the amount of fuel required to give the same energy result to the user. The extent of the efficiency effect depends on what happens to the price of the new equipment or building: if those price s rise in line with the fuel price, changes in the balances between fuel and capital or management will not occur. A new user technology , such as the development of the combined cycle gas turbine generator may increase efficiency and thus greatly reduce the quantity of primary fuel needed to produce the required output in this case electricity. If electricity prices had remained sticky, and the electricity and gas markets were not competitive, some of this advantages could have accrued to the gas suppliers in the form of an increase in price, because th4 unit of gas produces more output of electricity, it would have a higher value. In reality, the development of new economic competitive environment in both gas and electricity has tended to ensure that the benefits of such technical advanced accrue to the consumer through lower final prices. The same many apply in the case of improved efficiency in future non-manual driving auto vehicle development: the consumer's cost of motoring is reduced in new economic non-manual driven auto vehicle (Artificial intelligent vehicle) can replace manual driven vehicle , even electricity battery can replace oil energy to be used in vehicles. So, oil price may be influenced to reduce in future new economic development environment.

New and old economic theories explain oil is not main factor
to influence tourism income

● Can economic theory explain old price change to influence tourism income?

I shall attempt to apply old and new economic theory to explain whether oil changing price has direct relationship to influence global tourism indusry development or tourism income as below:

Is oil changing price the main to influence tourism income or tourism development or economic growth ? If oil price rises ar falls, it will or won't cause tourism income decreases or increases? If they have cause and effect relationship, what are the main factors to influence tourism income changes by oil price rises or falls ?

I aim to investigate how any why among oil price shocks will influence tourism income variables. We may distinguish between these oil price shocks: Supply-side , aggregate demand and oil specific demand shocks. I assume that oil specific demand shocks affect inflation and the tourism sector equity index. By constrast, I also believe that aggregate demand oil price shock exercisr an effect, either directly and indirectly tourism generated income and economic growth. So, in old economic theory, supply-side , aggregate demand view to oil specific demand shocks will influence tourism income varies. So, governments ought implement strategies against future oil price movements or plan for economic policy development.

In fact, instead of oil price changes will influence tourism income, it could also harm economic growth and tourism activities, due to the effect they expert on transporation, production cost, economic uncertainty.Because tourism activities is one important sector to influence any country's leisure consumption GDP income source. So, sudden fluctations in oil prices may also influence economic growth. It is based a hyphthesis known as the tourism led economic growth. So, it seems that they have direct or indirect relationship to case effect between oil price and tourism activities and development. So, increase on tourism income, the called " economic-driven tourism growth". In addition, high oil prices are affecting certain tourism industry segments , e.g. airlines, cruises lines, hotel, rent travelling car services etc. for oil, importing countries example, with reference to macro economic effects, higher oil prices generally lead to higher inflation, when they negatively influence to country's income.

Hence, from a micro-economic perspective, positive oil price shocks lead to a decline in disposable income. for low income people, it will bring an immediate and negative impact on tourism, mainly due to they feel tourism leisure is regarded as a luxury good, when oil price shocks to rise suddenly . It influences any airline or cruise entertainment service providers' costs are influenced to raise. Then, they need to increase air ticket or cruise ticket price. It will bring on negative tourism leisure demands-side the oil price increases low income group, potential tourism leisure consumers. Hence, it seems that oil price may have indirect relationship to influence tourism leisure consumers' needs.

● How the price of oil changes influences global tourism industry growth or recession?

In macro-economic view, sudden mid and long term oil price shock can influence global torusim industry growth or recession. For example, a oil price of US$180 per barrel was considered only a few years ago, now this has a realistic scenario to which all plaers in the T&T sector have to adapt. At such a high level, the price of oil will become even more critical to almost every part of the tourism value chain. Although, weak global demand, caused by global economic recesson, resulted in a steep oil price decline to US$45 per barrel by the fourth quarter of 2008 in the past low oil price occurrence history, this won't change the mid to long -term oil forecast.

In fact, the past oil price occurrence history of the dramatic structural had changed a high price imposed on airlines, travelers, and destination countries, all of which will have to navigate through times of shifting or even declining travel demand. I assume that a high oil price scenario is assumed in the long term in order to highlight the changes , such a senario would mean for consumer behavior and the competitiveness of several destinations.

Low oil price in the 1970 and early 1980 did not bring significant growth of international air travel, but its growth has been strongest between 1980 and 2004, a period with stable and relatively moderate oil prices. Also, the rapid development of the low-cost carrier business model in the 1990s further fueled air travel growth by capturing tourism leisure demand , such as weekend leisure travel to cities using mostly secondary airports in any big area countries, such as UK, US . However, the tourism growth is whole influenced by high oil prices, due to oil price had been continue rising in possible.

Basis of oil is shortage supply product, oil is assumed to be the main energy source for the aviation sector for the nest 30 years. Although, second-generation biofuels seem to be on the horizon, the economics as well as the production scalability and aviation biofuel shortage will be a main challenge to airline industry. So, I assume that oil price will continue rise up, if there have none any aviation biofuel can be reflected to oil to use for air plane energy.

Until 2004, the only factors to have affected air travel growth, negatively were in external shocks , such as 9/11, causes catching air plane crisis or US regional geopolitical conflicts. It brings some travelers feel fear to go to US travel, as well as until recently 2019, human mouth disease can influence air to have disease to anyone from mouth. So, global travelers number had been continue decreasing, because they are fear to get disease by air when many themselves every stranger travelers are sitting on the without windows air planes. Although, mouth human and air disease and US 9/11 air attack both matters may influence oil price falls effect, because air planes flying times will reduce. They won't need frequent to fly, to cause aviation oil energy need reduce. Consequently, oil price will decrease, due to travelers number reduces and air planes flying times are also influenced to reduce. (oil demand decreases cause oil price decrease). Although, air lines ' cost will also be influenced reduce, but oil price decrease can not bring travelers number increase , when air ticket price reduce because global many leisure and business trip travelers feel fear to catch air planes frequently when human mouth air disease occured in 2019. So, oil price decreases can not grow up tourism industry growth or rise tourism income.

However, the obvious impact of a high oil price is an increase in the operating costs of airline. Moreover, fuel cost as a percentage of airline operating costs vary significantly based on the length of the flight. The longer the flight, the higher the fuel costs as a percentage of the airline operating cost. So, from an online's perspective, long -hauel flights represent the most criticial challenge to profitable operation because the share of fuel on these flights, compared with other cost items, is largest, because of the unfacorable fuel economics, due to fuel costs even at high-load factors. For example, Thai airways dropped its non-stop Bongkok to US flights in the summer of 2008 for commercial reasons, because fuel reached operating cost levels of 55 percent on this route, a cost burden that could not be passed on to their customers. So, the estimated price elacticity of passengers demand at this Bongkok to US flights route is high, if Thai Airways rises less air ticket price, it will influence many travelers to choose other airlines to catch air plan to fly. Hence, due to Thai Airways can not make decision to rise air ticket price, because it believes that it will lose many travelers, so it only chooses to drop this non-stop Bongkok to US flights to avoid fuel cost rising economic loss.

However, although micro and macro economic theories may also that oil price variable or change, it may influence global tourism income. But, recently, on 2019, human mouth and air diseases, it can influence global individual leisure and business trip travelers feel fear to catch air plans to avoid their bodies get this kind of death sickness when they sit in the no fresh air supplying air planes. They feel that they reduce leisure travelling flying times or business trip flying times with strange travelers to sit in crowd air planes together. Then, they must many avoid human moth and air disease to avoid death crisis. Hence, in this global human mouth and air diseases threat environment occurrence, even oil price sudden reduces to low price, it brings airline's cost reduces and air ticke price reduces. However, when air ticket price reduce to be very cheaper, it can not still attract global many leisure or business trip travelers to buy air tickets to fly frequently. Why does air ticket reduction, it can not attract many leisure or businee trip travelers to buy air ticket to fly ? The main reason is because human mouth and air disease influences global many travelers feel fear to catch air planes frequently. In psychological view, this kind of human mouth and air sickness will bring long time negative influence to global traveles do not want to catch air planes for business trips or travelling leisure frequently. So, it implies that oil price changing to influence air ticket price reduction factor ought not main factor to influence tourism income. It may include traveler individual negative emotion psychological factor, such as human mouth and air disease or 2019 9/11 attack both cases, they can influence global travelers feel fear to catch air planes to fly to avoid death threat. So, oil changing price ought not be only one absolute main factor to influence global tourism income significantly.

On conclusion, in economic view, it seems that oil chang price may have indirect or direct relationship to influence tourism income, instead of some unpredicted external environment factors influence, such as US 9/11 attack crisis and human mouth and air disease factors, they may be main factors to influence travellers number to reduce in non-economic external unpredicted environment view.

COVID 19 human disease how influences global airline fuel manufacturers to rapid reach decline life cycle stage

Recently, since 2019 end, COVID 19 human disease confirms that any one can be gotten this kind disease by the COVID 19 patient individual mouth or air, hand, even things contact. This kind disease may hurt the heath person individual lung to let him/her to feel difficult to breathe, even death. So, this kind disease had influenced many people feel fear to catch airplanes, because when many passengers are sitting in the airplane, if one or more is/are COV19 human disease patient, then the patient has possible to bring this disease to let the health passengers to get his/her COVID 19 human disease in the none window airplanes environment easily. SO, when this kind of human disease is threatening global travellers to avoid to catch air airplanes to fly to travel frequently. Then, airplanes won't need to fly often. When airplanes do not need often fly in sky. Then gas fuel demand will be influenced to reduce to airlines because airplanes won't need often catch many travellers to go to different countries, due to travellers number reduces as well as many different countries' travellers had begun to reduce travelling times frequently and their airports restrict any high body temperature people to enter their countries, because they will have possible to bring COVID 19 human disease when they arrive any airports. Consequently, airplanes do not need to buy and use any more gas fuel to provide them to fly any more since COVID 19 human disease occurs.

How COVID 19 human disease influences global gas fuel sale number? Because travellers number had been decreasing, airlines do not any airplanes often catch many passengers to fly to any countries again. Surely, gas fuel demand to airplanes may be also influenced to reduce and it can also influence whole tourism leisure industry development will experience to the decline cycle life stage absolutely. Before , due to global has many travellers feel need to travel leisure activity. So, global travellers increasing number impacted to global needs to have many airplanes to be provide to fly every day frequently. Before average per day had above 10,000 times of airplane flying times in our earth every day, so it implied that gas fuel need must be influenced to increase to airlines, because airlines must need to buy a lot gas fuel to provide their airplanes to fly to different countries every day , when any countries have many travellers need to fly to different countries to travel. It is sure that airline gas fuel product must reach the maturity life cycle stage in this airplane gas fuel manufacturing industry, because travelling leisure activities are accepted to be on kind of popular habit leisure to global travellers, when air ticket price had been decreasing, it can also attract many travellers accept to spend money to buy air tickets to go to different countries to travel frequently.

So, cheap air ticket price and popular tourism leisure activity factors may influence global travellers number increases. When global travellers number increases, it impacts to global airplanes need to increase flying times to fly frequently and air tickets also increases purchase number. Consequently, airlines also are influenced to need to buy a lot gas fuel to provide to airplanes to fly. SO, due to gas fuel demand increases, but gas fuel supply number is not enough, then gas price can be influenced to raise, when airlines demand gas fuel number is more than gas fuel supply number.

It is based on economic theory, when demand to the product increases in the market, but the product has shortage to supply, then price may be influenced to bring sale price increasing chance. So, in this airline gas fuel demand and supply case, due to airplanes need to fly frequently, so global flying numbers had been influenced to rise and global airplanes need to buy many airplanes to catch passengers or travellers to fly to different countries. So, airlines must need to buy a lot gas fuel to provide airplanes to fly to different countries every day in this airline industry mature life stage. Thus, before 1029, it is gas fuel manufacturing industry and airlines travelling transport industry and tourism industry their maturity cycle stage period. Every day, global gas manufacturers need to attempt to find any lands have gas and explore any gas lands, than using technology to manufacture gas fuel in order to supply and satisfy any airlines' gas fuel needs every day. But, since COVID 19 human disease occurred in 2019 end, it influenced many airlines lose confidence the travellers number will increase, due to travellers number had been beginning to reduce every day and airplanes' flying times are also influenced to reduce , these both factors must influence gas fuel need reduces to any airlines their airplanes needs.

Hence, after 2019 end, it may be global tourism leisure industry decline life cycle stage, moreover, it may also be global airline transport flying service industry decline life stage both. So, global gas fuel need on airline sector must be influenced to reduce, when global airplanes did not often fly and global airplanes flying times had been influencing to reduce to per day 500 flying times, even less from the top level per day 10,000 flying times. SO, it can prove that they have relationship between tourism leisure industry and airlines' airplanes transport flying service industry and airline gas fuel product manufacturing industry. It means that when any unpredicted factors influence tourism leisure industry's life cycle stage changes, then the unpredicted factors may influence airline transport flying service industry and airline gas fuel product manufacturing industry life cycle service or gas fuel product stage change suddenly , such as this unpredicted COVID 19 human mouth disease, it can influence global tourism leisure industry and airline airplanes transport flying service industry and airline gas fuel product manufacturing industry had been beginning to experience the decline life cycle stage nowadays.

What COVID-19 human mouth disease can let airlines transport service providers and gas fuel manufacturers and tourism leisure service providers to learn? Airlines clearly have a lot on their airplanes at the moment, but since COVID-19 human mouth disease occurred in 2019 end. Many airlines had brought many airlines to prepare to catch global different countries travellers to go to different countries to travel, but nowadays, they do not need to be driven to fly to countries per day. These airplanes are staying on any countries' airports, but per day airlines need to pay high rent to the countries' airports when they are staying on the countries' airports. SO, their airport airplanes rent expenditure must be high, but their airplanes do not need to fly to different countries every day again , because COVID -19 human mouth disease influenced global travellers number had been reducing continue. With unpredicted consequences, many airlines will choose to sell their airplanes later, it none any one medicine can be invented to kill this kind of human mouth disease later, because if some airlines did not make decision to sell their airplanes, then they may nor regrow to growth life cycle stage from decline life cycle stage easily, due to passengers number reduces and it can influence their income reduces. But airline staffs still need to pay , e.g. pilots, airplane front line staffs and airports front line check in service staffs. Hence, sale of airplanes their assets may be the final strategic decision, when any airplanes can not continue to fly every day after 2020 year. Due to COVID 19 human disease can not be killed by any new medicine. If this kind of disease can not be filled for two or more years, then I believe that there are many airlines will experience to death life cycle stage from decline life cycle stage rapidly, otherwise if they can choose to sell some airplanes , they may keep cash available to prepare to reduce expenditure more easily. Although, some airlines made decisions to dismiss some airline service staffs, even pilots to achieve reducing salary expenditure in this decline life cycle stage. But, it will raise unemployment rate to bring social negative challenge. If later airlines choose to sell airplanes their assets to raise cash available strategy. However, it implies that gas fuel need must be influenced to reduce, due to COVID-19 human disease will continue to occur. So, it is the right time, gas fuel manufacturers ought not only concern how to manufacture more airplane gas fuel product to satisfy airlines airplanes transport flying need in this COVID-19 human disease occurrence stage. They ought find any new gas fuel users in this gas fuel market, if these airplanes gas fuel manufacturers expect to re-grow their gas fuel manufacturing and sale business to reach the growing life cycle stage from decline life cycle stage again in the future. Otherwise, many of gas fuel manufacturers will experience the death life cycle stage from decline life cycle stage within one to two years soon as possible.

Hence, if the gas fuel manufacturers can attempt to find other new kinds of gas fuel users in this gas energy market , instead of airline airplane gas fuel market and vehicle gas market main both markets. I believe that they can re-grow to growth life cycle stage from decline life cycle stage again in possible. Although, gas price must be influenced to reduce, because excess of gas supply to airline markets before 2019 end, but when airplanes do not need to fly frequently in this COVID -19 human disease occurrence environment. The COVID-19 pandemic human disease had had a significant impact on the aviation industry, due to travel restrictions and a significant full in demand among travellers. Significant reductions in passengers number have results in airplanes do not need to fly , airplanes feel price must drop, due to oil price war occurred. Hence, due to airline fuel price falls down, it causes many gas manufacturers' gas sale number also reduces to airline market. So, it is right time , any gas fuel manufacturers ought attempt to seek other new gas users, instead of airplanes users or cars users basic both gas users market. If they expect that they can change to experience regrowth life cycle stage from decline life cycle stage again and avoid to reach the final death life cycle stage within one to two years, due to COVID-19 pandemic human disease external environment factor influence.

In fact, on early assessment of the impact of COVID-19 on airline industry, it seems to have a more serve and more rapid impact on air traffic of fuel (oil price plummeted during the first quarter of 2020). It implies that global airline fuel price had been falling down due to COVID-19 human disease influences to global airplanes' flying times reduce. Moreover, COVID-19 impact on Asia-Pacific Aviation worsens, we have seen that first airline casually in the region, such as China , Singapore, Japan, Taiwan aviation fuel need has been influenced to reduce much significantly. Consequently, Asia-Pacific Aviation fuel price had been influenced to reduce much significantly. Then, it also influences Western Aviation, e.g. US, UK etc. Their flying times are also influenced to reduce, then fuel price sale to western Pacific Aviation can also influenced to fall down. Hence, it seems that COVID-19 human disease may also influence global aviation fuel price falls down. If the fuel manufacturers still only depend on sale aviation fuel income. I believe that the fuel manufacturers may reach to the death life cycle stage rapidly in short time. So, seeking new fuel users market is real need to any one fuel manufacturers , because global medicine scientists still can not guarantee when the kind of new medicine can be invented to kill COVID-19 human disease successfully. So, In this COVID-19 human disease threat environment, many experiencing mature life cycle stage airlines, such as US airline, Cathy airlines , UK airlines , Australia airline etc. they may be influenced to experience decline life cycle stage , even death life cycle stage within two year rapidly. Also, this kind of disease can also influence many travel agents' travelling leisure business development to experience decline stage cycle stage as well as it can also influence any airplanes fuel manufacturers to experience decline life cycle stage from mature life cycle stage in possible. Hence, it is right time , they need to change any new market users or service strategies in order to keep their businesses can continue regrow to the growth life cycle stage again.

CHAPTER FIVE

New economic society influences human right marginal social cost and benefit social analysis need

When our societies had been experiencing new economt societies, many people only concern on materialisam enjoyment aspect. Then,many stealing crimes, violences crimes number may increase in our societies. Is it right time to any countries policy decision makers need to spend time to evaluate whether their policies can bring marginal socical benefits or marginal social cost more? Because if the policy decision
maker's policy is not effective, it can not reduce social crime rate and social marginal cost will also increases consequently.

Economics provides a way to analyze the decision-making processes of work in social situations. Economists can also help when a social scientist wants to know the consequences of a country deciding to try a murder a case as a capital case in which the outcome may be the death penalty, when an international non-profit organization concerns what occurs in one of its target areas, when a travel considers the incidence of terrorism in a specific area.

However, each of these events relates to the decision makes themselves, the costs and benefits they face, and outcomes of those decisions. This process is called cost to benefit analysis. So, it explains that why it has relationship between economis and human rights, when one
organization or individual neesds to make any decisions which concern human right area absolutely. Hence, human right economic economic may

be explained by economists of human rights that economics is one way to analyze the choices being made in each area of human rights and indicates either positive or
negative incentives that can be used in policy-making to affect those choices.

However, human rights studies and economics are social sciences that study interactions within society. ON the other side, an economist must gain an understanding of the specific human rights topic in order to have an accurate perspective about the types of decisions, costs and benefits that exist within that area. So, economists are need to be train to step into an unfamiliar field will have more career and life opportunities as well as more tools to change the world.

Human rights may include those issues, such as freedom and equity, right to be recognition as a person before a court of law, freedom from discrimination before the law within each human right, violation, there are monetary and non-monetaty costs. When a country district attornoy makes the decision to try a care as a captial crime, the country is liable for the cost of the capital case. So, each of the violations of human rights
is the choices, based in part on costs to the decision maker.

Marginal cost is the cost of last unit produced or chosen in economic theory. IN human right marginal cost economic theory explanation aspect, for example, the number of times a person is convicted of a relatively minor illegal offence can add up to equal a relatively serious illegal offence, usually pubishable by imprisonment. Consequently, the more times the person is caught, the less chance , he will have to get a good job and bad things will be needed for survival in a community. The person decides to steal, the marginal cost increases. So, in society, the number of times food stolen increases,
than the social marginal cost of stealing food will also increases. So, our society needs to concern how to bring social net benefits of human rights violation, it means that when the number of times food stolen reduces, then the society will bring marginal benefit of reducing stealing food.

Hence, it is social decison-making maker individual duty to learn even when the stolen item is food. If theft is increasing in an area, policy-makers may look for incentives, which are positive or negative motivations used to modify behavior in order to avoid the stealing of food crime number increases. Increasing the penalty to theft or finding net ways to catch someone stealing increases the cost of someone choosing whether to steal

foods. It is a good method to reduce
social stealing food crimes occur. Also, costs to society increase in terms of increased needs for physical and mental health care, legal service, child care, housing counseling, violence prevention. If the society has many family violent crimes number increases. It will bring direct intangible cost (non- monetary value), such as pain and suffering, emotional loss of a loved one through a violent death, as well as indirect intangible costs, monetary cost may be unmeasured. These costs to the victim include lacks of self esteem, learned helpnesses, health problem, drud and alcholol abuse, depression etc.
socical cost raising problem.

Hence, in any countries decision makers ought consider how to reducing social marginal cost raising problem, due to family violence, stealing crimes number increases. For example, whether the country increases migrant number to increase in labor demand in itself labor supply market. It is one attractive
way or not. If the country permits many migrants immigrate to itself country, then it may influence the country itself native workforce job seekers feel difficult to find suitable jobs to do suddenly. Although, it will bring positive social benefit to employers when they may have enough labours to supply to them to work, but it mayalso bring negative socical costs, when many migrants immigration may raise the labour competition to itself local job seekers. So, any country's leaders must need to spend time to analyze whether migrants may help itself country to increase labor supply or raising job competition to itself country local job seekers or raising local unemlpyment ratio effect.

ON conclusion, future our society needs consider whether our policy can bring effect to real reduce social marginal costs more or raise social marginal benefits more when we need to implement any social decision in order to avoid social cost raises effect. It is our future new economic society will encounter marginal social cost raising occurrence challenges as well as our social policy decision makers need to spend time to research how to solve the social challenges and compare and evaluate its marginal cost and benefit relationship to them to our future societies' any social needs.

Environment Economy-Pollution and illness influences consumer behavior
How the economic consequences of outdoor air pollution influences consumer behaviors ? Air pollution can increase number of respiratory and

cardiovas cular diseases. How they can impact economic growth, e.g. on human health, mortality and morbidity and agriculture aspects ? Whether when this diseases are caused from outdoor air pollution, why it can influence consumer behavior or brings negative consumpton emotion?

The macroeconomic costs of these impacts of outdoor air pollution that are linked to economic activity, and it raises welfare costs related to activity morality and pain and suffering from illness to consumers. For example, market costs are those that are associated with biophysical impacts that directly affect economic activity, e.g. lower crop yields affect agricultural production . Non market costs may also include the monetised welfare costs of morality (premature deaths) , and of the disutility of illness (pain and suffering).

Raising emissions reflect the assumptions on economic growth with increasing GDP and energy demand, especially in fast growing economies, such as the high population countries, India and China. These large changes are due to the increase in the demand for agricultural products and energy (include transport and power generation). For continuousing increase in energy demand to China and India car drivers, when they need to drive their cars to go to anywhere often. The higher emission will bring serious pollution. The environment protecting householders will decrease to use emissions from energy demand for, with reflects technology improvement in energy efficiency, the use of cleaner fuels, and biomass in open fire to cleaner energy sources including LPG, ethanol or enhanced cooking stoves. Hence, when many people get the diseases from air pollution. It will increase the medical (healthcare) cost to governments or when government needs to give welfare assistance to patients.

The three different market impacts of air pollution may include: reduced labor productivity, increased health expenditures and crop yield losses. They may reduce the GDP pollution feedback on the economy. At the global level, the consequences of labor productivity and health expenditure may impact to market cost increases,because increases expenditure to labor productivity, health expenditure and value added generated in agriculture from low productivity changes in crop yields.

What is the welfare costs of mortality and illness ? It is possible to attribute a cost to non-market impacts, such as the premature deaths and the costs of pain and suffering from illness . The welfares cost of the premature deaths caused by air pollution are calculated using the value of a statistical life to any one. Large costs can also associated with the pain and suffering from illness. So, pollution causes diseases to bring welfare cost increases, they include hospital living day to every patient when he is caused illnesses from air pollution. Moreover, it will impact government pollution expenditure to raise welfare cost to assist the low income level pollution illness patients' hospital living welfacre cost when they need to live long days in hospitals.

How does air pollutin impact on consumer automobile choices ? Air pollution levels can bring negatively affect the sales of fuel inefficient cars to China or India car drivers. They will choose to buy electronic cars to drive to replace fuel cars, because electronic cars only need to charge battery and it can reduce air pollution. When China or India their big city people's income level is rising, they will have more money to buy electronic cars to drive to reduce air pollution. Moreover, they believe that electronic cars can have better car quality and reduced air pollution need to charge battery fuel efficiency to compare fuel cars, when they need to often drive cars on roads. Som electronic cars demand will be the preference choice battery fuel efficiency or green driving tools to compare general fuel cars to satisfy China and India car purchasers when they are living in serious air pollution environment cities.

When the high environment protection awareness car buyers number is increasing in the countries, environment protection awareness will influence their car choice decison on which car to buy , when they are living in more heavily polluted cities tend to buy less fuel-inefficient cars. So, the electronic cars number need will increase in China and India both car market, because these two countries have similar characteristics, they have high population and gardens and farms number is less and there are many people are living in cities and many people are high income level , they usually have one car at least. So, they must feel cities are serious polluted by their diving behaviors. So, their environment protection awareness are ususally higher to compare other countries , they have less cities. So high air pollution to cities can excite the environment protection awareness to China and India car purchasers as well as they will prefer to choose to buy electronic cars to replace fuel cars to drive in possible, because they do not hope to live a high car dirty cities to cause their poor health when they have high income level. Also, it implies that it has direct relationship between China and India cities have high income level people number increases and air pollution level increases and electronic car demand number increases and fuel car demand number decreases in China and India car market in micro economic China and India electronic car and fuel car demand and supply market.

I assume that each China and India car consumer makes a relatively fuel or electronic car choice among possible car transmissions, between the option of buying no car and buy car or between the option of buying electronic car and fuel car. However, air pollution will be one major factor to influence China and India car purchase demand number on electronic and fuel car supply number. If china and India's air pollution can reduce, then car purchase number will increase, as well as the fuel car demand number will also increase ,because China and India have many cities are polluted serious. It can influence car purchase buyers how to decide car choice to make car or no car purchase decision, even purchase either fuel car or electronic car decison.

● How consumer decisions are impacted on environment?

Environmental impacts may occur on households, when they need to buy food, mobility, house, household goods and appliances for home use in household consumer behavior view. It can bring direct impacts, that occue because of the use of householder products and services during householders are staying at home. When householders feel need to raise living quality, they will considerate how they use services and related household products. When minimizing the use of natural resources and toxic materials as well as the emissions of waste and pollutants over the life cycle of the service or household product, e.g. using electricity or fuel time at home, cooling time and bathing time at home activities. So, for on householder who has high environment protection awareness and energy protection awareness, he will reduce long time to use electricity or fuel use time for cooking, bathing, watching television, listening radio time activities at homes, because he does not hope energy waste and protect air fresh at homes.

So, consumption is concerned by environment factors, such as demographics, technology, income and prices, psychological, social , cultural environments, e.g. consumers economic behavior is influenced by habt, routines, conventions etc. different environment factors influence. So, economic assumptions of rational and regular behavior is based on long-established principles, such as utility maximization. For example, when one country is encountering serious air or water pollution, then consumers will spend long time to search any data (marketing research activities) when they need to make purchase decision on pollution environment as well as pollution environment is dependent on (e.g. attitude, intention to the consumers).

Because when pollution environment will influence consumption behavior, such as behavioral and experimental economic to consumers. It implies on pollution environment's psychological assumptions on individual consumption motives, such as on the role of mental habits, loss confidence. So, consumers usually feel to spend long time to make purchase choice or decison on pollution environment, exaggerated optimism, expectatons, avoiding miscalculation,short-sightedness more enjoyment etc. psychological factors. When they need to make purchase decision on pollution environment, e.g. when one car consumer will need to make choice to buy one car, when he is living in China city, city is polluted serious. So, he will need to spend long time to gather any car model and brand and quality and fuel quality air polluted level to achieve to choose to buy the most clean fuel and the most least air polluton car to avoid to cause air polluton when he is driving the car in the China's city. So, air pollution way causes the China environment protection awareness car consumers to spend long time to gather any less use fuel car information to avoid to cause air pollution when he needs often to drive the car on the city roads in the China cities.

Hence , air pollution may cause the China car purchasers feel need to spend more time to gather car information in order to decide whether he ought to buy one car or no car purchase choice on the air pollution environment. So, the car must use less fuel to avoid air pollution easily when he drives the car on the China's cities' roads.

Reference

Dimson, Marsh & Staunton, London Business School (2005) In The Global Investment Returns Year Book, ABN Amro.

Fiscal Policy And Long Term Growth, International Monetary Fund, IMF policy papers, Washington, D.C. Available from April, 2015, http://www.imf.org/external/pp/ppindex.aspx.

How artificial intelligence impacts energy
consumers using behaviours

Nowadays, many countries began to educate citizens who have responsibilities to use energy at homes or offices or public places or any indoor environments in avoiding to do energy wastage behaviours or misuse energy wastge attitudes as well as teaching them have responsibilities to protect their earth's natural environment to reduce air, water pollution in order to void rising temperature to bring globl warm challenge to influence our quality of life to be poor, even facing death threat, due to our natural environment is damaged and polluted by our energy wastage behaviours.

In fact, I feel the energy wastage eduction is not one efficient or effective method to persuade every energy consumers, such as householders, office workers, factories workers, any entertainment places workers or enjoyers, such as cinema service staffs, shopping center staffs etc. entertainment places to reduce to use any electricity for light or any entertainment aims to consider themselves working environment or entertainment environment to satisfy, e.g. cinema movie to satisfy customers' needs. For example, private vehicle drivers, public transportation tool drivers, householder energy users, businessmen energy users who still only consider themselves passengers comfortable aims, e.g. spending much electricity often to turn on light in buses, taxi, cars, trams, trains, underground trains in morning or afternoon time. So, these public transportation tools are popular to waste electricity because they expect their passengers to feel comfortable in summer , so they will often turn on air conditioners to keep colder in summer or turn on warmers to keep warmer in winnter all the transportation working hours. So, these drivers are doing energy wastage behaviours. Moreover, these private car drivers only expect to feel comfortable , so they will open air conditioners to keep colder in summer when they are driving cars, even they are stopping cars on the road. So, they are also waste energy.

Hence, they will be negligent to consider how to use energy in efficient attitudes or energy saving behaviors in order to avoid energy shortage challenge occurrence. However, since (AI) technology began be popular to be accepted to use by human. (AI) scientists began to carry on researching how to apply (AI) technologies, e.g. big data gathering , robotics to assist human to adapt or learn to use any kinds of energy in efficient and no wastage attitudes or using behaviours habitually.

I shall explain how to apply (AI) technology to assist human to adapt to use energy in order to avoid to do energy wastage behaviours easily to every energy users as below:

In consumer psychological view point, the behaviours of individuals can have a standard rational choice model, in which people, such as energy users objectively weigh up the costs and benefits of investing time and money into " greening" their homes or offices or any working places or entertainment places or transportation tools being more energy efficiently. So, the social, cognitive and behavioural factors are important in explaining why many energy users, such as householders, vehicles owners or public transportation tool drivers, office workers, businessmen who are neglient to avoid to spend much excessive energy to drive their vehicles on the roads , to turn on lights in offices or any working environment or entertainment places or at homes all days. When they feel that they need more enjoyment, raising productivity, raising service performance to satisfy customers' needs. So, when they weigh economic benefits and cost. They will choose to use more energy to achieve their profit growth or customer number growth or improving quality of life intentions.

Hence, it also explain why education method is not effective to achieve energy saving aim for every energy users, e.g. it has no reward to compensate to their losses, when they choose to reduce energy consumption to cause that they have economic losses. So, it seems any country's government or schools energy saving education method which won't achieve the best energy saving consequency nowadays.

Why does (AI) influence energy users to reduce and use more energy in order to achieve their energy -saving habitual impact easily than education method? I shall explain as below:

(AI) technology can be one auto-manual tool to help householders to protect their homes to be more green environment and be more energy efficient. For example, householders can install (AI) auto-energy efficient measurement tool to record whether they will spend how much money for energy . e.g. electricity , gas consumption at home every day. So, they can know whether they will pay how much money for electricity or gas fee. (AI) auto-energy efficient measurement tool can also change householders' energy consumption behaviours to save more electricity or gas when they discover that the day' electricity or gas using number is excessive to cause they will be pay more extra electricity or gas expenditure on the day. Then, they will find whether why or how or what reasons cause them to spend excessive electricity or gas energy at homes, then they will change their energy wastage behaviours to save energy more easily. So, their energy -saving behaviours are influenced by the (AI) auto-energy efficient measurement tool's daily electricity or gas using record at homes.

So, (AI) auto energy efficient measurement tool can help householders to save energy and money when they need to use electricity or gas energy at homes. But making the kind of improvements that have these effects is not always simple, they usually require some planning, time to prepare to adapt how to do avoiding energy wastage behaviours at home habitually . So, (AI) auto-energy efficient measurement tools can focuse on what householders might be able to do and further encourage the uptake of energy efficiently measures as well as it might be able to motivates householders to act through restructuring existing incentives and using collective rewards.

When, they discover that the (AI) auto energy efficient measurement tool shows either electricity energy or gas energy or both using energy number is excessive too much to compare the normal energy using number on the day suddenly. Then , they will attempt to find what reasons influence their energy spending number is excessive on the day, in order to change their energy using behaviours or habits and they will be more acceptable to adapt to do energy saving behaviours because they can earn energy expenditure saving rewrd and money saving reward in order to avoid further the excessive energy using number to be increased to pay more electricity or gas energy expenditure , due to they often do unnecessary energy using habitual behaviours at homes.

Hence, (AI) auto-efficient energy measurement tool will have much effort to persuade householders to choose to do energy saving behaviours habitually at homes, due to it can provide the more acceptable number concerns their daily electricity and gas energy using record at homes to let them to know how and why their energy expenditure changes to spend more suddenly in order to let they can understand the reasons why and how cause their needs to pay extra excessive energy expenditure at homes.

The main important reward is that the householders can be encouraged to measure their energy using number and find the reasons why and how their energy using behaviours cause their extra excessive energy using number on the day. Then, they can find what the factors are to cause their electricity or gas energy using number to be increased suddenly on the day and change their energy using behviours to avoid the energy using number to be continus increased in order to avoid to pay extra excessive electricity or gas fees on the month immediately.

6.1 How to apply (AI) technology to improve energy efficiency and better climate change and the security of energy supply as well a resource efficiency?

Increasing energy efficiency involves using a reduced quantity of energy to achieve the same or improved product, process or sevice. It is generally measured in a physical unit as the ratio between energy output and energy input. Similarly, resource efficiency refers to the ability to use a reduced quantity or volume of resources to produce the same or an improved service or product and it is measured as the ratio betweenn useful material output and material input, both measured in physical terms (Dahlstrom and Ekins, 2005).

Hence, if it was only (AI) technology can increase energy efficiency or reduce resource effifiency to improve service performance. Then, it will reduce energy wastage. So, it bring this question: How to apply (AI) tool to reduce resource consumptin indentified by analysis of historical resource efficiency?

It presents an historial analysis that seems have relationship between energy and resource efficiency improvements and resource consumption across a number of different sectors of activity, including iron, and steel production, electricity generation from coal, oil and natural gas and motor vehicle travel.

So, future(AI) technology needs to fight social and behavioural barriers to energy efficiency in the housing sector. If future (AI) technology can improve energy efficiency for home renovations and it can consider the social factors. It is a qualitative investigation technology of the decision making process guiding to teach householders hoe to use overall energy was reduced by the householders' house renovation. It will also bring another question: How can (AI) technology can help householders to do decision making to reduce overall energy consumption by householders' houses renovation, such as reducing energy using when the householder needs to renovate whose house's design, e.g. extensions and additional bedrooms or bathrooms . So, future (AI) technology can be needed to help low income householders to increae energy efficiency and reduce energy consumption when their homes need to renovate whose houses' design ,e.g. extensions and additinal bedrooms or bathrooms or bookrooms or children toy rooms at hoomes.

Due to low income householders were concerned about energy consumption for environment and economic reasons, upfront costs rather than life-cycle costs were considered more important when the low income householders need to renovate to extend extra bedrooms, bathrooms, studyrooms to buy extra electronic appliances to install them in these rooms to use. Then, they will be concerned energy awareness how will be more consume when the low income householders choose to renovate their homes design to extend more rooms to feel more comfortable, or large size, but they also need to consume or use more electrciity or gas energy for extra electronic appliances in these rooms possible as the same time.

Hence, future (AI) technology needs to assist these low income householders how to reduce or avoid to ue extra more energy, when they renovate their homes' designs to cause to need to buy extra more electric appliances to use more electricity or gas energy at homes. Moreover, future (AI) technology ought have effort to help any countries' buildings to be efficient energy saving buildings to be efficient energy saving buildings to help householders to use less energy to live in their builsing efficiently. When the country's overall buildings can use energy efficiently , it won't only bring energy saving benefits, even it can bring the country's economic cost to be reduced , due to any building' energy efficient using high technological method. So, future (AI) energy saving technology will concentrate on how to help any buildings to use energy efficiently , in order to achieve energy -saving efficient buildings to let the householders and office energy users to either live or work in energy -saving efficient buildings to avoid energy wastage aim.

Hence, future (AI) energy -saving technology needs to focus on how changing energy users' energy wastage behaviours to energy -saving behaviours. How to apply (AI) energy-saving technology to assist energy users change their behaviours to spend unnecessary excessive energy to use habitually daily.

I recommend that future (AI) robotic cans be such as energy-saving machines to help any factory workers to cooperate to work to achieve efficient energy -saving aim, but they can also raise productivities. So, factory robotic are as learning tools, allowing factory energy users (factory workers) to teach themselves how to use less energy to achieve the productivity won't be decreased intention. So, when the robotics and factory workers work in the factory environment together. The robotics can give feedback to let these factory workers how to cooperate to use lesser energy to work efficiently in factories.

Other information and advice achieving better understanding and control of energy use in factory. So, future factory robotic machine men are such as teachers teach students in classrooms or trainers provide training to train trainee in factories. It means that robotics and factory workers can learn how to understand to do every working steps to avoid to spend extra excessive energy , but they can also raise productivities as the same time in factories.

So , future (AI) robotics will be demanded to invent to be one energy-saving machines to assist factory workers to use lesser energy to manufacture any products in manufacturing process, but they can also have productivity and efficiencies won't be reduced in the efficient team work method. So, every factory robotic machine mman is needed to be designed to own the advanced manufacturing technological skills or manufacturing methods to assist the factory workers to manufacture the kind of products in team work together in order to shorten time and using the most efficient manufacturing methods to achieve and produce the best quality products and the highest productivity in energy-saving working environment in factories. For example, when every team watch factory's factory workers who need to operte with ten workers per team in the watch manufacturing factory. One robotic machine with ten workers per team will need to raise to manufacture at least fifty watchs number per hour to compare only ten workers per team can manufacture the maximum fifty watchs number per house, when the robotic machine participates to every team to work together.

The robotic machine must need to help them to use lesser time and electricity energy to manufacture more than fifty watches number pe hour in order to achieve long tem energy saving and time saving and efficient raising productive economic benefits to the watch manufacturing company. Hence, the watch factory's every watching manufacturing robotic machines can encourage the watch manufacturing firm to choose to use them to assist every team watch manufacturing workers to work in order to achieve high efficient productivities, high quality of watch manufacturing, reducing every watch manufacturing , reducing every watch manufacturing time and the important intention is energy -sving efficient benefit to reduce to spend more extra excessive electricity for long term expenditure.

So, in the future , every robotic machine will need have these benefits to satisfy manufacturers' every -saving needs in their participative manufacturing process in order to achieve energy expenditure to reduce for long term economic benefits to persuade them to use these energy-saving efficient robotics in factory attractively.

● Is the low income and rising price of modern fuels both factors best to influence Nigeria householders choose to use energy efficiently?

Firstly, for Nigeria householders energy consumption habit at homes example, it is richly with natural resources, modern energy resources which provide many householders with biomass (mostly firewood) and some other householders modern energy sources, such as kevosene, liquefied, petroleum, gas and electricity for their use. So, it is one country which can manufacture to provide energy for itself to use. It doesn't need to depend on other countries to import any kinds of energy to householders to buy to use at homes. But, it has social challenge, the poverty problem in Nigeria goes beyond low income, savings and growth rate, due to its low level of education, poor governamce, high level of unemployment factors influence. It is important to know how Nigeria householders meet their basic energy needs between poverty and energy can bde described in terms of quality and quantity of energy used. Generally, most poor householders use biomass fuels because of affordability and they (householders) do not have energy equipment (such as, gas cookers, electric cookers etc.) . So, it seems Nigeria householders won't demand their living quality to be improved. It implies that they will use any kinds of energy efficiently at homes, e.g. gas, electricity, due to they find themselves in energy poverty. Although, this country has enough nature resources to manufacture energy to provide to householders to use, but due to many people are low income group, so they won't spend too much expenditure to buy much energy to use at homes. So, the rising prices of modern fuels, such as liquefied, petroleum , gas (LPG) and electricity and their erratic supply have made many householders revert to the use of traditional fuel, such as firewood and charcoal.
It brings this questions: Is the low income and rising price of modern fuels both factors best to influence Nigeria householders choose to use energy efficiently?
The hypothes is predicated on the economic theory of consumer behavior. However, when income increases, householders not only consume more of the same goods, they also need higher quality . So, it applies economic theory to householder's energy consumption behavior at home. It explains why low living standards induce greater dependence on firewood and other biomass fuels owing to a combination of income and substitution effects, such as Nigeria low income household energy home users case. it explains why Nigeria householders can accept to use firewood and charaval traditional energy to replace liquefied, petroleum , gas (LPG) and electricity modern energy . So, economic theory explains the Nigeria household

energy users why they can accept to use traditional energy to replace modern energy and their energy useful or consumption behaviors are efficient at homes. Although, Nigeria has enough natural resource to manufacture modern energy to supply to householders to use at homes. But, due to these modern energy products prices are raised to the price level of householders who can not accept. it causes to Nigeria householders only choose to buy the cheap biomass, firewoods to replace high price of modern energy products to use at home often. So, they can accept their quality of living to be fallen down. So, expensive modern energy product price is one factor to influence some countries' householders to choose to buy cheap traditional poor quality of nature energy, e.g. firewood or biomass, to use at homes. Hence, they can raise energy efficiency to use when they choose to use traditional nature energy to replace modern nature energy at homes.

● Does season factor influence New Zealand householders' energy consumption behaviors at homes

Secondly, for New Zealand householders energy consumption habits at homes , for example, their living quality needs are general comfortable need feeling. Their countries' houses of space heating was found to average 34% of total housholder energy use. The relation to space heating includes low indirect temperature are associated with persistent under-heating , whether some space heating sources tend to be higher or lower in winter indoor temperature than others and winter indoor temperatures are compared to international benchmarks and established healthy temperature ranges. So, New Zealand occupant's perceptions of winter indoor temperature conditions are presented and explored in relation to heating patterns and household energy consumption. So, it seems that NZ winter temperature is low. Moreover, it will influence householders need to turn on heaters to keep more warmer feeling indoor. Then, they will use more electricity energy. In special, if the householders' houses spaces are large sizes . Hence, their heaters need long time to keep whole houses' areas or spaces or rooms temperature to be rised up in order to let they do not feel very cold in winter. So, NZ's winter extreme cold weather will influence householders' energy use or consumption to be increased in winter.

The electricity efficiency to every NZ householder is very high in winter to compare spring, summer, autumn seasons. Hence, if NZ electricity suppliers expected to forecast electricity consumption more accurate in NZ. In order to ease the life for both electric net designers and electricity suppliers, it was decided to find out, how the NZ weather conditions and every householder's house space size factors to influence the power consumption to NZ householders. If there is a clear trend observed , then this relation can be used for power consumption forecasts to NZ householders.

Why does NZ weather condition factor and householder's house space size factor can predict householders' electricity consumption at homes. Due to geographic location on the global the lowest south sets specific conditions for weather, such as NZ's south island geographic location is near to south ocean in our earth. It is a country where average annual temperatures are well between 10 degree to below 10 degree at NZ south island special geographic location to near to the sourth ocean in our earth at the same time.

However, large part of mankind is living in the conditions where there are four different seasons in NZ geographic location, dark winter, which is cold and snowy, spring with rising temperature and high precipitation, sunny , dry and rather hot summer, and windy and wet autumn. These conditions lead to different patterns in electric appliances use in NZ householders, in special, in NZ south island householders. If trends in electric energy use have substantial correlation with weather conditions, this can help NZ electric energy suppliers and producers to forecast electricity consumption and thus organize and manage production of electric energy.

Consequently, it will lead to much more stability in energy supply to NZ every householder. For example, when the NZ energy supplier gathers data concerns every householder's house space size data, e.g. the house has how many sleeping rooms, toilets, bath rooms, eating rooms and reading rooms number, even the house has how many family members are living in every NZ geographical location. Then if it can follow different location of NZ houses spaces sizes whether they are large or small space size as well as whethe every house has how many family members are living to evaluate whether how much electricity efficiency can satisfy their comfortable living needs in winter. Then, it can evaluate whether they will use how much electricity efficiency for their needs in different seasons. If in winter, many householders are living in the large space size house in the geographic location. Then, it is possible that the geographic location is householders will use much electricity efficiency and where geographic location hosueholders who will be possible to pay the most highest electricity fee to compare the other geographic location of small space size of house householders. Hence, weather factor is the most influential to change NZ householders ' electricity energy consumption behaviors at homes.

● Urbanization level and income per capita both tangible factors as well as temperature (weather variation factor) will have close relationship to influence China householder energy consumption or useful needs at home every day

For China householder energy consumption habit example, what factors can determine to impact this country's householders energy useful behavior at homes? Can the impacts of these factors be quntified? What are China householder energy consumption trends and characteristics? I shall explan as below:

I believe the influential factors include these three aspects to China householder energy users: Income per capita, urbanization level an annual average temperature (weather). These factors will influence any China householder energy useful or consumption behavior at homes.

Temperature (weather variation factor) is intangible from eastern region to western region of Chin, variances largely depend upon economic level and the provincial level. So, some regions were warmer and cooler temperature will influence the regional China householder how to use electricity. In addition, th influence of urbanization level varies according to income level as well as the urbanization level has more significant impact on the structure and efficiency of China householder energy consumption thatn on its quantity. So, the urbanization level and income per capita both tangible factors will have close relationship to influence China householder energy consumption or useful needs at home every day. Moreover, these two tangible factors (urbanization level and income per capita both factors) have the more influential to impact China any one of household family energy consumption or useful habit to compare temperature factor at home. Because temperature can only influence than to choose to turn on heaters to keep more cooler in summer or turn on air conditions (fans) to keep more warmer in winter.

The electricity energy needs for these equopment tools which will be influenced less. Otherwise, the urbanization level and income per family householder how to choose to spend more or less electricity or gas etc. energy at homes. Because in behavioral economy view point, when individual householder has more income and the urban in the China geographic location is lising many high income and high household families memebrs to every house. Then, the urbanization household energy household enery useful or consumption level will be raised. Such as China household electricity users case, e.g. large cities have many high income and many houses have more than four families members to live on one house together. Then, the electricity or gas energy efficiency will be influenced to rise. The city urbanization and per capita income level is high to these large cities have high to income population, who are living in these cities in China.

Moreover, the impact of lifestyle on energy use mainly reflects types and purposes of fuels are chosen by different China households factor which will influence the urbanization level of energy choice use. China is a country with typical binary economics and social diversity and these is significant difference in the consumption pattern between urban and rural regions. Urban residents consume high-quality energy, such as electricity, natural gas , heating power, solar energy and gasoline. For rural residents, usually use coal, and bismass energy because they are cheaper price energy products which requires much time and labor and are heavy indoor pollutants . The difference in energy consumption pattern between urban and rural China residents is closely related related to living of quality needs, building structure, e.g. steel or stone etc. different materials, manufacture, easily access clean and effective feels through the electric grid, natural gas network and district heating systems.

Therefore, it explains why urbanization level is as an integrated variable reflecting social progress situation to influence urban and rural regions, such as large cities , small cities and rural countryside regions' household energy consumption or useful behaviors which have differnet kinds of fuel useful demands and energy efficiencies qualify and quantity demand, or needs at homes. Consequently, it explains, urbanization level and income per captia level both factors are more influential to China household energy consumption at home to compare temperature (weather , seasonal) factor.

● Employment rates or gross domestic product macro economic variation factor, residential space size factor, and the government's implementation of energy labeling schemes provide significant impacts on Taiwan residential electricity consumption .

For Taiwan householder electricity consumption characteristics in the residential sector, which has different factors and pattern to compare China householder electricity householder electricity consumption habit at home.

Although, they are the same Asia country. I shall explain these reasons as below:

For Taiwan electricity householder factors influence their energy useful or consumption behaviors at homes. The main factors can influence their electricity energy useful patterns include: employment rates or gross domestic product macro economic variation factor, residential space size factor, and the government's implementation of energy labeling schemes provide significant impacts on Taiwan residential electricity consumption . However, the impacts of electricity raising price and the energy supply reducing shortage efficiency standards do not significant to influence the Taiwan residential electricity consumption behavior at sources.

It means that it won't influence Taiwan householders to use electricity or gas or any kinds of energy number to be reduced, even the Taiwan government energy suppliers sudden raise, any kinds of energy price and reduce to supply energy to satisfy Taiwan householders daily essential needs at homes.

In fact, Taiwan had improved gross domestic product (GDP) and it had raised employment rates recently. So, many Taiwanese has jobs to work, due to Taiwan economy had improved to be better. So, growth had also raised. The economy improvement causes many Taiwanese had enough jobs to work, due to new businesses are set up. Many consumers excit any kinds of businesses are invested to Taiwan from overseas or local investors. So, consumption is grown, the electricity consuming applicances are selected, as the household consumer focus grousp number if also influenced to be increased. So, Taiwan economy had improved to be better, it will encourage many electricity consuming applicances products are encouraged to excited to be selected to seel in Taiwan. Due to many different kinds of electricity consuming appliances are supplied to attract Taiwanese to choose to buy to bring to their homes for cooking, boiling water, or keeping rooms to be cooler or warmer temperature confortable feeling intention in winter or summer seasons. So, these electricity consuming appliances, e.g. rice cookers, heaters, air conditions, fans, bathing gas heaters etc. different home electricity consuming appliances will be increased to supply to satisfy Taiwan householders' needs. When they decide to buy any news electricity consuming applicances to bring to homes to use.

● Environment scientists' education message how to influence Greece householders home energy consumption behaviors from primary energy to change secondary energy

Finally , I shall indicate Greece, this western which will influence this country's householders have desires to do household energy conservation patterns or conservation energy consumption behaviors or energy conservation activities at homes. I shall explain the social economic variable, such as consumers' income and family size variation factor which can influence the different Greece family household members differences towards energy conservation preferences. IN addition, the variable, such as environmental information feedback and consciousness of energy problems are characteristics of the energy saver consumer.

Why and how can environmental pollution , environmental protection, energy conservation information message can influence Greece householders to choose to do energy use consumption conservation or less energy useful behaviors at homes. It is one interesting energy efficient use behaviors , due to Greece householders are influenced by energy conservation or environmental protection message.

In fact, scientists agree overconsumption of natural resources is a major threat to oue lives in earth. Environmental problems like greenhouse effect, ozone layer depletion, and acid rain effect are not any more problems of a specific region or environmental problem. Also, economic theory is indicated that in order to gain comfort and time households are becoming excessive energy users, neglecting the environmental impact of their choices.

Environment scientists bring these environment pollution message to influence Greeks (Greece householders) to change their energy consumption behaviors at homes. The environment scientists' message indicate that we are facing global warmth and natural resource and energy shortage challenges. Due to our Earth have limited natural resource numbers to supply to us to manufacture energy, but global population has been increasing every year. Thus, it is possible that we have energy shortage crisis. Also, manufactures are spending too much energy to waste to manufacture any products, the energy will cause air or water pollution in manufacturing process or drivers are driving their vehicles to pollute air on the roads.

Hence, environment scientists' message influence Greece householders began to consider these questions concern to reduce fossil fuel energy. Why do we need to Safety in using fuel and handle gas leaks? Why do we feel town gas smell? How is electricity located at electric station far away from town area? How to solve problems caused by the use of fossil fuels? How to reduce the use of fossil fuels?

Greece householders consider to solve the problems, the best way is to reduce thir used of fossil fuel. This helps prevent fossil fuels form being used up too quickly. Also, it helps them to reduce environmental problems because fewer pollutants are given out when less fossil fuels are used. Can human help to reduce the use of fossil fuels? Fossil fuels are mainly in power station. Although they use some fossil fuels for our gas cooker and car, it won't make much difference if I use less. Fossil fuel is not used renew primary energy. Most of energy Greece householders use come from fossil fuels, for example, the electricity we use is generated in power stations by burning fossil fuels. The buses they ride use diesel oil. Therefore, they can help reduce the use of fossil fuels by saving energy in Greece daily lives.

The actions that Greece householders can take such as: setting the air-conditioner to a higher temperature, walking instead of using lift, taking a short shower instead of a bath. This reduces the use of the hot water and thus the energy needed to heat the water. Thus, many people can help a lot to reduce our use of fossil fuels to avoid fossil fuel shortage risk occurrence.

Greeks (Greece householders) had been beginning to conern that they will face energy shortage challenge if they can not adopt more energy conservation actions. Because the Greece government began to bring negative environmental pollution and energy shortage challenge message if they often waste to use any kinds of energy, e.g. electricity , gas excessive number efficiency at homes. Then, they will be possible to fac energy shortage and environmental pollution challenge to their country in future one day. So, this energy shortage and environment pollution message has bring predictive negative worries to influence many Greece householder energy home users choose to reduce to avoid the waste of any kinds of energy use at homes.

So, their reducing energy use actions that had encouraged them to cause habits to avoid to waste excess energy to do any non essential electric appliances useful or consumption activities at homes often. Moreover, the environment protection and energy conservation message has changed many Greece householder to make decision and activities to change their lifestyle to b low living quality from high living quality. So, the environment protection and energy conservation message factor has much influential to change Greece household energy users' daily energy conservation or less energy use consumption activities at homes.

Greeks feel greenhouse energy can be environmental protection enegy.

A greenhouse can trap heat in the sunlight and keeps the air inside the greenhouse warm enough for plants to grow. The glass roof and walls of a greenhouse let in sunlight but prevent heat from escape, this makes the greenhouse warm inside. Similarly, some gases in the Earth's atmosphere can trap heat from the sun and keep the Earth warm. This is called the greenhouse effect. The gases energy that can trap heat from the sun are called greenhouse gases. It is future one kind of potential primary energy to reduce environmental pollution new energy products for human consuming. So, environmental protection message influence them to consume greenhouse enegy at homes.

So, environment scientists' environment pollution message had influence Greece householders concern to apply seconday energy (environment protection) to replace electricity energy to use at home. They will change energy to use at home. The scientists' messages have more influential Greece householders energy change consumption behaviors at homes. The messages are as below:

There are different forms of energy, e.g. light, heat, sound, wind, water, electrical kinetic, chemical and potential energy. Some form energy is primary energy and it can not renew to use, e.g. light, sound, wind, water, fossil fuel etc. Some form energy is secondary energy and it can renew to use in possible, e.g. nuclear, electric charge battery etc. Why does human need to concern how to manufacture secondary energy? Because it is possible that our natural resource will be consumed all, thus we will face primary energy shortage risk. If human can invent any new form of man-made secondary energy to renew to use in order to avoid primary energy shortage to supply to use to use, then human won't only depend on our Earth natural resource energy supply numbers. We can invent any new secondary energy to renew to use again either replaces primary energy or instead of primary energy limit number supply.

What is energy change? For television energy change power case. Firstly, electrical energy changes to television power to be used by television itself, then it changes to light power, next it changes to light power. How to choose fuel form to use? Due to energy can change to different form of powers to supply different form of power advantages to supply to human to use, so it is possible that we can also invent any secondary man made renew used energy to change different form powers to supply us to use, e.g. nuclear energy changes to light or sound or heat form of powers ; electrical charge batteries changes to light or sound or heat form powers to satisfy our daily life needs.

The environment scientists' energy consumption education influence Greece householders concern how to change to use secondary energy to replace primary energy at homes as below:

For primary natural resource fuel energy example, different fuel has different feature, e.g. easy to burn, safe to use, gives out a lot of energy, inexpensive, produces little air pollution, easy to transport and store. How can we use in different channels, such as heating food, hot pat, driving vehicles.

For example, although coal is not expensive to cause electricity energy for past transportation tool, e.g. traditional coal energy train or our daily home cooking, but it has negative influence to environment air pollution. Hence, we ought to follow the primary natural resource energy's feature to decide how to apply what aspects of our life needs.

For example, if the country's people hope to reduce pollution when who use any kind of energy, e.g. US , Europe energy markets. The energy entrepreneur ought concentrate on manufacturing the kind of energy which can reduce environment pollution to be the least level to supply the country people to use, e.g. electric charge battery supplies to these countries' drivers to drive their vehicles on the roads, wind energy or water energy to manufacture electricity power supply to reduce air or water pollution ; or if the country people hope to buy the inexpensive energy to use, even the energy's quality and performance is worse, e.g. China, India, Hong Kong markets. The energy entrepreneur ought concentrate on manufacturing the lowest cost and enough supply of natural resource to manufacture the kind of energy to sell cheap price to these countries to use, e.g. China, Africa can accept to use e.g. gas, coal, fuel energy to use to compare developed countries people, e.g. UK, US; or if the countries people who hope to use energy which can easy to transport and store, e.g. light coal. The energy entrepreneur can choose to concentrate on manufacturing much coal to supply to the countries people to use, e.g. China, Arica Thus, to choose to manufacture which kinds of energy supply to the countries market people to use, the energy entrepreneur how decides to manufacture which kind of energy, it depends on which kinds of fuel advantages of the countries people most concerning.

What is energy meaning? It is defined a dynamic quality, it is a fundamental entity of nature that is transferred between parts of a system in the production of physical change within the system, and it is usually regarded as the capacity for doing work, and it is usable power (such as heat or electricity) or the resources for producing such power.

Why does secondary energy own investment worth? Because the different forms of primary natural resource energy will have supply shortage crisis, such as natural resources coal, gas, solar, wind, water, geothermal, biomass(organic material) etc. However, human can attempt to explore any undiscovered Earth or Space resource to manufacture any kinds of secondary energies, e.g. nuclear energy, electric recharge battery energy to supply to electric vehicle or space robots transportation tools to use or satisfy our daily life needs in future one day. So any kind of undiscovered secondary man-made renewed used energy resources have potential commercial worth to any energy entrepreneurs, it is possible that they can replace traditional primary energy to supply to human to use for our different aspects of life needs. In the future, the secondary energy demand will increase, when primary energy supply number has decreased form natural exploration. So, it will cause the effect of any demand of secondary energy product to be raised and prices to be increased in possible. Due to global population has been growing up, considerably China and India both countries populations have been increasing rapidly. Scientists predict there are more than 1.2 billion people worldwide will lack access to electricity, and more than 2.5 billion still use wood, charcoal to cook and heat in the future when primary energy has no enough number to supply to us to use. Hence, the fact that demand is this much greater than supply to make energy a prime market for further growth.

Although, secondary energy will have much investment worth, but energy like all other investments will carry risks. The internal and external risk factors include such as: policy is always changing to prohibit which do energy trading more easily between the energy exporting and importing countries, the secondary energy manufacturer itself own abilities to invent and to manufacture any kinds of secondary energy, improved technology can quickly make an technology obsolete, geopolitical rifts can happen overnight, the country's energy consumer (user)'s preferable choice to use which either kinds of secondary energy or secondary energy. So, it seems that (man-made) renewed used secondary energy industry can provide above-average returns, but it can also bring high risk commercial investment.

Traditionally, energy supply companies will apply those methods to operate energy providing businesses. For Shell,. Exxon examples, which had own gas stations, explore and drill for gas on their own. Other companies specialize in a part of the energy market, e.g. leasing oil rigs for example, or operating a pipeline. Energy supplying companies can choose to manufacture any kinds of energy to supply, e.g. trade oil, gas, coal, uranium, electricity etc. Any energy price and supply is demanded on the countries energy users' which kinds of energy most choice need or certain energy commodities to be chose to use popularly. For example, if US most people prefer to use secondary man-made renew used energy more than primary energy. Then, US energy manufacturers ought concentrate on manufacturing much different kinds of secondary man-made renew used energy to prepare to supply to its domestic US market in order to raise secondary energy price to sell in its country. So, the energy manufacturer's energy manufacturing choice, it is depend on which the country's people prefer to use which kinds of energy for their daily life needs.

However, scientists predict secondary energy market will have large market share, due to primary energy will have shortage to explore to supply in our earth and future energy consumers(users) prefer to choose to use more efficiency, less energy consumption, none environment pollution cause, cost effectiveness, renew to use of any kinds of energy. For example, the electricity recharge battery secondary man-made renew used energy is one kind of reducing air pollution power to push any electric battery vehicles to be driven to compare gas energy during drivers are driving their cars on the roads. They can reduce noise and air pollution and drivers can drive safely, who only need to buy one electric recharge battery to recharge in any electric recharge battery stations on streets when the electric recharge battery has no enough power to push their cars and they need to recharge their electric recharge battery drive when they had driven between one to two days. Due to primary energy, e.g. fuel , gas, the kinds of primary energies will have shortage to supply to global drivers to drive their traditional cars. Thus, the electric recharge battery or any undiscovered secondary energy will be future driving market needs. So, man-made renew used secondary energy, e.g. biofuel, hydro-electric, nuclear, will be one kind of efficient, clean, less pollution cause, cost-effective of energy to supply to our global vehicle market, even any other undiscovered new markets. Supposing they are popular to be used for electric vehicle market globally in future one day, then their prices will be decreased and constructed to average car requires up to 1,700 gallons of oil. Also supposing that making average computer requires more than ten times or weight to fossil fuels, every calories of food eaten in the US requires roughly then calories of fossil fuels. Hence, cheap energy will be one successful factor to influence future potential energy consumer (user) individual choice needs. Conversely, ion good economic times, people are more willing to travel, to buy products, and all of which success demand and low process for energy.

In the future, secondary energy will be the best choice to food production market. The modern food production system is essentially a success of changing fossil fuels into food. So, raising energy prices are almost higher food costs and even shortage for fossil fuels energy. If one day, one kind of discovered secondary man-made renew used energy can supply to any restaurants or homes to be used to cook at the cheap price, then the profit is very high for this kind of food production energy. Thus, future food production secondary energy consumption market is large and because the primary energy inputs for agriculture are higher than the energy outputs of the food. However, future secondary man-made renew used energy for food production system is only one part of whole energy consumer in food industry. The food production is related to whole food consumption market which includes: household cooking energy market, agriculture or vegetable, rice, fruit etc. foods farming machines energy market, food manufacturing factories market, food machine package market, transportation food delivery market, supermarket or fruit/food sale stores market. They must need any energy inputs to achieve the food production or food transportation or warehouse / stores electricity supply or cooking energy needs. Hence, these food suppliers relate to any whole food factory manufacturers, food retailers, food wholesalers, farmers and home/restaurant cookers, all of them must need to use energy to carry on their food producing or food cooking or food transportation activities every day in overall food industry. Thus, it seems that undiscovered any second energy demand will be increased, when the primary energy supply number is decreasing. Also, when people can accept to use secondary energy to replace primary energy to be used for any cooking, transporting food, manufacturing food, food retail stores or warehouse food delivery energy need activities. Then, the secondary energy price will be fall down to attract many food energy consumers.

Nowadays, the food industry energy may includes primary nature resource gas energy or electricity energy for house house families or restaurants cooking needs, food delivering lorry drivers driving needs usually. If future second man made renew used energy is invented successful popular to be used, e.g. hydrogen, electric recharged battery energy for electric vehicles or restaurant/home families cooking needs or food factories machine maufacturing energy needs. Then, the seconday energy will have possible to replace primary energy to be food industry energy market.

Wiley, composition services graphics indicated that global primary energy consumption had been increasing 30 billion tons from 1830 year to 510 billion tons in 2010 year as well as global population size had been increasing from 70 billion 1830 yeat to 510 billion in 2010 year. Thus, it seems that global primary energy consumption will be needed largely after 2010 year. If future global nature resource primary energy is explored full number and it had not enough energy number to supply global human to use. Then, it will being many people feel uncomfortable and inconvenient,e.g. Some countries won't have enough energy to supply transportion tools to be driven, some homes and restaurants won't have enough energy to supply to cook to eat or to provide restaurant clients to eat etc. daily activies, due to human's much activities which are needs energy supply. Thus, it seems that global primary energy comsumption will be needed largely after 2010 year.

Wiley, composition services graphics also explianed that why the primary energy consumption demand can be needed to achieve the same level to the global population size increasing in 2010 year. The graph showed these reasons why cause the same level of global population size and global primary energy consumpion demand which may include: The graph showed that after a nation is developed, its per-person energy use hegins to level off. In North Ameruca and Europe, where energy demand has remained flat, or fallen dightly, in each of the past few years. But the 1.3 billion people on those two continents are far outweighted by the 5 billion people in Asia and Africa, e.g. Chinese and Indian. who currently have more energy need to comapre average per man to North America and Europe per man, ensuring that overall energy demand will rise for years to come.

Wiley, composition services graphics also predicted that the growth in primary energy demand. China will have 4,500 million tons in 2035 year. India will have 3,000 million tons in 2035 year. Other developing Asia will have 2,000 million tons in 2035 year. Russia will have 1,500 million tons in 2035, Middle East will have 1,300 million tons in 2035, other rest of world will have 1,000 million tons in 2035. Hence, it implied that China will be the largest primary energy need country in the future.

China will be future the primary potential energy consumer market. The primary energy includes water, coal, wind, fossil oil, gas ,solar, geothermal energy, biomass (organiz material) etc. different natural resource primary energy. Otherwise, US, UK, Europe will be secondary energy potential need market. For example, electrical recharge battery energy will be raised demand to supply to any future new design electrical charge battery vehicles in US, Europe, UK markets.

Due to US, Europe, UK people concern environment protection, so they will invent many electric charge battery vehicles to consume electrical charge battery to replace polluted gas energy to avoid air pollution when the drivers are driving cars on themselve countries' roads. For example, second man-made renew used nuclear energy can be applied to rockets to pusch them to leave our earth to fly to other space far away and consuming nuclear energy will be cost efficient, and nuclear energy saving will be more when nuclear to spcnd long time to be used in any long time space journey. Hence, nuclear energy and electric charge battery secondary energy will be popular to be applied to vehicles and rockets energy needs in US, Europe, potential marketss, even our daily energy needs in global second energy market.

Who are your energy business's competitors (peers)? How do they compare? How have your energy business company performed cyclically? How to choose to manufacture to sell which kinds of primary or secondary energy product(s), either manufactures only primary energy product(s) or manufactures only secondary energy products or both? Which countries do you plan to sell your energy product?

Illustration by Wilsey, composition services graphiss showed that these natural resources to energy product the world's electricity percentage, such as below:

41% of coal, 5% of oil, 21% of gas, 13% of nuclear, 16% of Hydro, 3% other renewable secondary man-made energy.

Hence, coal will be future the major natural resource to produce electricity. The energy entrepreneur ought attempt to explore any coal resources, when who choose to supply electricity power to consumers for future energy consumption country markets.

Wiley, composition services also predicted that the expectation is that North America coal will supply the expectation is that North America coal will supply Asian demand, Us export terminals have a total capacity of 173 million tommes output. China will drive 16% of the nations total output. China will drive the sea-born demand for coal over for the forcessable future. Chinese energy consumption will grow more than 12 % between 1980 and 2009 years. Though, China heads global demand, India is growing faster in terms of coal imports. Much of the global coal demand will be supplied by Indonesia and Australia. Colombia, Russia, South Africa and Mongolia are also players in global export coal energy resources.

Hence, environment scientists' education messages influence Greece householders believe that secondary energy will be one kind of new energy product to replace traditional primary energy product for human energy consumption market global needs. Hence, it is right time any energy entrepreneur needs to research how to explore any undiscovered man-made renew used secondary energy products to avoid primary energy shortage crisis occurrence. Greece householders will be the highest population number to choose secondary energy to replace primary energy to use at homes. it means that environment scientists had changed Greece householders' energy consumption behaviors at homes.

In conclusion, different countries will have different factors influence how the country's householders energy consumption behavioral changes. Hence, it seems that any country's householders' energy use of consumption behaviors will be possible influenced by extermal environment factors influence. Also, every country's energy providers can attempt to find whether the country has what kinds of unique factors to influence its householders' energy consumption efficiency to increase or decrease in order to find the methods to solve the energy efficiency demand reducing challenges successfully.

New economy society why and how changes to old economy society

● Reasons new economy society will experience old economy society

Although, our technological invention, e.g. artificial intellgent invention is developed to success, it may bring our societies to expereince new economy benefit, e.g. hospitals can apply robot to service patients, non-manual driving transport tools, e.g. taxi , robots can be applied to raise worker individual efficiencies and improve productivities to let businessmen to raise high profit and satisfy customers' needs. But, when our technological invention can create unlimited benefits to improve human living and raise global productivites and efficienies and raise talent workers when workers need to learn robotic technology to assist their tasks in any organizations in the future.

But, this global human disease occurrence from 2000 Dec. It influences global businesses go worse, e.g. tourism industry begun to decline, when global travelers feel fear to catch air planes when they need to sit in close air planes, because air plan windows can not open, if one human lung disease traveler sit in the air plane, he can let all the air plane passengers to get his lung disease from air plane air. Moreover, nowadays, many western people, e.g. US, UK, France, Germany, Italy etc. countries had many people had gotten this kind of new lung disease COIVD19. Consequently, it causes many travellers feel fear to travel these countries, even, Japan, Korea Asia countries, they have many people are alo got COIVD 19 lung diseases.

Moreover, this kinds of disease causes global tourism industry declines, then many airlines reduce many air planes flights, due to travellers number decreases, then they earn less profit, next they must need to fire some or many airlines front line staffs, e.g. pilots, air plane customer serice staffs, airport check in/out service staffs, even, clerical staffs etc. So, many airline staffs will face unemployment. Instead of tourism industry face declines, many travel agents also reduce air tickets sale number, then they also need to reduce staffs. So, airline and travel agent global staffs number will reduce due to COVID 19 human disease occurs.

Also, COVID 19 disease also brings taxi drivers income reduce, because taxi is small transport tool, when one COVID 19 disease passenger sits in the taxi, the taxi driver will need to contact the passenger in the small taxi. It is sure that the taxi driver will have high chance to get COVID 19 disease from the passenger. So, global will have many taxi drivers feel fear to drive taxi, even the health taxi passenger also feels fear to sit in the taxi when he feels the taxi driver has COVID 19 disease. Consequently, global taxi passengers number will also be influenced to reduce due to COVID 19 disease still occurs.

Also, COVID 19 influences many restaurants lose many eating clients in busy time, e.g. office lunch time, dinner time. Because many countries countries begin to limit eating clients number to all restaurants, they avoid many eating clients sit in the restauants, if one or more customers have COVID 19 disease, is/are sitting in the restaurants, then he/she/ they may bring COVID 19 disease to the eatting people when they are sitting in the restaurants. Consequently, global restaurants' tables may only perimt one person to sit, then global any restaurants eatting clients number must reduce.

All of these businesses must be influenced to reduce clients number, then their profits must reduce and clients number reduce, even staffs number is influenced to reduce. It is one good example to explain how we are facing global economic recession and global societies may be influenced to experience old economy society from new economy society in future.

● How to recover new economy society

Hence, it is only one way to help us to recover to experience new economy societies again. The way is that our old economy socical decline change will be disappeared when one kind of new medicine is invented to treat this kind of COVID 19 human disease. If our doctors or medicine inventors can not discover any new kind of medicine to treat this COVID 19 human disease successfully. Then, global will have many different kinds of businesses to cause decline. Consequently, their clients number will must continue reduce. So, COVID 19 human new kind of disease will be the main factor to influence our global new economic technological society to experience old economic traditional business model society, e.g. farming society, manufacuring industry characteristic. Because this kind of COVID human new kind disease will concentrate on influencing our future global different kinds of service businesses to experience decline business life cycle definitely. When our future societies lose many kinds of service industries, e.g. public transport, cinema movies entertainment activities, catching air plane travelling leisure activities due to we feel fear to catch air planes, enter cinemas, catch taxi ,even, bus, tram, train, ferry etc. public transport tools when we need to contact any strange people and we feel anyone will be the COVID 19 human disease patient, when our new economic activities will be reduced. Consequently, old economic activities, e.g. farming , manufacturing activities will be considered to any job seekers. Then, all businesses will only concentrate on farming and manufacturing industries only. It is future old economic society characteristic.